Debating Crime:
Rhetoric and Reality

David W. Neubauer

University of New Orleans

Wadsworth
Thomson Learning™

Australia • Canada • Mexico • Singapore • Spain • United Kingdom • United States

Criminal Justice Editor: Dan Alpert
Development Editor: Terri Edwards
Assistant Editor: Ann Tsai
Marketing Manager: Jennifer Somerville
Signing Representative: Charlotte Strasser
Project Editor: Jennie Redwitz
Print Buyer: Karen Hunt
Permissions Editor: Joohee Lee
Production Service: Linda Jupiter, Jupiter Productions

Text Designer: Rob Hugel, Little Hill Design
Copy Editor: Sarito Carol Neiman
Proofreader: Henrietta Bensussen
Indexer: Martha Osgood, Back Words Indexing
Cover Designer: Ross Carron
Cover Printer: Webcom Limited
Compositor: Thompson Type
Printer: Webcom Limited

Library of Congress Cataloging-in-Publication Data
Neubauer, David W.
    Debating crime : rhetoric and reality / David W. Neubauer.
        p. cm.
    Includes bibliographical references and index.
    ISBN 0-534-52711-6
    1. Criminal justice, Administration of—United States.
    2. Crime—United States. I. Title.

HV9950.N49 2001
364.973—dc21   00-032503

Wadsworth/Thomson Learning
10 Davis Drive
Belmont, CA 94002-3098
USA

For more information about our products, contact us:
Thomson Learning Academic Resource Center
1-800-423-0563
http://www.wadsworth.com

International Headquarters
Thomson Learning
International Division
290 Harbor Drive, 2nd Floor
Stamford, CT 06902-7477
USA

UK/Europe/Middle East/South Africa
Thomson Learning
Berkshire House
168-173 High Holborn
London WC1V 7AA
United Kingdom

Asia
Thomson Learning
60 Albert Street, #15-01
Albert Complex
Singapore 189969

Canada
Nelson Thomson Learning
1120 Birchmount Road
Toronto, Ontario M1K 5G4
Canada

To my wife, Carole

Brief Contents

Contents

Contents

Brief Contents

To my wife, Carole

Criminal Justice Editor: Dan Alpert
Development Editor: Terri Edwards
Assistant Editor: Ann Tsai
Marketing Manager: Jennifer Somerville
Signing Representative: Charlotte Strasser
Project Editor: Jennie Redwitz
Print Buyer: Karen Hunt
Permissions Editor: Joohee Lee
Production Service: Linda Jupiter, Jupiter Productions

Text Designer: Rob Hugel, Little Hill Design
Copy Editor: Sarito Carol Neiman
Proofreader: Henrietta Bensussen
Indexer: Martha Osgood, Back Words Indexing
Cover Designer: Ross Carron
Cover Printer: Webcom Limited
Compositor: Thompson Type
Printer: Webcom Limited

For permission to use material from this text, contact us by
Web: http://www.thomsonrights.com
Fax: 1-800-730-2215
Phone: 1-800-730-2214

Library of Congress Cataloging-in-Publication Data
Neubauer, David W.
    Debating crime : rhetoric and reality / David W. Neubauer.
        p. cm.
    Includes bibliographical references and index.
    ISBN 0-534-52711-6
    1. Criminal justice, Administration of—United States.
    2. Crime—United States. I. Title.

HV9950.N49 2001
364.973—dc21   00-032503

Wadsworth/Thomson Learning
10 Davis Drive
Belmont, CA 94002-3098
USA

For more information about our products, contact us:
Thomson Learning Academic Resource Center
1-800-423-0563
http://www.wadsworth.com

International Headquarters
Thomson Learning
International Division
290 Harbor Drive, 2nd Floor
Stamford, CT 06902-7477
USA

UK/Europe/Middle East/South Africa
Thomson Learning
Berkshire House
168-173 High Holborn
London WC1V 7AA
United Kingdom

Asia
Thomson Learning
60 Albert Street, #15-01
Albert Complex
Singapore 189969

Canada
Nelson Thomson Learning
1120 Birchmount Road
Toronto, Ontario M1K 5G4
Canada

Debating Crime:
Rhetoric and Reality

David W. Neubauer
University of New Orleans

 **Wadsworth**
Thomson Learning™

Australia • Canada • Mexico • Singapore • Spain • United Kingdom • United States

Introduction

- *12 students and one teacher are massacred at Columbine High School.*

- *21 police bullets kill West African immigrant Amadou Diallo.*

These two events, separated by three months and 3,000 miles, reveal much about debating crime in the United States. Varying reactions to these two tragedies highlight contrasting images and competing agendas.

In the aftermath of the shootings at Columbine High School in Littleton, Colorado, virtually all parts of the political spectrum immediately analyzed the causes of this national tragedy and offered up varying remedies.

- Calls for greater gun controls were countered by demands for stricter enforcement of existing gun laws (Issues 1 and 2).

- Social conservatives identified a morally lax culture as the culprit and demanded banning pornography on the Internet (Issue 18).

- Feminists called attention to the dominance of males in the incidents (Issue 12).

- Leaders of minority communities speculated that the societal reaction would not have been the same if the suspects were black (Issue 11).

- Perhaps above all, the deaths at Columbine High School fueled debate in Congress to drastically alter the nation's juvenile justice system (Issues 15 and 16).

Reactions to the killing of Amadou Diallo were vastly different. Diallo, an unarmed West African immigrant who did not speak English, was shot while he stood in the lobby of his apartment building. Neither the mayor of New York nor the New York Police Department explained why the four officers opened fire. Perhaps the reasons will emerge when the officers are tried for murder. But the immediate reaction from some segments of the nation was one of swift fury.

- Leaders of the local black community immediately condemned the shootings as the latest example of police brutality (Issue 3).

- Mayor Giuliani railed against cop bashers.

- Anticrime police tactics that fall most heavily on members of minority communities were questioned.

- NYPD officers denounced a TV ad for an anti-police brutality march as fueling the fire.

- Perhaps above all the shooting in New York City provoked another national debate over whether the criminal justice system unfairly discriminates against racial minorities (Issue 11).

The shootings in Littleton, Colorado, and New York City have now become part of the crime debate in the United States. Events like these, and the types of issues they raise, are the focus of this book. *Debating Crime: Rhetoric and Reality* has four objectives:

1. Examine the ongoing **debate** concerning crime in the United States.

2. Discuss how major **crimes** shape the national debate.

3. Probe the **rhetoric** of issues that have become the focal points of debating crime.

4. Explore the **reality** of policy options that often become blurred in the rhetoric of debating crime.

Let us briefly examine each of these objectives in turn.

The Crime Debate: Ongoing and Changing

In the modern era, crime became a significant issue during the 1964 presidential campaign. Republican candidate Barry Goldwater attacked the Democratic leaders for not doing enough about crime. Not to be outdone, after reelection President Johnson declared that "crime has become a malignant force" in our society and created a Presidential Commission to study the matter. All subsequent presidents have done likewise. Republican president Ronald Reagan, for instance, created a commission on crime victims. Republican president George Bush declared yet another war on drugs (Issue 17). Democratic president Bill Clinton campaigned to add 100,000 more police officers, build more prisons, and fund other anticrime initiatives, thus demonstrating that crime is no longer an issue solely for Republicans.

Although the political rhetoric during presidential campaigns is the most visible, crime has also become a defining political issue at all levels of government. Candidates for office, whether local, state, or national, fear the label of being "soft on crime" and therefore often go to great lengths to project an image of being "tough on crime." Indeed, crime issues often dominate urban elections (Heinz, Jacob, and Lineberry, 1983).

Although debating crime is an ongoing part of American society, the nature of the debate also changes over time.

- During the 1960s the call for "law and order" stood for a general sense of uneasiness about a prevailing "lawlessness" that for some meant antiwar protests (whether peaceful or not), and for others, crime on the streets.

- During the 1970s crime became identified with property offenses like burglary and theft.

- During the 1980s armed robberies, and later murders, dominated discussions.

- By the 1990s the words *drugs* and *crime* had become all but interchangeable.

Thus, the first objective of this book is to examine the ongoing and changing nature of debating crime in the United States. As we shall see, some issues are enduring. Gun control (Issues 1 and 2), racial discrimination (Issues 8 and 11), sentencing (Issue 9), and the death penalty (Issue 10) have been staples of discussion for decades. At the same time, new issues are added to the debate agenda. Thus over the last decade drunk driving (Issue 5), gender inequity (Issue 7), and domestic violence (Issue 6) have become important topics.

Debating: Crime Events As Focus

One reason that the crime debate is ongoing and changing in the United States is because new crimes become the focus of considerable national attention on a regular basis. Major events like the shootings in Littleton, Colorado, and New York City become part of the nation's memory bank of famous crimes and infamous criminals. To be sure some crimes have only a temporary impact on the nation's consciousness, quickly disappearing from popular attention. But other events endure in the nation's collective conscience. The acquittal of O. J. Simpson, for example, sparked a national debate over juries and jury nullification (Issue 8). In short, major crimes become intertwined with issues in the crime debate. In the same vein, the criminal and later civil trial of the Subway Vigilante became a national forum for debating self-protection, racism, and gun control (Part 1). In turn the events (and the debates that they spawn) have an impact on crime policy.

Thus, the second objective of the book is to discuss how crimes and criminals play an important role in debating crime. Throughout the book I use crimes and criminals to place issues in context, and at the same time explore varying reactions to these events. The trials of the police officers accused of beating Rodney King provide an introduction to Issue 3: "Is Excessive Use of Force a Systematic Problem?" Similarly, the acquittal of William Kennedy Smith provides a background for Issue 7: "Are Sexual Assaults Against Women Underprosecuted?"

The Rhetoric of Debate: Pro and Con Arguments

At the center of the crime debate, of course, is the often fiery rhetoric used to urge adoption of a particular action or alternatively to seek defeat of a proposed policy change. Pro and con arguments are worth examining for several reasons.

Perhaps most importantly, pro and con arguments shape the crime debate. Confronted with a crime issue, elected officials and spokespersons for interest groups offer a solution. Almost immediately other elected officials and spokespersons for other interest groups offer arguments for defeating the proposal. These pro and con discussions dominate media coverage, thus shaping public perceptions and reactions. In contemporary parlance, they provide a "spin" on crime events.

The pro and con format also has the advantage of probing a range of issues. Debating crime in the United States is a fragmented process. Individuals, groups, and elected officials are selective in the crime issues they rank as important. The twenty crime issues discussed in this book force the reader to move past his or her own select favorites and confront a variety of other issues. As we shall see, some crime issues tend to group with others. For example, those most concerned about police brutality (Issue 3) are also most likely to voice opposition to the death penalty (Issue 10). Conversely, these issues are of little interest to those whose agenda ranks highest the elimination of restrictions on police gathering of evidence (Issue 4) and the need for tougher sentences (Issue 9).

Pro and con arguments are also worth examining because opposing views challenge the reader to consider the other side. They force us to confront arguments made by the "opposition." This rarely happens to individuals because they have a strong tendency to hear only arguments that reinforce their own beliefs. Members of the NRA (National Rifle Association) are saturated with arguments opposing gun control (Issues 1 and 2). At the same time, citizens who favor gun control are most likely to hear only arguments favoring their currently held positions. As a result, in the public dialogue arguments raised by opponents tend to be dismissed out of hand. A systematic inquiry into the pro and con rhetoric can force the reader to at least consider the arguments posed by the other side.

Finally, the pro and con format forces the reader to systematically assess his or her own beliefs on an issue. Just as individuals are selective in the crime issues they rank as most important, they are often equally selective in why they hold those beliefs. Typically, for example, individuals have at their fingertips a fact or two that supports their position. Alas, this shallow reservoir of facts (and arguments) doesn't last long in a sustained discussion. The pro and con format can help the reader strengthen his or her own arguments.

Overall, the ultimate challenge of the pro and con format is to force students to begin thinking in different ways, moving beyond simplistic notions of good guys and bad. It can encourage them to think about the complexity of the issues under discussion and understand why different individuals, groups, or elected officials can legitimately offer competing solutions.

Thus, the third objective of *Debating Crime: Rhetoric and Reality* is to probe a number of contemporary issues that are focal points of debating crime in the United States. Because the number of topics is large (and growing) a book like this cannot discuss all the issues. Instead, I have chosen twenty of the most controversial issues. They have also been chosen because they are representative of the range of issues under discussion.

For each of these twenty issues (grouped in ten sections) I first seek to place the particular issue within a broader perspective. Next, a table presents, as objectively as possible, the major pro and con arguments sparked by the issue. To flesh out these arguments, the book provides articles by leading spokespersons for the respective sides. These pieces are variously drawn from press releases, advocacy pieces, magazine articles, testimony before Congress, and even Web sites. Some are quite fiery, providing a flavor of public dialogue. Others are more dispassionate but just as forceful.

The Reality Behind Debating Crime

Viewing the crime debate solely in an argument format, though, has it limits. The pro and con approach greatly oversimplifies complex matters. The rhetoric of debating crime portrays issues as simple; the reality is that crime involves a set of messy and often interrelated problems. Canvassing independent analysis of issues in *Debating Crime* is important for several reasons.

The rhetoric of pro and con falsely suggests that issues are binary. Indeed, solutions offered by various groups are portrayed as magic bullets: a simple policy change will produce major positive changes. Stripping aside the rhetoric, the reality of debating crime is policies reflecting compromise. Crime policy takes many forms. It includes laws passed by legislative bodies, decisions reached by courts, or strategies adopted by the executive branch (law enforcement agencies primarily). Typically these policies reflect compromises. As a result, neither side is completely happy, but most can at least live with the outcome. In turn individuals, groups, and/or elected officials who perceive that they were only partially successful will continue their efforts, often waiting for a more opportune moment to again urge adoption of more of their program.

Another major drawback of the pro and con format is how facts are treated. In debating crime, facts are thrown around to make the argument. Typically one side uses statistical data to argue that the problem is major. The opposition counters that the problem is overblown, and provides a very different set of numbers. The "facts" cited require careful scrutiny, beginning with a request for the source. It is amazing how often statistical assertions are made without bothering to provide the reader even rudimentary documentation. As we shall see, statistics defining the boundaries of a crime issue are often subject to debate.

Moreover, in debating crime a typical approach is the bold statement along the lines, "once all the facts are known you will agree . . ." Consider, for example, the debate over the war on drugs (Issue 17). The home page of the Partnership for a Drug-Free America (http://www.drugfreeamerica.org/) proclaims: "Much of the information available in cyberspace about drugs is not accurate. We have verified all information included in our site and have provided sources throughout." Translated, this seems to mean that the group rejects any "facts" raised by their opponents.

The polarized nature of the argument format can also result in a distortion of research and research findings. In debating crime, research findings play an important role. Proponents of a particular policy option are quick to point to research that supports their position. Just as quickly, opponents attack the study as flawed and unreliable. The debate over drunk driving (Issue 6) and mandatory arrest policies for domestic violence offenses (Issue 7) are but two cases in point. Independent analysis is important because often what organizations label "research" is no more than a selective rendering of favorable facts. Indeed, some research may be tainted by the fact that the organization has either done its own research, or paid others to provide "facts" that support their position.

Finally, independent analysis is important because all too often the rhetoric suggests that merely adopting proposal X will solve the problem. It is important to examine whether policies, once implemented, have the intended impact. Some do. Others don't. And to complicate matters further, some polices have unintended consequences.

Thus, the final objective of *Debating Crime: Rhetoric and Reality* is to stress the importance of moving beyond rhetoric to also examine the reality of crime policy. Toward that end, the book complements the pro and con articles with ones that provide analysis. These articles have been selected to reflect some of the best thinking of scholars who study these issues in depth. In addition, section openings and issue overviews contain guides to articles available on InfoTrac College Edition; the section termed *analysis* provides an analytical perspective on the issue in question.

A caveat is in order regarding the *reality* of the crime debate. A good part of the crime debate involves assessing what is reality. Alas, those seeking pure, unvarnished truth will likely be disappointed. An article reporting research may appear to one person, group, or elected official to be an independent, unbiased analysis but to other individuals, groups, or elected officials just a piece of biased propaganda. Indeed, scholars who study the same topic can and do reach differing conclusions. Nonetheless, a rational crime debate is far better off including research that attempts (to varying degrees of success) to understand reality, than relying simply on sometimes overblown rhetoric. Often, researchers are best at describing the complexity of issues, avoiding the moralistic simplicity being offered by opposing sides of the debate.

Debating Crime: The Importance of Perspective

As we emphasized earlier, tragedies like the massacre at Columbine and the shooting of Amadou Diallo provoke conflicting reactions.

- Conservatives demand harsher laws, while liberals call for more "people programs."
- Interest groups of all persuasions quickly attach their pet proposals to a recent crime.
- Some social scientists question whether societal reactions were appropriate or represented an overreaction.

Numerous academic disciplines are involved in the examination of crime issues. For our purposes, though, we will focus on three: law, political science, and sociology. The first section uses a major crime event—the Subway Vigilante—to introduce three perspectives on debating crime: individual attitudes, group activity, and societal reactions. These three perspectives will be used throughout the book to structure analysis.

World Wide Web Resources

Web Guides

http://dir.yahoo.com/Society_and_Culture/Crime/
http://dir.yahoo.com/Government/Law/Cases/

Searching the Web

crime, criminal justice, law

Useful URLs

Bureau of Justice Statistics: Provides easy access to a wide range of government statistics on crime and criminal justice.   http://www.ojp.usdoj.gov/bjs

Federal Bureau of Investigation (FBI): The nation's best known law enforcement agency.   http://www.fbi.gov/

Criminal Justice Resource Center: A good starting point for links to other criminal justice sites.   http://cj.wadsworth.com/

Legal Issues

FindLaw: The commercial leader of legal material on the internet.
http:/www.findlaw.com

Legal Information Institute (LII): Award winning site from Cornell Law School.
http://supct.cornell.edu

Today's Headlines

APB: http://www.apbnews.com/

Court TV: http://www.courttv.com/

Yahoo: http://dailynews.yahoo.com/headlines/cr/

Fun Sites

Famous American Trials: Offers a fascinating glimpse into trials, old and new, that have shaped U.S. society.
http://www.law.umkc.edu/faculty/projects/ftrials/ftrials.htm

Crime Library: Gallery of famous and infamous criminals.
http://www.crimelibrary.com/

InfoTrac College Edition Resources

InfoTrac College Edition is an online library that provides 24 hours a day, 7 days a week access to full articles from more than 600 scholarly and popular periodicals. The most general search terms are: **crime;** and **criminal justice, administration of. www.infotrac-college.com**

Part I

Perspectives on Debating Crime

Having been mugged twice, Bernhard Goetz, a 36-year-old electronics consultant now carried a gun to defend himself, and defend himself he did on December 22, 1984. Thinking that four black youth were trying to shake him down for $5 on the New York City subway, he fired several shots, wounding all four. The most seriously injured was 18-year-old Darrell Cabey, who was paralyzed and suffered brain damage.

Almost overnight the Subway Vigilante, as the case became labeled, became a focal point for debating crime. Some viewed Bernhard Goetz as a modern day folk hero because he dared to fight back. For those who had been helpless victims of crime, the Subway Vigilante was a character right out of the movies who stood tall and made a difference. But to others, Bernhard Goetz was a racist who had tragically overreacted. They stressed that after initially wounding Cabey, Goetz walked up to the bleeding youth and fired a paralyzing gunshot, proclaiming "You don't look too bad, here's another."

These competing images sparked national attention during the 1987 criminal trial. Eventually, the jury acquitted Goetz on all thirteen felony charges of attempted murder, assault, and reckless endangerment. They did, however, find him guilty of illegal possession of an unregistered handgun, a misdemeanor, and he served 8 months in jail.

These images were played out again during a nationally televised civil trial in 1996. During closing argument, Goetz's own lawyer admitted his client was a jerk. Nonetheless, he argued, Goetz acted in self-defense out of fear of becoming a crime victim again. Darrell Cabey's lawyer countered that Geotz was a racist, highlighting numerous inflammatory statements he made about Blacks, Hispanics and welfare mothers. He implored the jury to "award enough in punitive damages that you bankrupt every other bigot with a gun out there." The jury of four Blacks and two Hispanics apparently agreed, ordering Goetz to pay $43 million. It is unlikely, though, that Darrell Cabey will ever collect a dime—Goetz is bankrupt and unemployed.

Over the years, advocates of opposing views on issues like crime, race, and gun control have seized on the Subway Vigilante case to bolster their position. Later in this book we will explore these and other issues. In this opening section, though, we need to step back from the specific issues raised by the Subway Vigilante case to provide a perspective on debating crime. Three perspectives are helpful in understanding and analyzing specific issues in *Debating Crime*.

1. Individual attitudes are the subject of the section on the ideology of debating crime. The concepts of the due process model and the crime control model are better terms for analyzing competing beliefs than the popular terms liberal and conservative.

2. Group processes are the subject of the section on the politics of debating crime. Interest groups play an influential role in debating crime, as they attempt to shape governmental crime policy

3. Societal reactions are the subject of the section on the sociology of debating crime. Societal reactions (and overreactions) to crime and crime events have tremendous consequences for crime policy.

These three levels of analysis—individual, group and societal—are not mutually exclusive. Rather they are complementary. As we shall see, interest groups often reflect attitudes associated with either the due process model or the crime control model, and in turn use crime events (the Bernhard Goetz trial, for instance) as vehicles for trying to sway public opinion.

World Wide Web Resources

Useful URLs

American Friends Service Committee: A Quaker organization committed to social justice.   http://www.afsc.org/

Amnesty International: Works for the international protection of human rights. http://www.amnesty.org/

Cato Institute: The leading voice of libertarians.   http://www.cato.org/

Heritage Foundation: Nonpartisan research institute dedicated to the principles of free competitive enterprise, limited government, and individual liberties. http://www.heritage.org/

Human Rights Watch: Works to end a broad ranges of abuses. http://www.hrw.org/

Policy.com: The policy news and information source.   http://policy.com/

Public Agenda Online: Inside source for public opinion and policy analysis. http://publicagenda.com/

Today's Headlines

Atlantic Monthly: http://www.theatlantic.com/politics/crime/crime.htm

National Review: http://www.nationalreview.com/

New Republic: http://www.tnr.com/

Newsweek: http://www.newsweek.com/

Time: http://www.pathfinder.com/time/

U.S. News & World Report: http://www.usnews.com/usnews/home.htm

Fun Sites

Dumb Crooks: True Stories of Mentally Challenged Criminals
http://www.dumbcrooks.com/

Rate Your Risk: Series of tests that help realistically determine your chances of being a victim of a crime.   http://www.Nashville.Net/~police/risk/

Perspective 1

The Ideology of the
Crime Debate

In the public dialogue over controversial cases like the Subway Vigilante, conservatives quickly square off against liberals, hardliners accuse their opponents of "being soft on crime." While entertaining, this sort of terminology is not very helpful in understanding the debate on crime. Phrases like "soft on crime" attract our attention to questions about goals, but they are not useful for systematic inquiry because they are ambiguous and emotional.

In one of the most important contributions to systematic thought about debating crime, Herbert Packer articulates the gulf existing between two models of criminal justice. The "Due Process Model" proceeds from the premise that protecting the rights of the individual is primary, whereas the "Crime Control Model" holds that repressing crime is the key value. Moreover, these two approaches differ dramatically in their views as to the causes of crime. The due process model highlights the root causes of crime (poverty and racial discrimination primarily) while the crime control model points to a breakdown of individual responsibility.

Here is a short overview of ideological differences on some of the issues to be discussed in *Debating Crime*.

In reading this selection, as well as others later in this book, note that at times the Due Process Model and the Crime Control Model share important values. Both viewpoints, for example, seek to reduce crime but differ as to the best approach. Moreover, both sides recognize the importance of limiting governmental power but debate when and how to impose these restrictions on the power of the government to arrest, convict, and sentence.

Crime Control Model	Due Process Model
Most gun owners are law abiding.	Gun control will reduce crime.
Criminal sanctions are the best way to deter illegal drug use.	Rehabilitation is the best way to treat persons with a substance abuse problem.
Allegations of racial discrimination are unproven and irrelevant.	Racial minorities are disproportionately sanctioned by the criminal justice system.
The focus on gender diverts attention from important matters.	Gender inequity permeates criminal justice.
The exclusionary rule lets the guilty go free.	The exclusionary rule limits police abuse of power.
Punishment will deter crime.	Rehabilitation will prevent crime.
The death penalty deters crime.	Abolish the death penalty.
Juvenile offenders deserve adult penalties.	Juvenile court should emphasize rehabilitation.

World Wide Web Exercises

1. Using the search term, **"Bernhard Goetz"** search on yahoo.com, altavista.com, or the search engine of your choice for articles, web sites, etc. on the Subway Vigilante. Locate one article that defends Goetz and another one that condemns him. Hint: placing the search term in quote marks limits the search just to that phrase. Without the quote marks the search often yields sites that contain the word Bernhard or the word Goetz.

2. Examine four or more web sites that are active in the crime debate. Which web sites articulate values associated with the crime control model? Which web sites articulate values associated with the due process model? One way to locate web sites is to use the following yahoo search: http://dir.yahoo.com/Society_and_Culture/Crime/Organizations/

InfoTrac College Edition Exercises

1. Using the search terms **vigilante and crime** locate two or more articles that analyze the Subway Vigilante incident. Why does this case still stir such emotions? Would reaction to the incident be similar or different today? Hint: combining the two

terms (vigilante; crime) with the operative "and" will limit the search to articles that contain both words. Without the use of *and*, the searches often yield articles that contain one or the other word.

2. Using the search term **crime, causes of** locate one article that reflects the crime control model of criminal justice and another that is based on the due process model of criminal justice. How did you decide that the article belonged in one category and not another? Do these two articles make arguments similar or different from those discussed in this book? Despite their differences, what do these articles share in common?

Two Models of the Criminal Process

Herbert L. Packer

Two models of the criminal process will let us perceive the normative antinomy at the heart of the criminal law. These models are not labeled Is and Ought, nor are they to be taken in that sense. Rather, they represent an attempt to abstract two separate value systems that compete for priority in the operation of the criminal process . . .

I call these two models the Due Process Model and the Crime Control Model. . . . And, since they are normative in character, there is a danger of seeing one or the other as Good or Bad. The reader will have his preferences, as I do, but we should not be so rigid as to demand consistently polarized answers to the range of questions posed in the criminal process. . . . The attempt here is primarily to clarify the terms of discussion by isolating the assumptions that underlie competing policy claims and examining the conclusions that those claims, if fully accepted, would lead to.

Crime Control Values

The value system that underlies the Crime Control Model is based on the proposition that the repression of criminal conduct is by far the most important function to be performed by the criminal process. The failure of law enforcement to bring criminal conduct under tight control is viewed as leading to the breakdown of public order and thence to the disappearance of an important condition of human freedom. If the laws

Source: *The Limits of the Criminal Sanction* by Herbert L. Packer. Stanford University Press. © 1968 Herbert L. Packer. Used by permission.

go unenforced—which is to say, if it is perceived that there is a high percentage of failure to apprehend and convict in the criminal process—a general disregard for legal controls tends to develop. The law-abiding citizen then becomes the victim of all sorts of unjustifiable invasions of his interests. His security of person and property is sharply diminished, and, therefore, so is his liberty to function as a member of society. The claim ultimately is that the criminal process is a positive guarantor of social freedom. In order to achieve this high purpose, the Crime Control Model requires that primary attention be paid to the efficiency with which the criminal process operates to screen suspects, determine guilt, and secure appropriate dispositions of persons convicted of crime.

Efficiency of operation is not, of course, a criterion that can be applied in a vacuum. By "efficiency" we mean the system's capacity to apprehend, try, convict, and dispose of a high proportion of criminal offenders whose offenses become known. . . .

The model, in order to operate successfully, must produce a high rate of apprehension and conviction, and must do so in a context where the magnitudes being dealt with are very large and the resources for dealing with them are very limited. There must then be a premium on speed and finality. Speed, in turn, depends on informality and on uniformity; finality depends on minimizing the occasions for challenge. The process must not be cluttered up with ceremonious rituals that do not advance the progress of a case. Facts can be established more quickly through interrogation in a police station than through the formal process of examination and cross-examination in a court. It follows that extrajudicial processes should be preferred to judicial processes, informal operations to formal ones. But informality is not enough; there must also be uniformity. Routine, stereotyped procedures are essential if large numbers are being handled. The model that will operate successfully on these presuppositions must be an administrative, almost a managerial, model. The image that comes to mind is an assembly-line conveyor belt down which moves an endless stream of cases, never stopping, carrying the cases to workers who stand at fixed stations and who perform on each case as it comes by the same small but essential operation that brings it one step closer to being a finished product, or, to exchange the metaphor for the reality, a closed file. The criminal process, in this model, is seen as a screening process in which each successive stage—prearrest investigation, arrest, postarrest investigation, preparation for trial, trial or entry of plea, conviction, disposition—involves a series of routinized operations whose success is gauged primarily by their tendency to pass the case along to a successful conclusion.

What is a successful conclusion? One that throws off at an early stage those cases in which it appears unlikely that the person apprehended is an offender and then secures, as expeditiously as possible, the conviction of the rest, with a minimum of occasions for challenge, let alone postaudit. By the application of administrative expertness, primarily that of the police and prosecutors, an early determination of the probability of innocence or guilt emerges. Those who are probably innocent are screened out. Those who are probably guilty are passed quickly through the remaining stages of the process. The key to the operation of the model regarding those who are not screened out is what I shall call a presumption of guilt. The concept requires some explanation, since it may appear startling to assert that what appears to be the precise converse of our generally accepted ideology of a presumption of innocence can be an essential element of a model that does correspond in some respects to the actual operation of the criminal process.

The presumption of guilt is what makes it possible for the system to deal efficiently with large numbers, as the Crime Control Model demands. The supposition is that the screening processes operated by police and prosecutors are reliable indicators of probable guilt. Once . . . a determination has been made that there is enough evidence of guilt to permit holding [the suspect] for further action, then all subsequent activity directed toward him is based on the view that he is probably guilty. . . .

It would be a mistake to think of the presumption of guilt as the opposite of the presumption of innocence that we are so used to thinking of as the polestar of the criminal process and that, as we shall see, occupies an important position in the Due Process Model. The presumption of innocence is not its opposite; it is irrelevant to the presumption of guilt; the two concepts are different rather than opposite ideas. The difference can perhaps be epitomized by an example. A murderer, for reasons best known to himself, chooses to shoot his victim in plain view of a large number of people. When the police arrive, he hands them his gun and says, "I did it and I'm glad." His account of what happened is corroborated by several eyewitnesses. He is placed under arrest and led off to jail. Under these circumstances, which may seem extreme but which in fact characterize with rough accuracy the evidentiary situation in a large proportion of criminal cases, it would be plainly absurd to maintain that more probably than not the suspect did not commit the killing. But that is not what the presumption of innocence means. It means that until there has been an adjudication of guilt by an authority legally competent to make such an adjudication, the suspect is to be treated, for reasons that have nothing whatever to do with the probable outcome of the case, as if his guilt is an open question.

The presumption of innocence is a direction to officials about how they are to proceed, not a prediction of outcome. The presumption of guilt, however, is purely a prediction of outcome. The presumption of innocence is, then, a direction to authorities to ignore the presumption of guilt in their treatment of the suspect. It tells them, in effect, to close their eyes to what will frequently seem to be factual probabilities. The reasons why it tells them this are among the animating presuppositions of the Due Process Model, and we will come to them shortly. It is enough to note at this point that the presumption of guilt is descriptive and factual; the presumption of innocence is normative and legal. . . .

The criminal process thus must put special weight on the quality of administrative fact-finding. It becomes important, then, to place as few restrictions as possible on the character of the administrative fact-finding processes and to limit restrictions to such as enhance reliability, excluding those designed for other purposes. As we shall see, this view of restrictions on administrative fact-finding is a consistent theme in the development of the Crime Control Model.

In this model, as I have suggested, the center of gravity of the process lies in the early, administrative fact-finding stages. The complementary proposition is that the subsequent stages are relatively unimportant and should be truncated as much as possible. This, too, produces tensions with presently dominant ideology. The pure Crime Control Model has very little use for many conspicuous features of the adjudicative process, and in real life works out a number of ingenious compromises with them. . . .The focal device, as we shall see, is the plea of guilty; through its use, adjudicative fact-finding is reduced to a minimum. It might be said of the Crime Control Model that, when reduced to its barest essentials and operating at its most successful pitch, it offers two possibilities: an administrative fact-finding process leading (1) to exoneration of the suspect, or (2) to the entry of a plea of guilty.

Due Process Values

If the Crime Control Model resembles an assembly line, the Due Process Model looks very much like an obstacle course. Each of its successive stages is designed to present formidable impediments to carrying the accused any further along in the process. Its ideology is not the converse of that underlying the Crime Control Model. It does not rest on the idea that it is not socially desirable to repress crime, although critics of its application have been known to claim so. . . .

The Due Process Model encounters its rival on the Crime Control Model's own ground in respect to the reliability of fact-finding processes. The Crime Control Model, as we have suggested, places heavy reliance on the ability of investigative and prosecutorial officers, acting in an informal setting in which their distinctive skills are given full sway, to elicit and reconstruct a tolerably accurate account of what actually took place in an alleged criminal event. The Due Process Model rejects this premise and substitutes for it a view of informal, nonadjudicative fact-finding that stresses the possibility of error. People are notoriously poor observers of disturbing events—the more emotion-arousing the context, the greater the possibility that recollection will be incorrect; confessions and admissions by persons in police custody may be induced by physical or psychological coercion so that the police end up hearing what the suspect thinks they want to hear rather than the truth; witnesses may be animated by bias or interest that no one would trouble to discover except one specially charged with protecting the interests of the accused (as the police are not). Considerations of this kind all lead to a rejection of informal fact-finding processes as definitive of factual guilt and to an insistence on formal, adjudicative, adversary fact-finding processes in which the factual case against the accused is publicly heard by an impartial tribunal and is evaluated only after the accused has had a full opportunity to discredit the case against him. Even then, the distrust of fact-finding processes that animates the Due Process Model is not dissipated. The possibilities of human error being what they are, further scrutiny is necessary, or at least must be available, in case facts have been overlooked or suppressed in the heat of battle. How far this subsequent scrutiny must be available is a hotly controverted issue today. In the pure Due Process Model the answer would be: at least as long as there is an allegation of factual error that has not received an adjudicative hearing in a fact-finding context. The demand for finality is thus very low in the Due Process Model. . . .

Even if the discussion is confined, for the moment, to the question of reliability, it is apparent that more is at stake than simply an evaluation of what kinds of fact-finding processes, alone or in combination, are likely to produce the most nearly reliable results. The stumbling block is this: How much reliability is compatible with efficiency? . . . The Crime Control Model is more optimistic about the improbability of error in a significant number of cases. . . . The Due Process Model insists on the prevention and elimination of mistakes to the extent possible; the Crime Control Model accepts the probability of mistakes up to the level at which they interfere with the goal of repressing crime, either because too many guilty people are escaping or, more subtly, because general awareness of the unreliability of the process leads to a decrease in the deterrent efficacy of the criminal law. . . . All of this the Due Process Model rejects. If efficiency demands shortcuts around reliability, then absolute efficiency must be rejected. The aim of the process is at least as much to protect the factually innocent as it is to convict the factually guilty. It is a little like quality control in industrial technology, tolerable deviation from standard varies with the importance of conformity to standard in the destined uses of the product. The Due Process Model resembles a factory that has to devote a substantial part of its input to quality control. This necessarily cuts down on quantitative output.

All of this is only the beginning of the ideological difference between the two models. The Due Process Model could disclaim any attempt to provide enhanced reliability for the fact-finding process and still produce a set of institutions and processes that would differ sharply from those demanded by the Crime Control Model. . . . These values can be expressed in, although not adequately described by, the concept of the primacy of the individual and the complementary concept of limitation on official power.

The combination of stigma and loss of liberty that is embodied in the end result of the criminal process is viewed as being the heaviest deprivation that government can inflict on the individual. Furthermore, the processes that culminate in these highly afflictive sanctions are seen as in themselves coercive, restricting, and demeaning. Power is always subject to abuse—sometimes subtle, other times, as in the criminal process, open and ugly. Precisely because of its potency in subjecting the individual to the coercive power of the state, the criminal process must, in this model, be subjected to controls that prevent it from operating with maximal efficiency. According to this ideology, maximal efficiency means maximal tyranny. And, although no one would assert that minimal efficiency means minimal tyranny, the proponents of the Due Process Model would accept with considerable equanimity a substantial diminution in the efficiency with which the criminal process operates in the interest of preventing official oppression of the individual.

The most modest-seeming but potentially far-reaching mechanism by which the Due Process Model implements these antiauthoritarian values is the doctrine of legal guilt. According to this doctrine, a person is not to be held guilty of a crime merely on a showing that in all probability, based upon reliable evidence, he did factually what he is said to have done. Instead, he is to be held guilty if and only if these factual determinations are made in procedurally regular fashion and by authorities acting within competences duly allocated to them. Furthermore, he is not to be held guilty, even though the factual determination is or might be adverse to him, if various rules designed to protect him and to safeguard the integrity of the process are not given effect. . . .

In this concept of legal guilt lies the explanation for the apparently quixotic presumption of innocence of which we spoke earlier. A man who, after police investigation, is charged with having committed a crime can hardly be said to be presumptively innocent, if what we mean is factual innocence. But if what we mean is that it has yet to be determined if any of the myriad legal doctrines that serve in one way or another the end of limiting official power through the observance of certain substantive and procedural regularities may be appropriately invoked to exculpate the accused man, it is apparent that as a matter of prediction it cannot be said with confidence that more probably than not he will be found guilty. . . .

The possibility of legal innocence is expanded enormously when the criminal process is viewed as the appropriate forum for correcting its own abuses. This notion may well account for a greater amount of the distance between the two models than any other. In theory the Crime Control Model can tolerate rules that forbid illegal arrest, unreasonable searches, coercive interrogations, and the like. What it cannot tolerate is the vindication of those rules in the criminal process itself through the exclusion of evidence illegally obtained or through the reversal of convictions in the criminal cases where the process has breached the rules laid down for its observance. And the Due Process Model, although it may in the first instance be addressed to the maintenance of reliable fact-finding techniques, comes eventually to incorporate prophylactic and deterrent rules that result in the release of the factually guilty even in cases in which blotting out the illegality would still leave an adjudicative fact-finding convinced of the accused person's guilt. Only by penalizing errant police and prosecutors within the criminal process itself can adequate pressure be maintained, so the argument runs, to induce conformity with the Due Process Model.

Another strand in the complex of attitudes underlying the Due Process Model is the idea—itself a shorthand statement for a complex of attitudes—of equality. This notion has only recently emerged as an explicit basis for pressing the demands of the Due Process Model, but it appears to represent, at least in its potential, a most powerful norm for influencing official conduct. Stated most starkly, the ideal of equality holds that "there can be no equal justice where the kind of trial a man gets depends on the amount of money he has." The factual predicate underlying this assertion is that there are gross inequalities in the financial means of criminal defendants as a class, that in an adversary system of criminal justice an effective defense is largely a function of the resources that can be mustered on behalf of the accused, and that the very large proportion of criminal defendants who are, operationally speaking, "indigent" will thus be denied an effective defense. . . .

The norms derived from the premise do not take the form of an insistence upon governmental responsibility to provide literally equal opportunities for all criminal defendants to challenge the process. Rather, they take as their point of departure the notion that the criminal process, initiated as it is by the government and containing as it does the likelihood of severe deprivations at the hands of government, imposes some kind of public obligation to ensure that financial inability does not destroy the capacity of an accused to assert what may be meritorious challenges to the processes being invoked against him. . . . The demands made by a norm of this kind are likely by their very nature to be quite sweeping. Although the norm's imperatives may be initially limited to determining whether in a particular case the accused was injured or prejudiced by his relative inability to make an appropriate challenge, the norm of equality very quickly moves to another level on which the demand is that the process in general be adapted to minimize discriminations rather than that a mere series of post hoc determinations of discriminations be made or makeable.

Perspective 2

The Politics of the Crime Debate

In early June, 1998 the decapitated body of a 49-year-old black man, James Byrd, Jr., was found near Jasper, Texas. According to investigators, Byrd was driven to a logging road, beaten unconscious and then tied to the back of a pickup truck and dragged down the rural road. This murder drew immediate national attention, not just because of the grisly manner in which it had been committed but because two of the three white men accused of the crime had links to the Aryan Nation, a white supremacist group.

Testifying before the Senate judiciary committee a month later, the daughter of James Byrd, Jr. said she didn't want others to feel her family's pain. "Nothing that Congress does will bring my father back," said Francis Renee Mullins. "But I hope that by being here today I can help prevent any other acts of violence of this nature from occurring in America." Joined by officials of the National Association for the Advancement of Colored People (NAACP), she urged Congress to pass a hate crimes law that would expand federal law to include attacks based on gender, disability, or sexual orientation.

This vignette illustrates several important aspects of debating crime. First, individual cases, no matter how isolated or atypical, can become the rallying cry for policy changes. James Byrd, Jr. provided a face for the crime debate. Instead of considering criminal justice policy in the abstract, policy makers are now confronted with an emotional shorthand that is very difficult to oppose.

Second, the testimony before Congress illustrates how interest groups increasingly attach their long-standing policy preferences to specific crimes and crime victims. In large measure, the comments of spokespersons for interest groups go a long way toward defining an issue. As a result, the facts behind the latest rape, murder, or drug bust becomes less relevant than the spin that interest groups can apply to the event.

Finally, this tragic event illustrates the extent to which debating crime now involves both liberals and conservatives. For several decades crime was an issue dominated by conservatives that worked in favor of the Republican Party. But now liberal groups use crime issues to further their interest and help the Democratic Party.

Crime Control Model	Due Process Model
National Center for Policy Analysis	American Civil Liberties Union (ACLU)
National Rifle Association (NRA)	Handgun Control, Inc.
Mothers Against Drunk Driving (MADD)	National Restaurant Association
Partnership for a Drug-Free America	National Organization for the Reform of Marijuana Laws (NORML)
Fraternal Order of Police (FOP)	National Association for the Advancement of Colored People (NAACP)
National District Attorneys Association	National Organization of Women (NOW)

Listed below are some of the interest groups most prominent in debating crime, summarized along the ideological categories discussed by Packer in the last article. The introduction to the book discussed how crime has been a political issue since the 1960s. Voters have been alarmed about crime. Elected officials and those who wish to become elected officials have promised anxious voters that they will do something about the crime problem. In turn, legislators, executives and judges have taken innumerable actions to combat crime. The following article by David Neubauer (Professor of Political Science at the University of New Orleans) rounds out the discussion of the politics of debating crime by focusing on an often-neglected topic—interest groups.

World Wide Web Exercises

1. Examine the web sites of four or more interest groups which are active in debating crime. Use the categories in the following article by Neubauer to describe the key features of these advocacy groups.

2. Examine the web sites of several organizations actively involved in debating crime. Overall are the views of these groups closer to the crime control model or the due process model of criminal justice? Four possible groups are:

National Center for Policy Analysis   http://www.ncpa.org/bothside/crime.html

American Civil Liberties Union (ACLU)   http://www.aclu.org/

National Rifle Association (NRA)   http://nra.org/

National Association for the Advancement of Colored People (NAACP)
http://www.naacp.org/

InfoTrac College Edition Exercises

1. Using the search term **hate crimes, causes of** locate one article on either side of the issue. To what extent does the debate over passage of hate crimes legislation parallel ideological divisions between the crime control model and the due process model of criminal justice? What types of groups favor hate crimes legislation and what types of groups oppose such laws?

2. Using the search term **hate crimes, analysis** locate two or more articles. To what extent do these articles offer independent analysis, or do they more closely resemble advocacy pieces?

Interest Groups and the Crime Debate

David W. Neubauer

- The head of MADD testifies before a Congressional committee about the need to toughen the penalties for drunk drivers.
- An ACLU lawyer argues a death penalty case before the US Supreme Court.
- NOW demands legislative hearings about high rates of domestic abuse in the military.
- An NRA employee mails out campaign contributions to U.S. Congressmen who oppose gun control.

These activities illustrate how interest groups are active in the crime debate. An interest group, as defined by political scientists, is an organization whose members share common objectives and who actively attempt to influence governmental power.

A Variety of Shared Interests

The United States has often been called a nation of joiners. Indeed, public opinion polls reveal that two out of three Americans belong to a least one group or association. These groups go by a variety of names including association, alliance, coalition, community group, civil leagues, concerned citizens, foundation, committee, and the like. Many of these groups are mainly social, with little if any impact on public policy. But a number of groups are active in shaping public policy, crime policy included.

Interest groups are formed on the basis of members who share something in common. What members of the groups have in common can be quite varied.

Economic Interest Groups

Many interest groups, particularly those most active in the nation's capital, exist to promote the economic wellbeing of businesses. For example, the National Chamber of Commerce most often speaks for big businesses. Because economic interests focus primarily on government regulation of the economy, they seldom become involved in the crime debate.

Trade associations are a specific type of economic interest group, and occasionally are involved in the crime debate. Trade associations represent specific industries—booksellers, pharmaceutical companies, and the like. They become active in the crime debate when a specific issue directly affects the economic wellbeing of their members. A recent case in point is the National Beer Wholesalers, which fought to defeat efforts in the U.S. Congress that would require states to lower the limits for drunk driving (Issue 5).

Unions

Another type of interest group exists to advance the social and economic wellbeing not of employers but of employees. Most typically they are called unions in the private sector and unions, associations or benevolent groups in the public sector.

The largest national groups participating in the crime debate are the Police Benevolent Association (PBA) and Fraternal Order of Police (FOP). Their activities, locally and nationally, are directed toward increasing the pay of their members, advocating greater safety protections, and increasing the number of workers.

Citizen Groups

The steady expansion of interest groups promoting the economic wellbeing of their members has prompted a countertrend—the formation of citizen groups. Citizen groups are among some of the most active in the crime debate.

The best known citizen groups are based on race and ethnicity. The National Association for the Advancement of Colored People (NAACP) was established in 1909, and is best known for its efforts to end segregation. But organizational interests also extend to areas of the criminal justice system perceived to be biased against racial minorities. Thus the NAACP has filed suits against the death penalty (Issue 10), urged Congress to pass hate crimes laws, and campaigned against excessive penalties for possession of crack cocaine.

Other citizen groups are gender based. Following the success of the NAACP in achieving civil rights legislation, the National Organization of Women (NOW) was formed in the early 1960s to promote gender equity. NOW and other gender-based groups are very active in crime debate issues that directly affect women—domestic violence (Issue 6) and gender fairness in courts, for example (Issue 12).

Public Interest Groups

Concerned that many interest groups were narrowly focused on a specific economic self-interest, other groups, commonly known as "public interest groups" have been formed. Instead of being based on economic self-interest, public interest groups seek to promote the "collective good" (Berry, 1997). Many public interest groups seek to protect the environment and advance the rights of consumers.

Some public interest groups focus on Constitutional rights. The best known is the American Civil Liberties Union (ACLU) founded in 1920. According to its Web site, the ACLU works toward "transforming the ideals contained in the Bill of Rights into living, breathing realities." Through the years it has represented a host of unpopular cases, often engendering public scorn in the process.

How Interest Groups Are Organized

Interest groups vary not only in terms of the interests they share, but also on the basis of how they are organized. Size of the organization and the nature of its funding affect how an interest group participates in the crime debate.

Size

Interest groups range in size from the huge to the virtually miniscule. A few are large indeed. The behemoth in terms of criminal justice policy is the National Rifle Association (NRA) that claims over 2.5 million members with a staff of 550. Also big is NOW with 250,000 claimed members (32 staff members).

Another large organization very active in debating crime is Mothers Against Drunk Driving (MADD) that counts almost 3,000,000 members (staff of 260). From its initial focus on punishing drunk drivers (Issue 5) and helping victims of drunk drivers, it has now greatly expanded its scope to become the nation's leading advocate for the rights of crime victims.

On the other side of the ledger are interest groups that are small indeed. A homeowner's association, for example, may claim only a handful of members and of course, no paid staff. In addition, after examining some the home pages of interest groups that use electronic media to make known their views, the observer is left with the nagging question—is this anything more than a one-person band?

Funding

How interest groups are organized is largely dictated by financing. Many are membership organizations that receive the bulk of their funding from dues voluntarily paid by their members. Dues, for example, constitute 85 percent of the budget of the NRA. In turn, membership organizations devote a considerable amount of time showing their members that their dues are well spent.

Alternatively, some interest groups are financed by funding from foundations. For example, the Police Foundation is a privately funded, independent research organization created in 1970 through Ford Foundation funding. Interest groups funded by foundations enjoy a freer hand in making their views known on any given topic because they do not have to worry that their position will offend dues-paying members who might cancel their membership in protest.

Interest Group Involvement in the Crime Debate

Interest group involvement in the crime debate varies considerably. One way to look at interest group involvement in the crime debate is in terms of single-interest, multi-issue, and episodic involvement.

Single-Issue Interest Groups

Single-issue interest groups target one, and only one, issue. Thus, they use all of their resources to exert influence in one area. By concentrating their efforts on a single target, they can often have considerable influence, if for no other reason than the fact that over the years they have developed considerable expertise in the area. The crime debate tends to involve numerous single-issue groups. The National Organization for the Reform of Marijuana Laws (NORML), for example, has only one goal—the legalization of marijuana (Issue 17).

One of the most prominent interest groups active in the crime debate is a single-issue interest group—the National Rifle Association (NRA). This citizen group was established in 1871 with the primary purpose to protect the right to bear arms. Secondary purposes include public safety and promoting shooting sports (Marion, 1995). The NRA is the dominant actor in the area of gun control, becoming particularly more strident in its pronouncements over the last decade (Issues 1 and 2).

Multi-Issue Interest Groups

Multi-issue interest groups count multiple issues on their agenda. As a result, they are constantly shifting resources (staff time primarily) across an array of areas.

Some multi-issue interest groups involved in the crime debate are broad indeed. The NAACP, for example, includes on its agenda virtually all governmental issues that directly or even indirectly affect African-Americans. Similarly, the ACLU is involved in criminal justice issues like the death penalty (Issue 10) and searches by police (Issue 4), as well as freedom of speech, freedom of the press, etc. Note that the agenda of multi-issue interest groups typically contains a mix of crime and non-crime policy issues.

Episodic Involvement

Finally, some interest groups are involved in the crime debate only episodically. That is to say, most of their activity is engaged in other directions. But on occasion particular interest groups can become, for a time at least, a major force in the debate, committing considerable resources. Consider congressional efforts in 1998 to force states to toughen drunk-driving laws (Issue 5). Perceiving that important economic interests were threatened, various trade groups representing distillers, brewers, and the restaurant industry mobilized in opposition.

How Interest Groups Try to Influence Crime Policy

One of the core purposes of interest groups is attempting to influence governmental policy. Some of the most prominent strategies interest groups use toward this end are publicity, advocacy, litigation, and election activity.

Publicity

A basic way that interest groups attempt to influence public policy is through publicity. Many, for example, regularly publish journals, write newsletters or issue special alerts. These publications are meant not only to keep their members informed about important issues but are also aimed at presenting the interest group's views to outsiders. For example, the International Association of Chiefs of Police publishes *Police Chief* and the American Bar Association (ABA) publishes the *ABA Journal.*

In recent years the publicity efforts of interest groups has been made considerably easier by the advent of the Internet. Groups of all manner and persuasion now have home pages that provide their perspective on crime issues. Viewing home pages as an extension of interest groups' publicity campaigns helps the viewer understand the uneven nature of Internet information. In particular, Web sites have become an easy way for politically unpopular causes to make their views known. Allegations of police brutality are a case in point (Issue 3). Numerous national, state and local web pages are devoted to documenting and condemning police brutality. But to my knowledge not a single organization has come forward and directly condoned this practice.

Advocacy

Beyond merely keeping their members informed about current issues, interest groups also regularly engage in advocacy, trying to persuade others to adopt their perspective. Thus, interest groups will hold press conferences to draw attention to a problem. Just as importantly, when an event occurs their spokespersons are routinely quoted in the press, expressing their organization's "slant" on a given issue (spin control, in modern parlance). By commenting in this way, interest groups attempt to define issues in a manner favorable to the group.

One specific type of advocacy is lobbying, which is the attempt to influence the passage or defeat of legislation. Lobbying on broad pieces of legislation can be extensive. For example, 218 individuals and interest groups provided testimony on proposals to reform the federal criminal code. Most groups appeared only once or twice, but twelve groups testified three or more times (Melone and Slagter, 1983).

Litigation

A third strategy that interest groups employ in efforts to influence criminal justice policy is litigation. On a regular basis, interest groups go to court to gain victories before judges that they lost before legislatures or executives. Alternatively, interest groups find themselves in court defending hard fought battles won in the legislative or executive arenas. Here are but three examples:

- The National Rifle Association (NRA) challenged the National Instant Check system required by federal law before buying a gun (Issue 2).

- The National Association for the Advancement of Colored People (NAACP) financed cases like *Gregg v. Georgia* opposing the death penalty (Issue 10).

- The American Civil Liberties Union (ACLU) led successful efforts to have the Supreme Court declare unconstitutional the federal law outlawing pornography on the Internet (Issue 18).

One litigation strategy used by interest groups is direct sponsorship of cases. Beginning at the trial stage, interest groups will recruit litigants and provide lawyers in an effort to shape the case for a favorable legal victory in high courts. Direct sponsorship of litigation often involves the filing of a class action lawsuit, which is a lawsuit brought by one person or group on behalf of all persons similarly situated. For example, a lawsuit arguing that conditions in prison violate the Eighth Amendment would seek legal relief not just for the individual prisoner(s) filing the suit, but for all prisoners at that prison.

Another litigation strategy used by interest groups is the filing of an *amicus curiae* (friend of the court) brief. A group that is not a direct party to a lawsuit may be allowed to make its views known to the court by filing an amicus curiae brief. By way of illustration, the ACLU filed an amicus brief in *Mapp v. Ohio,* urging the Court to hold that the exclusionary rule should be made mandatory on the states, a position the Court indeed adopted (Issue 4).

Election Activities

One of the most direct ways that interest groups attempt to influence governmental policy is through election activities. Most immediately, interest groups encourage their members to vote for candidates who are supportive of their position; alternatively, interest groups actively seek the defeat of candidates who oppose their position.

How successful interest groups are in affecting elections is partly the product of size. Large organizations can potentially turn out more people to the polls than smaller ones. Perhaps the NRA is the best case in point, because it can turn out tens of thousands of angry voters across the nation literally overnight. But numbers alone are not necessarily the key. A second factor is intensity. Interest group leaders often threaten to turn out large number of voters come election day but are seldom successful because they can not find a way to motivate their constituents. Overall, a broad, indifferent majority has less election day clout than a narrow, intense minority. The clearest example is gun control: although a majority of citizens support gun control an intense minority represented by the NRA has stymied most efforts.

Beyond seeking to mobilize their members, interest groups can attempt to influence election outcomes through monetary contributions. Indeed, many interest groups have formed Political Action Committees (PACs), which can legally contribute money to candidates running for office. In other political areas (particularly governmental regulation of business) campaign contributions are a major issue. On many key criminal justice issues, though, campaign contributions play only a minor role. But on occasion, contributions to candidates supportive of the position of the interest group are part of the political equation. The NRA, for example, handed out millions in campaign contributions during the 1994 election to candidates opposing gun control. Besides the issue of gun control, the only areas where large sums of money are potentially available involve government regulation of "sin" (alcohol, gambling, and pornography) (Fairchild, 1981). For example, the National Beer Wholesalers, the National Restaurant Association, and the Wine and Spirits Wholesalers and other alcohol beverage organizations contributed over a million dollars to various political organizations and candidates in an attempt to defeat the 1998 legislative proposal to force states to reduce BAC to .08, the blood alcohol content that defines drunk driving.

Debating the Role of Interest Groups

Even though interest groups have become an integral part of American political life, average citizens remain skeptical. Average citizens and some political analysts express concern that decisions made by government are biased in favor of special interests at the expense of the interests of the general public. The undue influence of interest groups is typically mentioned as the cause. Thus, terms like "narrow" and "special" denote these groups perceived to be opposed to the public good. Organized interest groups respond, on the other hand, that they do represent the general interest.

In this vein, interest groups are sometimes referred to as "special interests." Political actors, though, typically use this phrase to refer to those interest groups that disagree with them and do not support their programs. Conversely, pubic interest groups that claim to speak for the "entire public" in reality address issues of concern to only some segments of the public.

It is useful, therefore, to view politics as involving conflict among competing groups with different ideas of what constitutes the general interest or public good. Consider the debate over gun control. Some believe that the public interest is best served by gun control, a position that draws angry response from groups like the NRA that vehemently state that gun control will not reduce crime.

Conclusion

One important consequence of interest group involvement in the crime debate is the fragmentation of policy. Topics are debated in isolation from one another. Pressures to crack down on drunk drivers, substance abusers, wife beaters, and repeat offenders proceed independent from one another. These single-issue interest groups proceed on the assumption that theirs is the *only* issue facing the criminal justice system. All assume that government resources are infinite, and if the police would just crack down, the courts sentence more severely and jailers do the same, their problem will go away. Alas, it is very difficult to interject into this interest group debate dialogue to address real-world limitations. For example, groups that call for the jailing of more drunk drivers (or drug addicts or wife beaters) seem not to care that by doing so there will be fewer prison cells for drug addicts or wife beaters.

Another consequence of interest group activity in the crime debate is the shift in attention away from local communities (where crimes are committed) to the corridors of Washington, D. C., where national policy is made. Interest groups concentrate on influencing national policy because it shows their members that they are doing something for them. Even more importantly, it is easier to show victories. Given limited resources, interest groups understandably prefer to try to achieve at least a partial victory at the national level rather than diluting resources by fighting battles in the fifty state capitals.

Perspective 3

The Sociology of
the Crime Debate

In August, 1983, Judy Johnson complained to the police that her son had been sexually molested by Ray Buckey, who worked at the McMartin preschool owned by his wife and mother-in-law. Although there was no physical evidence or confirmation from other children at the school, Ray was arrested but because of lack of evidence the DA decided to not prosecute.

The chief of the Manhattan Beach Police then created a local panic by circulating a "strictly confidential" letter to parents of present or past McMartin students. The letter specified that Ray might have forced the children to engage in "oral sex, fondling of genitals, buttocks or chest area, and sodomy." The parents were urged to question their children, seeking confirmation. A local TV station soon reported that the preschool might be linked to child pornography rings and various sex industries in nearby Los Angeles.

In March, 1984, 208 counts of child abuse involving forty children were filed against Ray Buckey and six other adults associated with the school. Over the next six years a series of trials resulted in not guilty verdicts against most defendants, and hung verdicts for others. In 1990 the prosecutor decided to drop all remaining charges, finally ending the longest U.S. criminal trial in history. It was also the most expensive; the state spent $15 million, although no convictions were obtained.

Were the concerns of the parents and some law enforcement officials justified? Or did citizens and criminal justice officials alike overreact? Asking these questions about the McMartin Preschool case highlights the importance of societal reactions to crime. In studying crime, sociologists and criminologists examine not only crime and criminals, but also try to understand how society reacts to these events.

In this tradition, the concept of moral panic is one of the more useful concepts to have emerged in recent years. A moral panic is characterized by a wave of public concern, anxiety, and fervor about something perceived as a threat to society. The distinguishing factors are a level of interest totally out of proportion to the real importance of the subject, some individuals building personal careers from the pursuit and magnification of the issue, and the replacement of reasoned debate with scapegoating and hysteria.

Past examples of moral panics include the witch-hunts in Europe during the Renaissance and the Salem witch-hunts in Salem, Massachusetts, during the colonial period. More recently, scholars have used the term "moral panic" to analyze public concerns about Satanic rituals, missing children, date rape, drugs and cyberporn (Wilkins, 1997).

The McMartin Preschool case has likewise been described as a moral panic. The prosecution was inspired not by actual evidence but by worries about what happens in day care, out of parents' view. The conflict was over wanting to maintain parental control while having to leave the child with strangers because of work (de Young, 1997).

In the following article, Erich Goode and Nachman Ben-Yehuda offer the provocative argument that the contemporary war on drugs can be at least partially understood as a moral panic.

World Wide Web Exercises

1. Using the search term **McMartin preschool** locate further information about this case. Were the reactions to this case warranted or unwarranted? Would the reactions be similar or different today?

InfoTrac College Edition Exercises

1. Using the search term **moral panic** find two or more articles that use this concept to analyze a crime topic other than drugs. To what extent are the arguments similar to those raised in the article by Goode and Ben-Yehuda? In what ways do the arguments differ?

2. Using the search term **McMartin preschool** locate and read two or more articles that analyze this case. Do these articles support or refute arguments that the case represented a moral panic?

The American Drug Panic of the 1980s

Erich Goode and Nachman Ben-Yehuda

Over the decades of the twentieth century, drug use has gone through cycles of intense public awareness and concern, and relative indifference. For some of these decades, reformers, the public, the media, or legislators focus on a specific drug, which stands in for or represents the drug problem generally. The late 1980s witnessed a drug "panic," "crisis," or "scare." Public concern about drug use, although it had been building throughout the 1980s, fairly *exploded* late in 1985 and early in 1986. And the drug that was the special target of public concern was cocaine, more specifically, crack, a cocaine derivative. Drug use generally came to be seen as a—some say *the*—social problem of the decade. Drug use, abuse, and misuse emerged into the limelight as perhaps never before. . . .

In many ways, the drug panic of the late 1980s is interesting because it was so unexpected. The 1970s represented something of a high water mark in both the use and the pubic acceptance and tolerance of illegal drugs. . . .

The Decade of the 1980s: Measures of Public Concern

. . . Beginning roughly in the first year of the decade of the 1980s, public tolerance of the use of illegal drug use declined, belief that the use of illegal drugs is harmful increased, belief that use, pos-

session, and sale of the currently illegal drugs should be decriminalized or legalized declined, and the use of these illegal drugs declined.

Periodically, the Gallup poll asks a sample of Americans the question, "What do you think is the most important problem facing this country today?" Drug abuse declined among the most important problems named by the public in Gallup polls between the early 1970s . . . and the late 1970s . . . , a period, ironically . . . when drug use among the American public was at an all-time high. . . . Between 1979 and 1984, drug use and abuse did not appear at all in the Gallup polls among the most often mentioned problems facing the country, indicating a relatively and consistently low level of concern about the issue.

This changed in the mid 1980s. In . . . 1985, the proportion of those polled mentioning drug abuse as the nation's number one problem fluctuated from 2 to 6 to 3 percent. In July 1986, this figure increased to 8 percent, which placed it fourth among major American social problems. . . . The figure continued to grow through nearly the remainder of the 1980s until, in September 1989, a whopping 64 percent of the respondents in the *New York Times*/CBS News poll said that drug abuse represented the most important problem facing the country; this response is one of the most intense preoccupations by the American public on any issue in polling history. The concern at that time had been fueled by a barrage of network news programs on drug abuse and a major speech by President George Bush declaring a "war on drugs" . . . In short, by the late 1980s, drug abuse had attained a "celebrity" status. . . .

Source: *Moral Panics: The Social Construction of Deviance* by Erich Goode and Nachman Ben-Yehuda. Blackwell. ©1994 by the authors.

The 64 percent figure for September 1989 proved to be the apex of public concern about drugs; it is unlikely that a figure of such magnitude will be achieved for drug abuse again. After that, said one media expert, intense public concern simply "went away." . . .

Why? There is something of a social problems marketplace . . . in which different issues must compete for public attention and concern; there is something of a "carrying capacity" or saturation point of public attention: Only so many issues can rank near the top, and, obviously, only one can be number one. Late in 1989 and into the early 1990s, two additional problems overshadowed the drug issue in the public consciousness—the economic recession and the crisis and war in the Persian Gulf. By the early 1990s, "other issues [aside from drugs] came in. The media stopped covering it [the drug story], and the public stopped thinking about it as much" (Oreskes, 1990). Just as social problems can be constructed, they can also be "deconstructed"! . . .

Why the Drug Panic?

The question is, Why? What generated such intense public concern about drug abuse between 1986 and 1989? Did this issue emerge as a consequence of objective factors—that is, did changes take place late in 1985 or early in 1986 to make drug use even more threatening, dangerous, or damaging than it had been prior to that period? Had even more dangerous drugs emerged and come to be used more frequently in the mid to late 1980s than was true in the late 1970s and early 1980s? Were they used via more damaging and dangerous methods or routes of administration? Were more people dying during the "panic" period than before and after?

Or, on the other hand, was this concern solely a consequence of subjective factors—an illusory issue, perhaps, generated by politicians to get elected in the 1986 campaigns? If so, why in 1986, but not in 1984 or 1982? . . .

Kerr (1986) falls just short of declaring the intense concern over drug abuse which had begun building throughout the first half of the 1980s, and fairly exploded in 1986, "all hype." . . .

Levine and Reinarman (1987, 1988) take the argument a step further and claim that in the late 1980s, America was "in the throes of a drug scare . . . [that] takes a kernel of truth and distorts and exaggerates the facts for political, bureaucratic, or financial purposes. During a drug scare all kinds of social problems are blamed on the use of one chemical substance or another—problems which have little to do with the drug" (1987). Citing the surveys conducted by the National Institute on Drug Abuse (NIDA), which show tens of millions of Americans to have used illegal drugs once or more, they argue that the "vast majority" of individuals who try drugs "do not become addicts—they do not end up in emergency rooms, or on the streets selling their mother's TV for a fix." They conclude that there are many problems that are objectively far more important than the illegal use of drugs. The "just say no" administration, Levine and Reinarman argue, "has just said no to virtually every social program aimed at creating alternatives for inner city youth." The drug scares of the twentieth century, they conclude, "do not aid public health; they may actually hurt it, and they give a very distorted sense of priorities and problems. This drug scare, like the others before it, is drug-abuse abuse" . . .

Again, the question is, Why? Why a scare about a virtually nonexistent threat—or, more precisely, why a scare about a threat whose current and potential damage is less than other, far more serious, conditions? And, presumably, which causes significantly fewer deaths than it did a decade earlier, when drug use was at a strikingly higher level?

The "latest drug scare," Levine and Reinarman say, "has been concocted by the press, politicians, and moral entrepreneurs to serve other agendas"; it is, "quite simply, scapegoating" (Levine and Reinarman, 1988). It appeals to "racism, bureaucratic self-interest, economics, and mongering by the media." In addition, "the issue of illicit drug use . . . focuses attention away from structural ills like economic inequality, injustice, and lack of meaningful roles for young people. A crusade against drug use allows conservative politicians to be law-and-order minded; it also permits them to give the appearance of caring about social ills without committing them to do or spend very much to help people." . . .

Some additional factors that have been cited by others as contributing to the construction of drug abuse as the major social problem in the mid to late 1980s include:

The Explosion of Crack Cocaine Use

At the beginning of 1985, crack, a potent crystalline form of cocaine, was practically an unknown—and unused—drug in the United States. By late 1985, the drug was beginning to be used extensively in urban areas, and the press accorded prominent coverage to it. Its previous obscurity, the seeming suddenness of its widespread use—although it had been used on a smaller scale since the early 1980s—and the degree to which it caught on in some neighborhoods made the crack story newsworthy and gave the public the impression that a major drug crisis had erupted practically overnight. Actually, the drug was and is used in large numbers only in some urban areas and, in those, only in certain neighborhoods. The 1986 national high school senior study asked a question about crack cocaine for the first time; about 4 percent in the study said that they had used the drug at least once. Thus, it was not simply the greater danger that new patterns of crack used posed but the drama of a new, previously almost unknown, and potentially destructive, drug type on the drug abuse stage that helped generate the panic.

The Death of Athletes from Cocaine Abuse

In June 1986, barely a week apart, two popular young athletes died of a cocaine overdose—on June 19, University of Maryland basketball forward Len Bias, and on June 27, Cleveland Browns defensive back Don Rogers. Bias's death was felt to be especially devastating, to some degree, because of the proximity of Maryland's campus to the nation's capital. Said one member of the House of Representatives, "Congress is predominantly male and very sports-minded." With Bias's death, he said, "you were hit with a devastating blow" (Kerr, 1986). More generally, a nation, such as the United States, that glorifies sports figures is one which will tend to treat the death of a famous athlete as not only a catastrophe, but will see the source of that athlete's death as more *common* and *representative* than it actually is.

The Role of the Media

The drug-related events or developments mentioned above, which would have received a great deal of media attention in any case, were even more nationally prominent because they occurred in close proximity to major media centers—Bias's death in the Washington area, and the emergence of crack cocaine use specifically in neighborhoods in New York City and Los Angeles, "only blocks from the offices of major national news organizations" (Kerr, 1986).

The General Political Climate

Although not specific only to the 1986–9 period, one factor that helped to highlight the drug issue as a major social problem was the generally conservative political climate of the 1980s. Whether a cause or a consequence of this climate, the election of Ronald Reagan as President of the United States in 1980 set the tone for much of what was to follow throughout the decade, especially in the areas of sex, family, abortion, pornography, homosexuality, civil rights and civil liberties, and, of course, drugs . . . . In short, "it was in this general setting of conservativism that drugs could emerge as the leading social problem" facing the country in the 1980s.

The 1986 Congressional Election

The 1986 elections must be counted as a source of heightened concern about the drug issue, and the 1988 election, too, must be mentioned as a factor stirring up end-of-the-decade concerns as well. There is something of a dialectic or give-and-take relationship between public concern and attention by politicians to a given issue. On the one hand, we see a "bandwagon" effect here: politicians sense that public concern about and interest in a given topic are growing and they exploit this—in other words, "Congress smells an issue . . . When the media started talking about it, it lit a fire . . . Senators, once they started talking, realized they were all hearing similar things from their local officials" (Kerr, 1986). On the other hand, while politicians took advantage of an issue that was in the incipient problem stage, once they got on the bandwagon, public concern escalated even further. We need not accuse politicians of being scheming Machiavellians on the drug issue. It is their job to get elected, and they try to do it the best way they know how. Moreover, they would argue, it is their job to address the needs and concerns of their constituencies; dealing with the drug issue, or seeming to—that is, only in speeches, is one way of doing just that. This also does not mean that the drug crisis was "fabricated," "engineered," or "orchestrated" by politicians who stirred up an issue in the face of public indifference. The public is not that gullible, and politicians cannot usually create feverish concern where none previously existed simply by making speeches. Many political campaigns have fallen flat, failing completely to capture the public imagination—witness the stress on the "family values" theme, which was unsuccessfully touted by the 1992 election campaign of President Bush. In contrast, the drug issue tapped genuine widespread (though, in large part, erroneously based) concerns on the part of the American public, even though they were helped along by politicians who "smelled an issue."

The Role of Prominent Spokespersons

Soon after Ronald Reagan took office in 1981, his wife, Nancy Reagan, began making speeches stressing the anti-drug theme. It was from her office as First Lady that the "Just say no" slogan emerged. Some observers (Beck, 1981) have suggested that Mrs. Reagan chose the issue in part out of public relations considerations. Initially, she had been portrayed by the media as a "cold and insensitive person, whose chief concern seemed to be her wardrobe." Her choice of the drug issue could very well have been made to boost her public image, to suggest that she was a compassionate

and concerned human being. Regardless of her initial motivation, her campaign, while, again, little more than words, bore fruit some five years after it was launched. The drug crisis of the late 1980s has to be set in the context of Mrs. Reagan's immensely publicized campaign. It was she who took the first steps toward galvanizing public concern and media attention. While other spokespersons, before and since, have "spoken out against drugs," she, possibly more than any single individual, is responsible for the success of the drug panic.

Is the Objectivist Perspective Irrelevant?

As we see, the drug panic was constructed for a variety of reasons; a number of these reasons are subjective factors and have little, if anything, to do with the concrete damage or harm inflicted on the society by the use of illegal psychoactive substances. In this sense . . . the 1986–9 outbreak of concern over drugs was a moral panic. On the other hand, we should not dismiss the objective dimension as completely irrelevant. Simply because a problem or crisis is constructed does not mean that it is imaginary. Because the media, politicians, and the public do not necessarily react to the objective features of a particular condition does not indicate or imply that they do not exist. . . . As measured by the human toll, drug use was *not* the most serious condition facing the country in the late 1980s. And recreational illegal drug use was actually declining at the precise period when public hysteria reached an all-time high. . . . At the same time, while *occasional recreational* drug use declined throughout the 1980s, heavy, frequent, chronic use—specifically of powdered and crack cocaine—during this period actually increased. And it is among heavy users that major medical and social damage is most likely to occur, such as lethal and nonlethal overdoses and violent crime.

While drug use may not be the number one problem in American society by any conceivable measure—nor, possibly, among the top ten problems—its contribution to the devastation of some neighborhoods and communities, and victimizing behavior of users and dealers cannot be denied. . . .

1986–1989: A Moral Panic over Drug Abuse?

Was the concern generated by illegal drug use, especially crack, in the United States in the late 1980s a moral panic? Our answer to that question has to be a qualified yes. In the sense that an increase in this concern actually was accompanied by an increase in measurable harm (caused in part by an increase in heavy, chronic use), this concern cannot be referred to as a panic. On the other hand, crusaders and activists did not make a sober or systematic assessment of the facts; the concern over drugs in the late 1980s *was* a panic in the sense that claims-makers made use of arguments and facts that *were, in fact,* in excess of the available facts. (An example: the famous "This is your brain. This is your brain on drugs. Any questions?" ad campaign.) The fact that overdoses increased during this period, while relevant to the *drama* of the drug panic, was irrelevant to *whether or not* the concern constituted a moral panic, since the data to demonstrate that fact were ignored by major claims-makers in this drama. Moreover, this increase did not cause the concern—indeed, had nothing to do with it—because, again, key actors seemed to be unaware of their existence (or relevance to their arguments). They were not reacting to simple matters of body count and overdoses but to the usual array of constructionist factors discussed earlier—the novelty of crack, its seeming powers of enslavement, the overdoses of a few prominent athletes, the role of prominent moral entrepreneurs, and so on. Thus, the fact that some measures of concrete harm rose in concert does not deny the existence of a moral panic over drugs in the United States in the late 1980s. Indeed, a close inspection of its dynamics emphasizes its panic-like quality. . . .

In addition—and this is a matter for debate, not one of clearly verified fact—it is entirely possible that both a law enforcement crackdown and the crisis mentality that such concern generates may actually have contributed to the seriousness of the problem, rather than alleviated it.

Part II

Debating Crime and Guns

- *New Orleans mayor Marc Morial files suit against the handgun industry, seeking millions of dollars in damages to reimburse hospital and police costs due to gun related violence (Suro, 1998).*

- *A woman stalked by her husband's ex-girlfriend stands in line at a Virginia police station seeking a permit for carrying a concealed weapon (Gest, 1995).*

- *Eleven-year-old Andrew Golden steals his grandfather's deer rifle and kills five people and wounds ten others at a Jonesboro, Arkansas, school.*

- *In a rite of passage, a father gives his son a .22 rifle for his thirteenth birthday (Epstein and Zaneski, 1998).*

- *Following a drug deal gone bad, the police arrest a local drug dealer who admits he bought the murder weapon on the illegal market.*

These are some of the multiple faces and events that fuel the longstanding and increasingly acrimonious gun debate. In turn, these multiple realities explain why the nation's efforts to deal with the correlation between guns and crime are both limited and contradictory.

The most recent development in the gun-control debate is lawsuits brought by an increasing number of big cities targeting the manufacturers of handguns. These legal actions have been inspired by the success of anti-tobacco lawsuits, under which forty plus states have received tens of millions of dollars in out-of-court settlements from tobacco manufacturers to cover the medical costs of treating diseases related to smoking. It is too early to tell whether the cities bringing these lawsuits will ultimately receive any money, but along the way big cities hope to force gun makers to put safety devices on their products. Thus, whether successful or not, gun lawsuits have clearly ratcheted up the debate.

This section considers two aspects of the gun debate. The first focuses on an individual's constitutional right to bear arms. The second examines gun control itself.

World Wide Web Resources

Web Guides

http://dir.yahoo.com/Society_and_Culture/Firearms/Firearms_Policy/Gun_Control/

Searching the Web

gun control; right to bear arms

Useful URLs

American Firearms Industry: World's largest and oldest professional firearms retailers' association.   http://www.amfire.com/

Bureau of Justice Statistics: "Firearms and Crime Statistics"
http://www.ojp. usdog.gov.bjs/guns.htm

Handgun Control, Inc. and The Center to Prevent Handgun Violence: Pressing for more rational, commonsense gun laws.   http://www.handguncontrol.org/

Gun Owners of America: Bills itself as the only no-compromise gun lobby in D.C.
http://www.gunowners.org/

National Rifle Association of America (NRA): Fighting for your right to keep and bear arms.   http://nra.org/

Potomac Institute: "It's not about guns; it's about citizenship."
http://www.potomac-inc.org/index.html

Second Amendment Committee: Protesting the abolishment of our states, the disarming of the nation and its citizens, plans to bring foreign soldiers to our nation, and the increase in socialism.   http://www.libertygunrights.com/

U.S. Department of Treasury: Bureau of Alcohol, Tobacco, and Firearms—Firearms programs.   http://www.atf.treas.gov/core/firearms/firearms.htm

Violence Policy Center: National educational foundation working to reduce firearms violence in America.   http://www.vpc.org/

Today's Headlines

http://fullcoverage.yahoo.com/Full_Coverage/US/Gun_Control_Debate/

http://community.cnn.com/cgi-bin/WebX?13@@.ee7b396

Fun Sites

Gun Laws in the U.S.: Interactive map of gun laws in various states.
http://www.cnn.com/SPECIALS/1998/schools/gun.control/

Jews for the Preservation of Firearms Ownership   www.jpfo.org

Online Gun Show   http://www.onlinegunshow.com/

World Wide Web Exercises

1. Summarize the basic statistical information on guns and crime. What types of statistics are gun-control advocates most likely to cite? What types of statistics are gun-control opponents most likely to cite? The major sources of statistics collected by the government are:

   Bureau of Justice Statistics: "Firearms and Crime Statistics"
   http://www.ojp.usdog.gov.bjs/guns.htm

   Bureau of Alcohol, Tobacco, and Firearms—Firearms Programs:
   http://www.atf.treas.gov/core/firearms/firearms.htm

2. Using the search term **gun lawsuits,** search using excite.com, altavista.com, or a similar search engine. What is the current status of lawsuits against gun manufacturers?

InfoTrac College Edition Resources/Exercises

Basic Searches

gun control, right to bear arms, second amendment

1. Using the search term **gun lawsuits,** find one article that supports lawsuits against gun manufacturers and one that opposes such legal action. Summarize the major arguments on either side.

Issue 1

Does the Constitution Create a Right of Individuals to Bear Arms?

- *A woman stalked by her husband's ex-girlfriend stands in line at a Virginia police station seeking a permit for carrying a concealed weapon (Gest, 1995).*

- *In a rite of passage, a father gives his son a .22 rifle for his thirteenth birthday (Epstein and Zaneski, 1998).*

These two vignettes illustrate why few topics stir as much passionate debate as gun control. The touchstone of the longstanding gun debate hinges on the interpretation of the Second Amendment, which reads:

> A well regulated Militia being necessary to the security of a free State, the right of the people to keep and bear Arms shall not be infringed.

In the public debate surrounding gun control, the "right to bear arms" is constantly invoked, especially by gun-control opponents. It is ironic that in the debate over gun control, the U.S. Constitution is very salient while the U.S. Supreme Court has been very silent. The Court last addressed the issue in 1939 and shows no inclination to revisit the matter. The Court, though, has considered other legal dimensions of federal gun control and has, by and large, been unsympathetic to governmental efforts to regulate guns.

The debate over the interpretation of the Second Amendment illustrates an important feature of the crime debate. Notions of rights under the Constitution operate on two distinct levels. One centers on rights as interpreted by courts. The other involves rights as understood by individuals. In the realm of the Second Amendment there is a clear disjuncture. No matter what lawyers and others might say about the Second Amendment, individuals persist in believing that the Second amendment bestows on individuals the right to bear arms. And since these citizens are also voters, candidates for public office promise to support the right to keep and bear arms.

Pro	Con
Opponents of gun control stress that the Second Amendment applies to individuals. Thus when the amendment says "the right of the people" it means just that, and is not limited to the militia.	Advocates of gun control view the Second Amendment as applying not to individuals but the militia. In the modern context, militia is best viewed as the National Guard.
Statements from the National Rifle Association repeatedly stress that owning a gun or rifle is a constitutionally protected right.	Merely repeating a proposition does not mean that the courts agree.

The first article, "Bending Second Amendment . . . ," typifies the fiery rhetoric of gun-control opponents. The author, Wayne LaPierre, Jr. (executive vice president of the National Rifle Association) articulates why the Second Amendment includes individuals.

Often lost in the often nasty rhetoric of the gun debate is the Court's decision in *U.S. v. Miller,* holding that the Second Amendment applies not to individuals, but to the militia.

World Wide Web Exercises

1. Examine Web pages that are directly related to the right to bear arms. Are there more Web sites on the pro side or the con side? To what extent are arguments about the right to carry concealed weapons similar to or different from arguments about possessing hunting rifles, etc.? Here is one useful Web address: http://dir.yahoo.com/Society_and_Culture/Firearms/Firearms_Policy/Gun_Rights/

2. Would the U.S. Supreme Court interpret the Second Amendment today the way it did in *U.S. v. Miller*? Find *Law Review* (or equivalent) articles that discuss this point. A useful starting point is the Second Amendment Law Library: http://www.2ndLawLib.org/

InfoTrac College Edition Exercises

1. Using the search term **gun rights** locate two additional articles that adopt different viewpoints about interpreting the Second Amendment. Do these articles offer similar viewpoints or different ones from those in the book?

2. Using the search term **gun rights** locate additional articles that analyze the right to bear arms. Do these analysis pieces support or refute one side? Ultimately, is this issue a legal one or a political one?

Bending Second Amendment Will Put Clinton Under the Gun

Wayne R. LaPierre, Jr.

If you have an extra copy of the Bill of Rights, you may want to send it to the White House. Bill Clinton either hasn't read it or he just doesn't get it!

This week, Clinton is taking another outrageous step in banning an entire class of firearms, ordering a halt of the importation of legal, self-loading (semiautomatic) firearms. Make no mistake: The banning of self-loading firearms by country of origin does not camouflage the fact that the real agenda of the Clinton administration is to ban self-loading firearms in general.

And this president will use every means available to deny Americans the right of firearms ownership. "We are taking the law and bending it as far as we can to capture the whole new class of guns," White House official Jose Cerda boasted last week.

This time, the White House is bending the law to ban firearms that the Clintonists themselves admit are legal and not banned under Clinton's own 1994 ban on self-loading firearms.

Why does the president want to ban these firearms that function exactly like those another president—Teddy Roosevelt—used for hunting? Because Clinton just doesn't like the way some firearms look. He would have you believe that polyurethane stocks are evil, and that lug nuts on gun barrels are a menace to society. But the truth is a Remington 7400 semiautomatic deer rifle shoots the same way, whether it has a plastic stock or one made of oak. And the same principle applies to the semiautomatic firearms the president wants to ban.

The logical next step for Clinton is to ban that Remington. And to ban the Benelli semiautomatic shotgun he hunted with last year. They all function the same. They all shoot the same. The only difference is in their looks, and it seems that Clinton, Sen. Dianne Feinstein of California and Rep. Charles Schumer of New York, all Democrats, and the rest of the gun-banners have not seen a firearm they don't want to ban. It's just a matter of time before they find more firearms to "capture" under another manufactured guise.

The tragic irony is that none of this has anything to do with crime. According to FBI Uniform Crime Reports covering the last decade, only about three percent of homicides involve a rifle of any kind—let alone a self-loading model. In fact, again according to the FBI, more people are killed each year by "fists and feet" than by so-called "assault weapons." Obviously, banning self-loading firearms will have no impact on violent crime—especially the 71 percent of violent crime that doesn't involve firearms at all.

What actually reduces crime is simple: prosecution and incarceration. Law-enforcement experts tell us that about 70 percent of violent crime is committed by about seven percent of repeat, violent offenders. These habitual criminals walk in and out of a revolving-door criminal-justice system and commit the overwhelming majority of violence in our nation. Yet, the administration that "bends the law" to "capture a whole new class of guns" is the same administration that has decreased federal prosecutions of gun crimes by 33 percent during the Clinton term. And it is this same Clinton administration that has jailed just three people in four years under their much-heralded Brady gun-control law.

To achieve real crime reduction, Clinton should start jailing criminals and leave law-abiding American gun owners alone. But that's not going to happen.

If a self-loading firearm doesn't appear "sporting" enough (whatever that means), the president wants it banned. And if it looks okay today, there is no guarantee it won't be the next target tomorrow. The president's action this week is a clear, decisive step toward banning all self-loading firearms. Or in the words of Clinton's aide, it is an effort to "capture a whole new class of guns."

The nearly three million members of the National Rifle Association and the more than 65 million gun owners nationwide all know something the president seems to have forgotten. That is, that the Second Amendment is not about sport. It's about individual freedom and the basic liberty to protect one's self, family and nation.

Unlike the overwhelming majority of Americans, Clinton just doesn't respect that sacred freedom guaranteed to us by our Founding Fathers. The president should read the Bill of Rights rather than twist the law to deny us our rights. If the president wades into the pool of banning lawful ownership of firearms by the American public, he'll find the waters much deeper and much rougher than he can imagine.

United States v. Miller

307 U.S. 174 (1939)

Mr. Justice McReynolds delivered the opinion of the Court.

An indictment . . . charged that Jack Miller and Frank Layton "did unlawfully, knowingly, willfully, and feloniously transport in interstate commerce from the town of Claremore in the State of Oklahoma to the town of Siloam Springs in the State of Arkansas a certain firearm, to-wit, a double barrel 12-gauge Stevens shotgun having a barrel less than 18 inches in length . . ."

[The District Court held that Section 11 of the 1934 National Firearms Act] violates the Second Amendment. It accordingly . . . quashed [dismissed] the indictment . . .

In the absence of any evidence tending to show that possession or use of a "shotgun having a barrel of less than eighteen inches in length" at this time has some reasonable relationship to the preservation or efficiency of a well regulated militia, we cannot say that the Second Amendment guarantees the right to keep and bear such an instrument. Certainly it is not within judicial notice that this weapon is any part of the ordinary military equipment or that its use could contribute to the common defense. . . .

The Constitution as originally adopted granted to the Congress power "To provide for calling forth the Militia to execute the Laws of the Union, suppress Insurrections and repel Invasions; To provide for organizing, arming, and disciplining the Militia, and for governing such Part of them as may be employed in the Service of the United States, reserving to the States respectively, the Appointment of the Officers, and the Author-ity of training the Militia according to the discipline prescribed by Congress." (U.S. Constitution Article 1, Section 8) . . . With obvious purpose to assure the continuation and render possible the effectiveness of such forces the declaration and guarantee of the Second Amendment were made. It must be interpreted and applied with that end in view. . . .

The sentiment of the time strongly disfavored standing armies; the common view was that adequate defense of country and laws could be secured through the Militia—civilians primarily, soldiers on occasion.

The signification attributed to the term *Militia* appears from the debates in the Convention, the history and legislation of Colonies and States, and the writings of approved commentators. These show plainly enough that the Militia comprised all males physically capable of acting in concert for the common defense. "A body of citizens enrolled for military discipline." And further, that ordinarily when called for service these men were expected to appear bearing arms supplied by themselves and of the kind in common use at the time . . .

Adam Smith's *Wealth of Nations* . . . contains an extended account of the Militia. It is there said: "Men of republican principles have been jealous of a standing army as dangerous to liberty. In a militia, the character of the laborer, artificer, or tradesman, predominates over that of the soldier: in a standing army, that of the soldier predominates over every other character; and in this distinction seems to consist the essential difference between those two different species of military force. . . ."

The General Court of Massachusetts, January Session 1784 . . . provided for the organization and government of the Militia. It directed that the Train Band should "contain all able bodied men, from sixteen to forty years of age, and the Alarm List, all other men under sixty years of age. . . ." Also, "That every non-commissioned officer and private soldier of the said Militia not under the control of parents, masters or guardians, and being of sufficient ability therefor in the judgment of the Selectmen of the town in which he shall dwell, shall equip himself, and be constantly provided with a good fire arm, &c."

By an Act passed April 4, 1786 . . . the New York Legislature directed: "That every able-bodied Male Person, being a Citizen of this State, or of any of the United States, and residing in this State, (except such Persons as are herein after excepted) and who are of the Age of Sixteen, and under the Age of Forty-five Years, shall, by the Captain or commanding Officer of the Beat in which such Citizens shall reside, within four Months after the passing of this Act, be enrolled in the Company of such Beat. . . . That every Citizen so enrolled and notified, shall, within three Months thereafter, provide himself, at his own Expense, with a good Musket or Firelock, a sufficient Bayonet and Belt, a Pouch with a Box therein to contain not less than Twenty-four Cartridges suited to the Bore of his Musket or Firelock, each Cartridge containing a proper Quantity of Powder and Ball, two spare Flints, a Blanket and Knapsack . . ."

The General Assembly of Virginia, October, 1785. . . . "The defense and safety of the commonwealth depend upon having its citizens properly armed and taught the knowledge of military duty."

It further provided for organization and control of the Militia and directed that "All free male persons between the ages of eighteen and fifty years," with certain exceptions, "shall be enrolled or formed into companies." There shall be a private muster of every company once in two months. . . ."

Most if not all of the States have adopted provisions touching the right to keep and bear arms. Differences in the language employed in these have naturally led to somewhat variant conclusions concerning the scope of the right guaranteed. But none of them seem to afford any material support for the challenged ruling of the court below. . . .

Reversed and remanded.

Issue 2

Should Gun Control Be Adopted?

- *Eleven-year-old Andrew Golden steals his grandfather's deer rifle and kills five people and wounds ten others at a Jonesboro, Arkansas, school.*

- *Following a drug deal gone bad, the police arrest a local drug dealer who admits he bought the murder weapon on the illegal market.*

These vignettes show one side of the gun-control debate—weapons are often used in the commission of crimes, particularly violent crimes. Unconvinced, groups opposed to gun control respond with bumper stickers that proclaim: "When guns are outlawed, only outlaws will have guns." (Walker, 1998).

The public is profoundly ambivalent about gun control. A majority of Americans supports gun control in some form. But at the same time a majority also believes that citizens have the right to own guns. The two sides, of course, cite different poll numbers in an effort to make their case.

Public ambivalence over gun control is reflected in the variety of measures that have been debated, and in some cases adopted, in the last decade. Among the most frequently mentioned proposals are: bans on assault weapons; outlawing Saturday night specials; restrictions on who can carry concealed weapons; requiring safety locks on handguns; mandatory sentences for use of a gun during the commission of a crime; and prohibiting persons convicted of domestic violence from owning a gun.

As the above proposals indicate, it "is a myth that the United States has no gun-control laws." (Walker, 1998). Rather, the nation has lots of gun-control measures but they lack consistency from state to state. Given public ambivalence, the nation seems unwilling to adopt major and draconian measures that would be effective.

Pro	Con
No other country in the world is as permissive about the ownership of guns as the U.S. As a result, no other country has as much violent crime. Half of all murders are committed with handguns. Two-thirds of all police officers killed in the line of duty are slain by handguns.	Millions of Americans own guns and never violate the law, much less commit a violent offense. Indeed, many citizens own guns to protect themselves from criminals.
Gun control will reduce crime, particularly violent crime, by reducing the supply of guns used by criminals.	Violent crime rates are high in the U.S. because criminal justice officials are not aggressive enough in prosecuting and punishing criminals who use weapons.
Gun control will also reduce injuries caused by accidental use of weapons.	Outlawing weapons will not reduce the supply of guns used by criminals because they can obtain weapons through illegal markets.

The first article, "An 'Anti' Perspective . . . ," argues for a ban on carrying concealed handguns. The author, Michael Beard (President of the Coalition to Stop Gun Violence) concludes that the National Rifle Association blocks efforts to reduce societal violence.

The second article, "Ten Essential Observations on Guns in America," argues that guns are a vital part of American culture. The author, James D. Wright (a sociologist at Tulane University), concludes that gun-control efforts are largely symbolic exercises.

World Wide Web Exercises

1. Select four (or more) groups that focus on the gun-control issue, and analyze the contents of their Web pages. Ask yourself the following questions: From the title of the organization (or Web page) is it immediately obvious where the group stands on the issue or do they attempt to disguise their position? What types of arguments do these Web pages make? Do they tend to rely on emotional arguments, or support their position with facts? Irrespective of your personal preference on the topic, what Web page do you find most persuasive and why? One easy way to locate groups actively involved in the gun-control debate is the following: http://dir.yahoo.com/Society_and_Culture/Firearms/Firearms_Policy/Gun_Control/Organizations/

2. Examine the Web pages of groups on various sides of the gun-control debate. What additional arguments do they raise beyond those discussed in *Debating Crime?* Do

interest groups opposed to gun control agree on all issues, or do they disagree on some matters? Similarly, do interest groups supporting gun control agree on all issues, or do they disagree on some matters? For this assignment you may wish to use the term **gun control** for an altavista.com or excite.com search.

InfoTrac College Edition Exercises

1. Using the search term **gun control, analysis** or **gun control, laws,** locate one article arguing in favor of gun control and another opposing gun control. What additional arguments do they make about the topic?

2. Using the search term **gun control, political aspects,** locate two or more articles that analyze the debate over gun control. In particular, why do some elected officials back gun control and others oppose it?

3. Using the search term **gun control, research,** locate two or more articles that analyze the impact of gun control. Do the findings tend to support gun control, or oppose it?

An 'Anti' Perspective
(The Right-to-Carry Trend)

Michael K. Beard

Claiming "an armed society is a polite society," the National Rifle Association (NRA) lobbies for state laws allowing citizens to carry concealed handguns. These laws allow almost everyone to receive a permit to carry a handgun. This legislation preys upon people's fear of violent crime while distorting the real meaning of the Second Amendment. And these laws do nothing to lower the crime rate; in fact, they increase the danger that citizens face.

Before I lay out the facts, let us consider the reality behind the NRA's rhetoric. On May 26, the three-year-old daughter of two D.C. police officers climbed on top of a piece of furniture, got her father's loaded service pistol, and killed herself with one shot. Even a highly trained police officer with over six years on the job can make a devastating mistake. In an instant, their lives changed forever.

By bringing a gun into your home or carrying a gun on your hip, you greatly increase your risk of becoming a victim of tragedy. Are you willing to live with the consequences of carrying a gun? The NRA extols the virtues of carrying weapons as a quick fix to the problem of violence, but an examination of the facts proves otherwise.

Based on data collected from five urban areas in three states, University of Maryland researchers found that homicide rates did not significantly drop following the states' adoption of concealed carry laws. Instead, in three of the five cities studied, these researchers found a significant increase in the rate of gun-related homicides—74 percent in Jacksonville, Florida; 43 percent in Jackson, Mississippi; and 22 percent in Tampa, Florida. Arguably, concealed weapons laws may cause criminals to behave more violently. A criminal may anticipate a victim is armed and shoot first.

Despite the fact that the U.S. is heavily armed, less than one percent of all victims of violent crime use a firearm to defend themselves, according to the Department of Justice. The FBI and Centers for Disease Control report that there were 90 handgun homicides, suicides and unintentional deaths for every one justifiable handgun homicide by a civilian in 1994.

If anything, carrying a concealed weapon makes you more vulnerable. Even with their extensive training and expertise, law enforcement officers are at risk of having their own weapons used against them. The *American Journal of Public Health* reports that 20 percent of all police officers shot and killed over the last 15 years were killed with their own guns.

The gun lobby perpetuates myths about sexual assault. They paint a picture of a lone woman at night, attacked by a stranger. The truth is the vast majority of sexual assaults occur between people who know each other and in a private residence. A 1992 study found that 75 percent of all rapists are known by the victim, including neighbors, friends, husbands, boyfriends, and relatives.

Furthermore, the presence of a gun in a violent situation frequently causes the escalation of violence against the victim. Virtually all self-defense experts specifically advise against owning

Source: From *Campaigns & Elections* by Michael K. Beard. August, 1996 V17, N8. Reprinted by permission.

a gun for self-defense because guns are so frequently used against victims.

Handgun sales have been declining. The market for handguns is saturated. The gun industry is promoting concealed-carry laws to revive their ailing sales. Advertisements by the gun industry reveal a marketing strategy of using the rhetoric of concealed-carry laws to sell handguns and accessories such as holsters and purses. The gun industry is out for their profit, not the safety or well being of Americans.

Despite the NRA's claims, not one gun-control law brought before the Supreme Court or any other federal court has ever been overturned on Second Amendment grounds, including several local statutes outlawing handguns. The gun lobby, firearms industry, and the politicians that serve them must quit hiding behind their false interpretation of the Second Amendment. This contrived debate blocks honest efforts to curb gun violence and costs America too much in money and lost lives.

Arming society does not create civility nor produce solutions to gun violence. We cannot solve our society's violence problem by putting a gun on everyone's hip.

We must consider the message concealed-carry weapons laws send to our children. We have a responsibility to ourselves, our nation, and our children to stop wasting time on these dangerous bills and start examining real solutions to gun violence in America.

Ten Essential Observations on Guns in America

James D. Wright

Increasingly, the ammunition of the gun-control war is data. Pro-control advocates gleefully cite studies that seem to favor their position, of which there is no shortage, and anti-control advocates do likewise. Many of the "facts" of the case are, of course, hotly disputed; so too are their implications and interpretations. Here I should like to discuss ten essential facts about guns in America that are not in dispute—ten fundamental truths that all contestants either do or should agree to . . .

1. Half the households in the country own at least one gun. . . . This is probably not the highest gun ownership percentage among the advanced industrial societies (that honor probably goes to the Swiss), but it qualifies as a very respectable showing. We are, truly, a "gun culture. . . ."

    [I]t is frequently argued by pro-control advocates that the mere presence of guns causes people to do nutty and violent things that they would otherwise never even consider. In the academic literature . . . this is called the "trigger pulls the finger" hypothesis. If there were much substance to this viewpoint, the fact that half of all U.S. households possess a gun would seem to imply that there ought to be a lot more nuttiness "out there" than we actually observe. In the face of widespread alarm about the skyrocketing homicide rate, it is important to remember that the rate is still a relatively small number of homicides (ten to fifteen or so) per hundred thousand people. If half the households own guns and the mere presence of guns incites acts of violence, then one would expect the bodies to be piled three deep, and yet they are not. . . .

2. There are 200 million guns already in circulation in the United States, give or take a few tens of millions. It has been said, I think correctly, that firearms are the most commonly owned piece of sporting equipment in the United States, with the exception of pairs of sneakers. In any case, contestants on all sides of the gun debate generally agree that the total number of guns in circulation is on the order of 200 million—nearly one gun for every man, woman, and child in the country.

    It is not entirely clear how many acts of gun violence occur in any typical year. There are 30–35,000 deaths due to guns each year, perhaps a few hundred thousand nonfatal but injurious firearms accidents, maybe 500,000 or 600,000 chargeable gun crimes (not including crimes of illegal gun possession and carrying), and God knows how many instances in which guns are used to intimidate or prey upon one's fellow human beings. Making generous allowances all around, however, the total number of acts of accidental and intentional gun violence, whether fatal, injurious, or not, cannot be more than a couple of million, at the outside. . . .

    Because of the large number of guns already in circulation, the violence-reductive effects of even fairly draconian gun-control measures enacted today might well not be felt for decades.

3. Most of those 200 million guns are owned for socially innocuous sport and recreational purposes. Only about a third of the guns presently in

Source: *Society,* March–April, 1995 v32. Reprinted by permission of Transaction Publishers. All rights reserved.

circulation are handguns; the remainder are rifles and shotguns. . . .

Unfortunately, when we seek to control violence by controlling the general ownership and use of firearms among the public at large, it at least looks as though we think we have intuited some direct causal connection between drive-by shootings in the inner city and squirrel hunting or skeet shooting in the hinterland. In any case, this is the implication that the nation's squirrel hunters and skeet shooters often draw; frankly, is it any wonder they sometimes come to question the motives, not to mention the sanity, of anyone who would suggest such a thing?

4. Many guns are also owned for self-defense against crime, and some are indeed used for that purpose; whether they are actually any safer or not, many people certainly seem to feel safer when they have a gun. There is a fierce debate raging in gun advocacy circles these days over recent findings by Gary Kleck that Americans use guns to protect themselves against crime as often as one or two million times a year, which, if true, is hard to square with the common assumption of pro-control advocates that guns are not an efficacious defense against crime. Whatever the true number of self-defensive uses, about a quarter of all gun owners and about 40 percent of handgun owners cite defense against crime as the main reason they own a gun, and large percentages of those who give some other main reason will cite self-defense as a secondary reason. Gun owners and gun advocates insist that guns provide real protection, as Kleck's findings suggest; anti-gun advocates insist that the sense of security is more illusory than real.

5. The bad guys do not get their guns through customary retail channels. Research on both adult and juvenile felons and offenders has made it obvious that the illicit firearms market is dominated, overwhelmingly, by informal swaps, trades, and purchases among family members, friends, acquaintances, and street and black-market sources. It is a rare criminal indeed who attempts to acquire a gun through a conventional over-the-counter transaction with a normal retail outlet. It is also obvious that many or most of the guns circulating through

criminal hands enter the illicit market through theft from legitimate gun owners. . . .

Since felons rarely obtain guns through retail channels, controls imposed at the point of retail sale necessarily miss the vast majority of criminal firearms transactions. It is thus an easy prediction that the national five-day waiting period will have no effect on the acquisition of guns by criminals because that is not how the bad guys get their guns in the first place. . . .

6. The bad guys inhabit a violent world: a gun often makes a life-or-death difference to them. When one asks felons—either adult or juvenile—why they own and carry guns, themes of self-defense, protection, and survival dominate the responses. Very few of the bad guys say they acquire or carry guns for offensive or criminal purposes, although that is obviously how many of them get used. These men live in a very hostile and violent environment, and many of them have come to believe, no doubt correctly, that their ability to survive in that environment depends critically on being adequately armed. Thus the bad guys are highly motivated gun consumers who will not be easily dissuaded from possessing, carrying, and using guns. . . .

7. Everything the bad guys do with their guns is already against the law. That criminals will generally be indifferent to our laws would seem to follow from the definitions of the terms, but it is a lesson that we have had to relearn time and time again throughout our history. So let me stress an obvious point: Murder is already against the law, yet murderers still murder; armed robbery is against the law, yet robbers still rob. And as a matter of fact, gun acquisition by felons, whether from retail or private sources, is also already illegal, yet felons still acquire guns. Since practically everything the bad guys do with their guns is already against the law, we are entitled to wonder whether there is any new law we can pass that would persuade them to stop doing it. . . .

8. Demand creates it own supply. That "demand creates its own supply" is sometimes called the First Law of Economics, and it clearly holds whether the commodity in demand is legal or illegal. So

long as a demand exists, there will be profit to be made in satisfying it, and therefore it will be satisfied. In a capitalist economy, it could scarcely be otherwise. So long as people, be they criminals or average citizens, want to own guns, guns will be available for them to own. . . . What alcohol and drug prohibition should have taught us (but apparently has not) is that if a demand exists and there is no legal way to satisfy it, then an illegal commerce in the commodity is spawned, and we often end up creating many more problems than we have solved. . . .

9. Guns are neither inherently good nor inherently evil . . . Benevolence and malevolence inhere in the motives and behaviors of people, not in the technology they possess. Any firearm is neither more nor less than a chunk of machined metal that can be put to a variety of purposes, all involving a small projectile hurtling at high velocity downrange to lodge itself in a target. We can only call this "good" when the target is appropriate and "evil" when it is not; the gun itself is immaterial to this judgment.

Gun-control advocates have a long history of singling out "bad" guns for policy attention. At one time, the emphasis was on small, cheap handguns—"Saturday Night Specials"—which were thought to be inherently "bad" because no legitimate use was thought to exist for them and because they were thought to be the preferred firearm among criminals. Both these thoughts turned out to be incorrect. Somewhat later, all handguns, regardless of their characteristics, were singled out (as by the National Coalition to Ban Handguns); most recently, the so-called military-style assault weapons are the "bad guns of the month. . . ."

10. Guns are important elements of our history and culture. Attempts to control crime by regulating the ownership or use of firearms are attempts to regulate the artifacts and activities of a culture that, in its own way, is as unique as any of the myriad other cultures that comprise the American ethnic mosaic. . . .

[G]un control deals with matters that people feel strongly about, that are integral to their upbringing and their worldview. Gun-control advocates are frequently taken aback by the stridency with which their seemingly modest and sensible proposals are attacked, but from the gun culture's viewpoint, restrictions on the right to "keep and bear arms" amount to the systematic destruction of a valued way of life and are thus a form of cultural genocide.

Guns evoke powerful, emotive imagery that often stands in the way of intelligent debate. To the pro-control point of view, the gun is symbolic of much that is wrong in American culture. It symbolizes violence, aggression, and male dominance, and its use is seen as an acting out of our most regressive and infantile fantasies. To the gun culture's way of thinking, the same gun symbolizes much that is right in the culture. It symbolizes manliness, self-sufficiency, and independence, and its use is an affirmation of man's relationship to nature and to history. The "Great American Gun War," as Bruce-Briggs has described it, is far more than a contentious debate over crime and the equipment with which it is committed. It is a battle over fundamental and equally legitimate sets of values.

Part III

Debating the Limits of Police Power

Awakened in the middle of the night by the sounds of police sirens, George Holiday pointed his newly purchased video recorder toward the unfolding scene nearby. The 81-second video showed a white LAPD officer repeatedly striking a black motorist while numerous other white officers looked on. Excerpts of this video would be shown countless times on TV over the next year, producing a lasting impact on the Los Angeles Police Department and on policing across the nation.

The validity of complaints of police brutality is typically difficult to verify because the evidence is contradictory: the testimony of the police officer differs dramatically from the person arrested. Thus, what marked the Rodney King case as very unique was the presence of compelling visual evidence. But if the video established the "facts" of the encounter, interpretations differed nonetheless.

To a good deal of the nation, the video convincingly showed excessive use of force. "At some point you have to look at the video and say enough is enough," implored the deputy district attorney. Those who concluded that the LAPD used excessive force emphasized the part of the video that showed a prone Rodney King being struck over 45 times.

To the arresting officers, the video overwhelmingly depicted the necessary use of force. "I was scared to death that if this guy got back up, he was going to take my gun away from me," testified one of the officers. Those who interpreted the video as showing proper use of police force zeroed in on the three seconds of tape that showed Rodney King charging the officers.

These conflicting interpretations carried over to two criminal trials. (The City of Los Angeles settled the civil lawsuit out of court for $3.8 million).

A state jury (drawn from a predominately white suburb) acquitted the four white police officers. The not guilty verdict was the spark that ignited long simmering tensions between minority communities and the LAPD. What followed was the deadliest race riot since the Civil War; in the end, 54 people were killed, thousands injured and nearly $1 billion in property destroyed. An article in *Jet* expressed the views of black leaders across the nation: "Nation Voices Outrage, Shock, Despair over King Verdict."

The not guilty verdict in state court resulted in a very unusual development— a second trial was held, this time in federal court. Officers Laurence Powell and Stacey Koon were convicted of violating the civil rights of Rodney King. Police officers and others were outraged that the federal trial violated the constitutional ban on double jeopardy. The *National Review* denounced the federal prosecution as political, and wondered sarcastically whether Los Angeles was safer after the verdict.

The contrasting verdicts and equally contrasting reactions to the verdicts underscore difficult issues about policing in a constitutional democracy. In totalitarian governments there are no limits to police power (at least in the short term). Police can use whatever means they choose to enforce the edicts of the government. Thus, arresting, torturing, and occasionally killing opponents of the government does take place. But in the long run, such actions often work to undermine the legitimacy of the regime. That is why American democracy insists on placing limits on police (which is to say governmental) power. This section considers two controversial issues surrounding the limits of police power.

Issue 3 focuses on the police use of force. Because the police are often called upon to deal with the seamier side of society, it is understood that the police use of force is a fact of life. Although the public, and therefore jurors, sympathizes with police officers dealing with events in the line of duty, they also perceive limits.

Issue 4 focuses on limits on police powers to search a person or a place. There is little doubt that the most controversial legacy of the Warren Court is the decision to not allow illegally seized evidence into a court of law. Law enforcement critics argue that the exclusionary rule undermines police ability to arrest and convict criminals. Civil libertarians respond that without the exclusionary rule, police would be free to violate the U.S. Constitution at will.

World Wide Web Resources

Web Guide

http://dir.yahoo.com/Society_and_Culture/Crime/Law_Enforcement/

http://dir.yahoo.com/Government/U_S_Government/Military/Army/Units/
Military_Police/

Searching the Web

The basic search term is **police** but this will yield so many results as to be virtually useless. It is better, therefore, to use more specific search terms like **police brutality, police stress, racial profiling,** and the like.

Useful URLs

Federal Bureau of Investigation (FBI): Best known national law enforcement agency.   http://www.fbi.gov/

Fraternal Order of Police (FOP): The world's largest organization of sworn police officers dedicated to issues of safety and improving working conditions. http://www.grandlodgefop.org/

International Association of Chiefs of Police: The world's oldest and largest organization of police executives.   http://www.theiacp.org/

Police Executive Research Foundation: Leading force in law enforcement innovations.   http://www.policeforum.org

Today's Headlines

http://dailynews.yahoo.com/headlines/cr/

http://www.apbnews.com/cjprofessionals/behindthebadge/
index.html?s=apbnews_homepage

Fun Sites

Heavy Badge: Explores the effects of stress on law enforcement. http://www.heavybadge.com

National Center for Women and Policing: The first nationwide resource for women in policing.   http://www.feminist.org/police/ncwp.html

National Law Enforcement Officers Memorial Fund: Pays tribute to officers killed in the line of duty.   http://www.nleomf.com/

National Organization of Black Law Enforcement Executives: Dedicated to increasing diversity in law enforcement and ensuring equity in delivery of services. http://www.noblenatl.org/

InfoTrac College Edition Resources

Background

Encyclopedia and reference books provide excellent background on the history of policing and contemporary problems.

Basic Searches

The basic search terms are **police** and **law enforcement.** Each contains numerous subdivisions.

Related Searches

criminal investigation; law enforcement; police questioning; searches and seizures; police misconduct; police, complaints against.

World Wide Web Exercises

1. Examine the Web pages of several law enforcement organizations and analyze them in terms of the categories discussed in the article "Interest Groups and the Crime Debate." In addition, analyze the ideological tone of these organizations. Do these organizations appear to focus primarily on the improving the position of law enforcement officers, or are they primarily focused on issues involved in the crime debate? One easy way to identify some law enforcement organizations is through the following Yahoo search: http://dir.yahoo.com/Society_and_Culture/Crime/Law_Enforcement/Organizations/

2. Using the search term **Rodney King** conduct a search using excite.com (or another search engine of your choosing). Select two or more contemporary articles about this incident and discuss why this case remains newsworthy. In addition, discuss how this case illustrates the themes developed in the introduction to *Debating Crime*.

InfoTrac College Edition Exercises

1. Select a nation other than the United States and explore the types of issues facing their police departments. Use the search term **police** and then locate a subheading to find two or more articles on policing in the nation of your choice. Are the problems facing these police departments similar to or different from those in the U.S.?

2. Using the search term **Rodney King** or **Rodney King, analysis,** select two or more articles that discuss the aftermath of the Rodney King case. In addition, analyze the ideological tone of each article. Does the author appear to support the crime control model, or the due process model of criminal justice?

Issue 3

Is Excessive Use of Force a Systemic Problem?

- **New York detectives fire 41 shots, killing Amadou Diallo.**

- **Chicago patrolman James Camp is fatally shot in the face by a stolen-car suspect.**

The killing of Amadou Diallo, an immigrant from West Africa who spoke little English and was unarmed, set off an explosive series of confrontations in the nation's largest city. In a biting opinion piece ("Storm Brewing Over Killing by Police") *New York Times* columnist Bob Hubert (1999) wrote "I don't know if Mayor Rudolph Giuliani realizes it, but there are limits to the amount of abuse that black New Yorkers will accept from violent and racist police officers." The controversy was fueled by the lack of a public explanation for the police action. During the criminal trial a year later, the officers testified that they thought Diallo had a gun and they fired only in self-defense. The jury acquitted all four officers, which in turn set off another round of public protests decrying criminal injustice.

About a month later 34-year-old Chicago policeman James Camp was patrolling Cottage Grove Avenue, "where cocaine road begins, stretching . . . through dead neighborhoods killed by the drug trade." Camp and his partner pulled over a stolen car driven by a man wanted for auto theft and threatening to kill a police officer. During a scuffle, Camp lost his service revolver and the suspect shot him in the face. In a poignant opinion piece ("And You Wonder Why Police Officers Become Embittered") *Chicago Tribune* columnist John Kass (1999) wrote "If Camp had shot first, he would have been accused of brutality. But he didn't. He lost his gun and he died for it."

Statistics on police use of force are notably unreliable, but the most recent numbers do help to place these two tragedies in perspective.

- 11 of every 100 law enforcement officers in the nation were assaulted (with three out of 100 injured); 67 were killed in the line of duty

- 332 justifiable homicides by law enforcement officials occurred during the same year.

Defining excessive use of police force is difficult. Police are authorized by law to use necessary force to arrest a suspect. In a typical year, one in five persons 12 or older has a face-to-face contact with a police officer. Most typically the civilian needed help, or reported a crime. Nonetheless, in about one percent of these encounters (500,000) the police used or threatened to use force during the contact (BJS, 1997 Police Use of Force). But is this force necessary, or excessive? Complaints about excessive use of force run the gamut from verbal abuse (name calling and racial slurs, for example) to slight use of force (an unnecessary shove) to major force (bruises and broken bones) to the use of deadly force.

Allegations of excessive use of force strain public confidence in the police. Because of declining crime rates, public trust in the police has increased. Well publicized incidents of police brutality (Rodney King and Amadou Diallo, for instance), though, erode public confidence in the police. While opinions held by blacks and whites are adversely affected, the magnitude of change is much greater for blacks than for whites. Moreover, the experiences of minorities have greater staying power in shaping attitudes (Tuch and Weitzer, 1997).

The debate over excessive use of force runs along the following lines.

Pro	Con
Police use of excessive force is pervasive.	Police use of excessive force is isolated.
Excessive use of force falls heaviest on minorities and erodes community support.	The concentration of crime and criminals in minority areas explains police vigilance.
The blue wall of silence makes it hard to root out bad cops who use excessive force.	Existing internal reviews effectively remove the occasional bad cop.
Juries in civil cases often find police departments liable when officers use excessive force.	Juries in criminal cases rarely convict police officers of using excessive force.
Highly publicized cases are only the tip of the iceberg.	The media distorts a few cases, thus badly undermining law enforcement.

The article "Established: A Pattern of Abuse" argues that the report published by Amnesty International proves that police brutality is a common problem in the U.S. The author (Barbara Dority, president of Humanists of Washington) concludes that people have been killed by excessive use of force, or misuse of a variety of weapons.

The article "Black and Blue: New York Erupts Over A Race-tinged Killing—Again" argues that recent police brutality allegations in New York City have been covered in a one-sided fashion by the media. The author, John O'Sullivan (a writer for *National Review*) concludes that often, so-called racial profiling is a necessary reaction to experience.

World Wide Web Exercises

1. Using the search term **Amadou Diallo** find two articles that provide different perspectives on the shooting of Amadou Diallo. To what extent do these differences parallel the crime control versus due process models of criminal justice?

2. Search for Web pages that discuss **police brutality.** What types of arguments do these Web sites raise? What definitions of police brutality do they employ? Are the number of pages balanced, or do they tilt toward one side of the debate rather than another? If so, why? The following Web site features some sites devoted to the topic: http://dir.yahoo.com/Society_and_Culture/Crime/Crimes/Police_Brutality/

InfoTrac College Edition Exercises

1. Using the search term **police misconduct, analysis** or **police misconduct, social aspects** find two or more articles that articulate different perspectives on the topic. Do these articles offer similar arguments or different ones than the pieces in *Debating Crime?*

2. Using the search term **police misconduct, laws** or **police misconduct, prevention** read two or more articles in scholarly journals that analyze the problem of police misconduct. How does the academic perspective differ from the public debate? Are there realistic solutions, or are proposals wishful thinking?

Established: A Pattern of Abuse

Barbara Dority

There is a widespread and persistent problem of police brutality across the United States. Thousands of individual complaints about police abuse are reported each year and local authorities pay out millions of dollars to victims in damages after lawsuits. Police officers have beaten and shot unresisting suspects; they have misused batons, chemical sprays, and electro-shock weapons; they have injured or killed people by placing them in dangerous restraint holds.

This is the first paragraph of an unprecedented and historic report, "USA: Rights for All," issued by Amnesty International (AI) . . . Simultaneously, the organization announced the theme of its U.S. education campaign: "Human rights aren't just a foreign affair."

For many—myself included—this is a long-awaited and irrefutable confirmation of the alarming state of human rights in America. Indeed, this report leaves no doubt whatsoever that American law enforcement agencies—including the Immigration and Naturalization Service, the Federal Bureau of Investigation, and the prison system— must be immediately reined in, fundamentally reformed, and held accountable to the citizens who literally entrust them with their lives.

AI's report confirms that the overwhelming majority of victims of law enforcement abuses are members of racial and ethnic minorities, while most police departments remain predominantly white. Relations between the police and members of minority communities—especially young black and Latino males in inner-city areas—are often tense, and racial bias is reported or a factor in many instances. The report continues:

> Unarmed suspects have been shot while fleeing from minor crime scenes; mentally ill or disturbed people have been subjected to excessive force; police have shot distraught people armed with weapons such as knives or sticks, in circumstances suggesting that they could have been subdued without lethal force; victims have been shot many times, sometimes after they had already been apprehended or disabled.

AI issues a strong warning:

> Police officers are responsible for upholding the law and protecting the rights of all members of society. Their job is often difficult and sometimes dangerous. Experience from around the world shows that constant vigilance is required to ensure the highest standards of conduct—standards necessary to maintain public confidence and meet national and international requirements. . . . be made more accountable for their actions by the establishment of effective monitoring mechanisms. National, state, and local police authorities should ensure that police brutality and excessive force are not tolerated.

Despite reform programs in several major U.S. police departments, the report documents that

Source: *The Humanist*, January, 1999 v59 p5. Full text ©1999 American Humanist Association. Reprinted with permission from the author.

authorities still fail to deal effectively with police officers who have committed abuses. The disciplinary sanctions imposed on officers found guilty of brutality are frequently inadequate, and officers are rarely prosecuted for using excessive force. The "code of silence" still commands widespread loyalty, contributing to a climate of impunity. . . .

Predictably, most complaints of police brutality involve excessive physical force by patrol officers during the course of arrests, searches, traffic stops, the issuing of warrants, and street incidents. Common forms of ill treatment are repeated kicks, punches, or blows with batons or other weapons—sometimes after a suspect has already been restrained or rendered helpless. There are also complaints involving various types of restraint holds, pepper spray, electroshock weapons, and firearms.

AI's investigation confirms—as many civil libertarians already knew—that there are no accurate national data on the number of people fatally shot or injured by police officers—data which are essential for meaningful peacemaking. AI states:

> Most law enforcement agencies maintain that abuses, when they occur, are isolated incidents. However, in the past eight years, independent inquiries have uncovered systematic abuses in some of the country's largest police departments, revealing a serious nationwide problem. . . . The emphasis on the "war on crime" in recent years has reportedly contributed to more aggressive policing in many areas. . . .

Physical abuse and harassment of gay men and lesbians by police officers is also endemic in many areas. In addition, gay and lesbian victims of crime (including victims of homophobic attacks) frequently find their complaints to the police are not treated seriously and, in some instances, are met with verbal or physical abuse. . . .

It is particularly significant that AI's report specifically references two of the worst instances of abuse by federal law enforcement in the past forty years:

> FBI agents have also used unnecessary levels of force. In 1995 the government paid $3.1 million in a wrongful death claim to the family of a white separatist whose wife and son were shot dead by FBI sharpshooters during a siege in Idaho in 1992. A Justice Department inquiry found that senior officials in charge of the siege had violated federal policies on the use of deadly force. While several senior officials were demoted, no officers were prosecuted. And during a 51-day standoff with members of an armed religious sect—the Branch Davidians—in Waco, Texas, in 1993, federal agents pumped CS gas into a compound known to hold children as well as adults for three and a half hours. The siege ended when fire engulfed the compound, killing over 70 men, women, and children.

The report confirms that victims of law enforcement abuse include not only criminal suspects but also bystanders and people who question police actions or are involved in minor disputes or confrontations. Abuses in response to challenges to police authority (widely known as "contempt of cop") have been widely documented.

Also confirmed is the fact that suspects have been tortured or ill-treated inside police stations by methods such as electroshock and having plastic bags placed over their heads. There have also been numerous deaths in police custody following restraint procedures known to be dangerous. Suspects have died after being placed facedown in restraints, usually while "hog-tied" or after pressure has been applied to the neck or chest.

The police also have a variety of so-called less-than-lethal weapons at their disposal, including chemical sprays, electroshock weapons, and batons. At least 3,000 U.S. police departments authorize the use of oleoresin capsicum (OC) spray. An inflammatory agent derived from cayenne peppers, OC spray inflames the mucous membranes, causing closing of the eyes, coughing, gagging, shortness of breath, and an acute burning sensation on the skin and inside the nose and mouth. Since the early 1990s, more than sixty people in the United States are reported to have died in police custody after being exposed to OC spray.

Patrol officers in some police departments are authorized to use stun guns or tasers. The stun gun is a hand-held device with two metal prongs that emit an electric shock. The taser is a hand-held device that shoots two barbed hooks into the subject's clothing from a distance; the current is transmitted through wires. In both cases, a high-voltage jolt, typically 50,000 volts, incapacitates the suspect. There have been several reported deaths following the use of such weapons.

The problems are not confined to inner cities. AI cites reports from human rights groups documenting longstanding brutality by law enforcement agents toward people of Latin American origin in states with large immigrant populations, such as California and Texas. There have also been complaints of brutality and discriminatory treatment of Native Americans, both in urban areas and on reservations.

The report refers to an agreement reached with the Justice Department in April 1997 to improve procedures in the Pittsburgh Police Department, which AI considers a model program. The agreement includes proposals for a computerized record of each officer's disciplinary training and complaints history (including unsustained complaints and data on civil lawsuits), as well as data on arrests, traffic stops, and use-of-force incidents. The agreement provides for regular independent audits and reviews of the data for potential racial bias or other patterns of concern and establishment of independent oversight of the complaints process in all U.S. police departments.

AI calls for federal, state, and local authorities to take immediate action to halt human rights violations by police officers:

> They should make clear that abuses including torture, brutality, and other excessive force by police officers will not be tolerated; that officers will be held accountable for their actions; and that those responsible for abuses will be brought to justice. Victims of abuse by

police officers should be guaranteed effective and timely reparation. International human rights standards should be fully incorporated into police codes of conduct and training.

> Review boards must be given full subpoena powers and have the authority to make recommendations on policy.

AI also recommends that Congress should provide adequate funding to enable the Justice Department to fulfill its mandate under the Police Accountability Act provisions of the Violent Crime Control and Law Enforcement Act of 1994. All allegations of human rights violations and other police misconduct should be fully and impartially investigated. All officers responsible for abuses should be adequately disciplined and, where appropriate, prosecuted.

Traditionally, Americans have appropriately viewed Amnesty International's reports of human rights violations in the developing world as symptomatic but dismissed them as anecdotal here at home. However, as Eleanor Roosevelt, former chair of the United Nations Human Rights Commission, said:

> Where, after all, do human rights begin? In small places, close to home—so close and so small that they cannot be seen on any maps of the world. Such are the places where every man, woman, and child seeks equal justice, equal opportunity, equal dignity, without discrimination. Unless these rights have meaning there, they have little meaning anywhere.

With this report—a first-ever detailed account of the state of human rights in America—AI has conclusively validated my longstanding fear that the United States may become a tyranny if present trends continue. In fact, for many minorities, gays, people of color, and inner-city citizens, America is already a police state.

Black and Blue: New York Erupts Over a Race-tinged Killing—Again

John O'Sullivan

Whenever a crime with racial overtones hits the newspapers, a highly predictable scenario is acted out. If the crime is, say, a mugging of a white person by a black person, the news media take immediate pains to establish that the crime had nothing to do with race. It was simply an isolated act of thuggishness. The law must take its course—but no more need be said about the matter. If, on the other hand, a black man is attacked by a white person or gang of whites, then it becomes the occasion for wider social theorizing about the persistence of racial attitudes in American society. Perhaps it was an attempted lynching; very likely, it was a hate crime; almost certainly it indicates racism in the community. And if the crime is one of police brutality against someone belonging to an ethnic minority, then it is held to demonstrate widespread ill-treatment of minorities by the police, the entrenched racism of social institutions in general, and the need for their reform along "affirmative action" lines.

If this account seems exaggerated, consider the media's treatment of two New York crimes that occurred within four months of each other in 1989: the murder of Yusuf Hawkins, a black youth, by a white member of a street gang in Bensonhurst and the rape and near-fatal beating of a white investment banker by a gang of black and Hispanic youths in Central Park. "Black Youth Is Killed in Brooklyn by Whites in Attack Called Racial," is how the *New York Times* headlined the

Source: *National Review,* April 19, 1999 v51. ©1999 by National Review, Inc., 215 Lexington Ave., NY, NY 10016. Reprinted by permission.

Yusuf Hawkins murder. Only a few months before it had given the Central Park rape a more racially dispassionate introduction: "Youths Rape and Beat Central Park Jogger."

No one suggested that the people of Schomburg Plaza, where the jogger's attackers lived, bore any responsibility for the assault on her. Indeed, the *New York Daily News* solemnly warned against any such lapse into racial stereotyping: "the simple truth [is] that dreadful things are done by individual thugs to individual victims—not by or to a race." But the Hawkins murder produced exactly the opposite reflection: that it was the inevitable result of the racial hostility allegedly felt by the Italian-American inhabitants of Bensonhurst towards blacks. A Daily News editorial duly intoned: "despite the protests of some Bensonhurst residents, the attack was based on race . . . wrong to dismiss it as a bunch of neighbor rowdies going too far . . . The motivation was deeper, more insidious." Connoisseurs of double standards will especially enjoy the titles of the two News editorials. They were, respectively, "Stay Calm, New York" and "Dare to Attack Racist Violence."

This discrepancy in journalistic treatment might be understandable if most crimes in which the victims and perpetrators are of different races were committed by whites against blacks, or other minorities. But, as statistics amply demonstrate, this is not the case. In light of the sad reality, it is not racism but prudence that prompts a white person to cross the street at the approach of black youths. Merely consider the trade-off. If the white's fears are misplaced and the youths are decent, respectable persons, they will at worst suffer feelings of rejection and humiliation at being mistaken for criminals. If his fears are correct, however, then he has saved himself from something terrible. These considerations weigh very differently in the scales of justice: It is perfectly reasonable to risk hurting others' feelings in order to avoid being murdered. And when that trade-off is multiplied thousands of times, it is more than reasonable for a city police force to risk hurting the feelings of those who fit a criminal "profile" by frisking them for guns in order to save hundreds of people from being murdered.

Split-Second Decision

Which brings us to the case of Amadou Diallo in New York. On February 4, four New York cops searching for a serial rapist in the Bronx followed Diallo into the foyer of his tenement building and shot him 19 times, firing 41 bullets in a matter of five seconds. Diallo was unarmed, and the cops have since been charged with second-degree murder. The most common explanation, drawn from a lawyer for the four and other policemen, is that Diallo fit the profile of the rapist and the cops thought he was going for a gun. In a split-second decision, they shot him to save themselves. But since the cops have not yet given their account of the incident and there were no eyewitnesses, no one else really knows what happened.

That has not prevented New York's media mavens like the *Times* columnist Bob Herbert, on-the-make liberal politicians like Mark Green, failed mayors like David Dinkins, racial hucksters like "the Rev." Al Sharpton, and almost-famous people like Susan Sarandon from deciding not only that the cops are guilty of a serious crime but that such an outrage is the inevitable result of the policing tactics adopted under Mayor Rudolph Giuliani. In a left-wing version of debutantes being presented at court, various celebrities turn up outside City Hall to be arrested, appear briefly in court, and then head off to receive congratulations on their extremely civil disobedience over Park Avenue cocktails. Media coverage since the shooting (the *New York Post* excepted) has generally hewed to the line "Dare to Attack Racist Policing" rather

than "Stay Calm, New York." We are continually reminded, for instance, that "four white cops" killed Diallo by newspapers that generally criticize references to the race of criminal suspects; so is journalistic etiquette thrown out the window.

Unusually for such ideologically charged cases, however, there seems to be broad agreement on the facts. All agree that under Giuliani the New York Police Department has conducted a remarkably successful war against crime—though people differ about the alleged costs of that success. How did this astounding improvement take place? Not because the NYPD has been shooting more people, as the agitprop campaign over Diallo might suggest. The rate of police shootings in New York is low and declining. In the last three years, it has fallen from 344 shootings to 249. Fatal police shootings have declined still more dramatically, from 30 to 19 over the same period—the second-lowest figure since 1973, when records began to be kept. Indeed, such shootings in New York are now more rare than in other major cities. Diallo's murder was not an indication of how the NYPD operates, as the protesters allege; if anything, it runs counter to the trend of policing under Giuliani.

Crime has declined because the NYPD has waged an aggressive campaign to stop it before it happens, in particular by conducting searches for illegal handguns in high-crime areas. The Street Crimes Unit—to which the four policemen who shot Diallo belong—is one important element in this campaign. Although it constitutes only about one percent of the NYPD, it accounts for 40 percent of all gun arrests. It has accomplished this by conducting street frisks of those whom cops have a "reasonable suspicion" are armed and dangerous. But its critics charge that this has led to the frisking of too many people. A *New York Times* report, for instance, gave the numbers frisked in 1997–98 as 45,084, of whom only 9,546 were arrested for gun possession—which led the *Times* reporter to complain that "nearly 40,000 people were stopped and frisked . . . because a street crimes officer mistakenly thought they were carrying guns."

What that means, of course, is that about one in five of those stopped was in fact carrying an illegal gun. One wonders what percentage the

Times would consider reasonable—30 percent? 50? 75?—before it blessed such searches. And since 20 percent is apparently too low, how does it justify allowing 9,546 armed criminals to wander round New York to mug, murder, and rape merely to avoid embarrassing about 17,500 people annually?

The answer is, of course, that, like mainstream media opinion in general, the *Times* would raise no serious objection if those frisked and arrested were an ethnic cross-section of society. What raises its hackles is that they are mainly black or Hispanic, which in turn raises its suspicions that they are the victims of police "racial profiling." This the NYPD strongly denies—taking someone's race into account when conducting a search is illegal to begin with. Its own explanation is that, if you are conducting searches mainly in high-crime areas, then you will inevitably end up frisking mainly black and Hispanic suspects. As a former commander of the Street Crimes Unit said, "In the precincts that we worked in, it would be difficult to find a white guy." But does anyone seriously suggest that the police should concentrate on low-crime areas?

Liberal Racism

In the end, the objection to the NYPD's successful anti-crime policy amounts to a desire to ignore racial disparities in crime and to escape their implications. Liberals in particular are unhappy fighting crime if they seem to be fighting mainly black crime. Their favorite offenses are "hate" and white-collar crimes where, they hope, more of the "perps" will turn out to be white. And they shrink from police tactics that, though they may greatly benefit the black majority by increasing their safety, may undermine liberal myths of pervasive white racism and black victimhood. It is this liberal racism that forms the emotional backdrop to the Diallo case in New York . . .

But the glue that holds all liberal critics together is the conviction that white America is fundamentally racist and has to be continually restrained from its punitive racist impulses. Hence the trends in media coverage and political rhetoric noted above: White-on-black crimes must be highlighted to shame white America out of its racism; black-on-white crimes must be downplayed lest they encourage white America in its racism; and any broader social indicators—whether crime statistics or police tactics—must be judged by the test of whether they serve to encourage or restrain white racism.

As with almost all liberal policies, of course, the unintended consequences are likely to prove more important than those intended. Hastily recruited minority cops will be more likely to act, and shoot, as hastily (the Detroit and Washington forces, which have higher numbers of minorities, also have much worse records of police brutality); uniformed cops will be unable to surprise criminals; and monitoring "racial" friskings will waste police time and discourage the frisking of manifestly dangerous suspects when the relevant quota has been filled. Even while these reforms are still in the discussion stage, the number of street-crime arrests in New York has fallen by 60 percent since the Diallo killing, and the murder rate has ticked up slightly. Once they are implemented, crime will resume its increase, including black crime; white racism will then have more to feed on; and—oh yes—the number of black victims will rise disproportionately too. But what will that matter to comfortable middle-class liberals as long as "the work goes on, the cause endures, the hope still lives, and the dream shall never die"?

Issue 4

Should the Exclusionary Rule Be Abolished?

- *The exclusionary rule exacts a high price from society in the form of the "release of countless guilty criminals" (Chief Justice Burger,* **Bivens v. Six Unknown Federal Narcotics Agents,** *1971).*

- *"A court which admits [illegally seized evidence] manifests a willingness to tolerate the unconstitutional conduct which produced it." (Kamisar, 1978).*

These two quotes summarize the ideological differences over how the courts should respond to an illegal search and seizure. Both sides agree, though, that applying the Fourth Amendment (drafted in the 18th century) to the complexities of the 21st century is difficult. The framers provided that "the right of the people to be secure in their persons, houses, papers and effects against unreasonable search and seizure, shall not be violated." But they did not spell out what might constitute an illegal search and seizure. Nor did the drafters suggest what should happen if the police do indeed conduct an illegal search and seizure.

Through the 19th century the rule was straightforward: "If the constable blunders the crook should not go free." This began to change in 1914 when the Supreme Court first applied the exclusionary rule *(Weeks v. U.S.)*. The exclusionary rule is a rule created by judicial decisions holding that evidence obtained through violations of the constitutional rights of the criminal defendant must be excluded from trial. Initially, this rule applied only to federal law enforcement officials. But in 1961, in one of the most important (which is also to say most controversial) Warren Court decisions, the exclusionary rule was extended to apply to state and local police *(Mapp v. Ohio)*.

Conservatives quickly blamed Supreme Court decisions like *Mapp* for the nation's rising crime rate. Thus, the crime control model quickly became a major political issue. Forty years later the debate continues. There has been an important shift, however. Initially, conservatives called for the outright abolition of the exclusionary rule. More recently, they have stressed giving the cops greater leeway by creating a "good faith exception" or allowing for an "honest mistake."

The ideological debate masks important changes that have occurred. Both state and federal courts are reluctant to hold that evidence is inadmissible. This is particularly true when the police seize large quantities of drugs. Thus some say that today the Fourth Amendment has been rewritten to include a preamble: "Except in drug cases, the right of the people to be secure . . . "

The contemporary debate runs along the following lines.

Pro	Con
Minor police errors can throw a case out of court, no matter how guilty the defendant.	A court of law should never tolerate illegal and unconstitutional conduct.
Letting the crook go free serves no useful purpose.	Letting the crook go free is the only effective way to deter police misconduct.
Existing remedies work; internal disciplinary actions and civil lawsuits effectively control illegal conduct by the police.	Alternative remedies are unworkable; internal review boards cover up and juries will not award damages in civil suits.
Minor, technical mistakes are treated the same as egregious violations.	The police will abuse any "good faith" exception or honest-mistake doctrine.
"Countless" guilty suspects are released each year because of the exclusionary rule.	Less than one out of 100 police arrests are declined for prosecution because of exclusionary rules.

The debate over the exclusionary rule typically pits advocates of the crime control model against proponents of the due process model of justice. The following two articles, though, reflect divisions among conservatives.

The article "Why Stop Halfway?" argues the exclusionary rule allows criminals to go free and does not effectively restrain police conduct. The author, Morgan O. Reynolds (director of the Criminal Justice Center of the National Center for Policy Analysis and professor of economics at Texas A&M University), concludes that the exclusionary rule should be repealed rather than reformed.

The article "Congress and the Exclusionary Rule: Would Killing the Exclusionary Rule Repeal the Fourth Amendment—or Restore It?" argues that the Exclusionary Rule Reform Act of 1995 would destroy Fourth Amendment prohibitions against unreasonable searches by allowing police to conduct searches without a warrant. The author, Robert E. Bauman (a retired Republican U.S. Congressman) concludes that keeping the exclusionary rule supports the principles of the Fourth Amendment.

World Wide Web Exercises

1. The U.S. Supreme Court adopted the exclusionary rule in *Mapp v. Ohio* 367 U.S. 643 (1961). Read the majority and the dissenting opinions. Are the arguments made then similar to, or different from, those expressed by the justices? The opinion can be found on the Internet at http://findlaw.com/casecode/supreme.html. Then type in the case name **Mapp v. Ohio.**

2. Select the search engine of your choice. Using the search term **exclusionary rule** or **search and seizure,** locate two or more articles that discuss issues related to the topic. What kinds of issues are currently under discussion?

InfoTrac College Edition Exercises

1. Use the search term **searches and seizures, laws** and read one article on either side of the issue. Are the issues discussed similar to or different from those argued in the readings?

2. Using the search term **exclusionary rule (evidence), analysis,** find and read two or more articles that analyze the actual impact of the exclusionary rule on police practice and court outcomes. Do these findings tend to support arguments for (or against) abolition of the exclusionary rule?

Why Stop Halfway? (Need to Repeal the Exclusionary Rule)

Morgan O. Reynolds

A motorcycle cop stops a speeding car. Without a search warrant but suspicious, the policeman demands that the driver open his trunk, and discovers the corpses of a woman and two children. The man later walks out of court scot-free because the evidence was inadmissible. The criminal's Fourth Amendment rights had been violated.

This miscarriage of justice supposedly improves the protection of our civil liberties, but it does no such thing. The entire theory of suppressing illegally obtained evidence in criminal court is misguided.

The exclusionary rule was concocted by an imaginative Supreme Court in *Weeks v. United States* in 1914. Until then, little had been heard about reckless abuse of citizens' constitutional rights by federal law enforcement officials. The agitated justices declared that, without their little creature, the Fourth Amendment was "of no value" and "might as well be stricken from the Constitution."

In 1961, Earl Warren and company initiated their do-good revolution in criminal privileges by imposing the exclusionary rule on all state courts in *Mapp v. Ohio,* a breathtaking expansion of power considering that more than 90 percent of criminal cases are prosecuted by the states. Between 1920 and 1960, half the states had allowed pertinent evidence into criminal proceedings, even if it had allegedly been obtained illegally, on a case-by-case basis. The remaining states, either through statute or through appellate court decisions, emulated federal suppression. Advocates of quashing had succeeded in twenty states during the 1920s, usually as a device to soften the impact of Prohibition.

Not only does the exclusionary rule have a wholly suspicious origin—the twentieth-century federal judiciary—but it defies common sense and lacks empirical evidence in its favor. As former Chief Justice Warren Burger points out, "There is no empirical evidence to support the claim that the rule actually deters illegal conduct of law-enforcement officials." The exclusionary rule remains unique to American jurisprudence. Our celebrated civil-libertarian neighbor to the north, for example, relies on the tort system to correct overzealous police searches and compensate victims.

Like the rest of the Warren Court revolution, the rule excluding illegally obtained evidence makes so little sense that the courts and Congress have tried steadily to narrow its application. Yet allowing an exception to the exclusionary rule for evidence seized illegally but in good faith is a defective cure. It allows police officers to blunder in good faith again and again. Government agents now routinely conduct unconstitutional searches and seizures with impunity.

Expanding the legal liability of police departments and setting up compensation funds for money damages would make the police respect constitutional liberties and avoid illegal searches and seizures for which they might be sued.

The exclusionary rule has benefits only in the eyes of those who judge laws strictly by their intentions rather than their actual effects. The rule offers no civil-liberties benefits, only social cost. It

Source: *National Review,* May 15, 1995 v47. © National Review Inc. 1995. Reprinted by permission.

artificially impedes justice by freeing at least 20,000 criminals each year. Statistical studies show that exclusionary rules, all else equal, are associated with a 15 percent increase in crime rates. The Warren Court has the blood of thousands of crime victims on its hands.

While most policemen honestly try to follow Fourth Amendment directives, current law is so tortured that even experienced lawyers and judges do not know if particular searches will be upheld by the courts. The exclusionary rule has done more to undermine the Fourth Amendment than to protect it. As District of Columbia Circuit Judge Malcolm Wilkey once wrote: "If one were diabolically to attempt to invent a device designed slowly to undermine the substantive reach of the Fourth Amendment, it would be hard to do better than the exclusionary rule."

The exclusionary rule makes it more difficult to convict the guilty, including police officers who commit crimes. The rule makes it easy for corrupt cops to protect favored criminals from prosecution by simply making an illegal seizure.

The exclusionary rule dooms many criminal prosecutions. Prosecutors have limited budgets and avoid prosecuting cases with serious search and seizure problems. Their reasoning: Why risk a prolonged struggle over the technicalities of the exclusionary rule?

The exclusionary rule does not punish overzealous or criminal police conduct because officers and police departments are typically rated on overall arrest clearance rates rather than conviction rates. The police practices attacked by the courts have increased since the do-good rule was imposed nationwide in 1961.

The irony of the exclusionary rule is that the public, not the culpable police, bears the costs of freeing the guilty criminals. Considering the liberal sociological view that "society" is to blame for crime rather than the criminal, this is an ironic success for this theory of justice. Under exclusion of evidence, the criminal freed on a technicality is free to punish society again.

Rather than trying to "gut" the exclusionary rule through good-faith exceptions, it would be better to repeal it in a straightforward way. Montesquieu wrote, "We must not separate the Laws from the End for which they were made." The courts have lost their way, and both they and the public know it. However, the corrective efforts to date, including the Republican expansion of the good-faith exception, are misguided. Let's start over. At least allow federalism: let the state legislatures and courts decide whether they want to retain the exclusionary rule or substitute more rational means to make the police respect constitutional liberties.

Congress and the Exclusionary Rule: Would Killing the Exclusionary Rule Repeal the Fourth Amendment— or Restore It?

Robert E. Bauman

"The greatest dangers to liberty lurk in the insidious encroachment by men of zeal, well-meaning but without understanding." It's almost as if, way back in 1927, Supreme Court Justice Louis D. Brandeis foresaw the advent of the 104th Congress and the so-called anti-crime provisions of the "Contract with America."

Brandeis's eloquent dissent was rendered in a case interpreting the Fourth Amendment, that revered provision of the Bill of Rights that for 204 years in theory has prohibited an American police state by forbidding unreasonable searches and seizures.

One can imagine the reaction of the late Justice had he returned to witness the scene in the House of Representatives when, by a roll-call vote of 303 to 121, the crime-busting congressmen rejected the actual language of the Fourth Amendment, after the chief sponsor of the "Exclusionary Rule Reform Act of 1995," Bill McCollum (R., Fla.) made the astounding claim that its inclusion would "gut the bill."

The bill in question, HR-666, now pending in the U.S. Senate, went on to sail through the House by a vote of 289 to 142, even though it eviscerates the traditional guarantees of personal privacy and freedom. A subsequent *New York Times*/CBS News poll showed 69 percent of Americans opposed to warrantless searches such as the bill permits, suggesting that Congress is out of step with both the Constitution and the people.

The Fourth Amendment has two parts—a prohibition against "unreasonable" police search and seizure, and a specific requirement 1) that police may obtain a search warrant from a judge only after a showing of "probable cause," and 2) that warrants must particularly describe the place to be searched and the things to be seized. This is the heart of the Amendment—forcing police to convince a neutral magistrate that the totality of the circumstances indicates that evidence of a crime exists.

As James Jackson Kilpatrick [noted conservative writer] observed in opposing the bill, while most Americans will rarely if ever avail themselves of most other constitutional protections, "the Fourth Amendment is the one provision of the Constitution more vital to human liberty than all the rest . . . [because it] embraces us all." Our home really is our castle. Representative McCollum's deplorable bill effectively repeals the constitutional duty of police to obtain a search warrant. Instead, any rookie cop or eager DEA or FBI agent is empowered to kick down your door if he personally has formed "an objectively reasonable belief" that his action is "in conformity with the Fourth Amendment." The constitutional interpretation of your right to privacy would be delegated by Congress to that well-known local civil libertarian—the cop on the beat.

As a conservative, a Republican, and a former member of Congress viewing the capricious and driven atmosphere of Gingrich's reign of terror, I wonder if any of these "representatives" have read any American history.

The First Congress of the United States, on September 25, 1789, forwarded to the states

Source: *National Review,* May 15, 1995 v47. © National Review Inc. 1995. Reprinted by permission.

twelve Amendments to the new Constitution. This was done, in the words of Congress, because the states had "expressed a desire, in order to prevent . . . abuse of power, that further declaratory and restrictive clauses should be added," among which was the Fourth Amendment. The ten Amendments ratified became our "Bill of Rights."

The 1789 prohibition against warrantless searches and seizures was rooted in very real contemporary history. The Amendment was the direct product of the fear and humiliation experienced by thousands of colonial Americans at the hands of King George III's agents.

Crown revenue agents were issued blanket "writs of assistance" empowering each officer at his own discretion to search suspected places for smuggled goods. So widespread and brutal were these police actions that the fiery James Otis, an early leader of the Revolution, denounced the writs in a February 1761 speech as "the worst instrument of arbitrary power," since they placed "the liberty of every man in the hands of every petty officer." No less a witness to history than John Adams characterized Otis's denunciation with the opinion: "Then and there the child of Independence was born."

In *Weeks v. United States,* the 1914 decision that established the so-called "exclusionary rule," Chief Justice Edward D. White of Louisiana recalled this hallowed history as a unanimous Court held that evidence illegally obtained by police in violation of the Fourth Amendment would no longer be admissible in federal courts. In 1961 this rule was extended to state courts as well. The main purpose of the rule is to deter police misconduct, and except for this mild sanction, little does. As Justice Robert Jackson put it in a 1948 case: "[To justify] officers in making a search without a warrant would reduce the Fourth Amendment to a nullity and leave the people's homes secure only in the discretion of police officers."

Attacks on the Amendment

As politicians have frantically tried to outbid each other in "wars" on drugs in particular, and crime in general, the exclusionary rule has been ritually denounced as a "legal technicality" allowing criminals to go free. This was the demagogy codified as part of the GOP's Contract with America. This scare tactic is pure myth. Various studies by the General Accounting Office, the American Bar Association, and the National Institute of Justice have shown that possibly less than one percent, and at most 2.35 percent, of criminal cases are dismissed because of the rule. As they should be.

In the last twenty years warrantless raids and ransackings have become standard police procedure and, except in the most outrageous instances, the courts give routine approval for exceptions where evidence is in plain view, police are in hot pursuit, or evidence might be destroyed. The big break for unbridled police power came in 1984 when the Supreme Court held that illegally obtained evidence could be admitted if based on "good faith" use of a warrant later determined to be defective. The Republicans now want to go one better and remove even the need for the warrant.

Proponents of curtailing the exclusionary rule argue that internal police disciplinary measures will curb any misconduct (ask Rodney King about that), or that injured citizens can sue police for civil damages, presumably after these aggrieved citizens have been convicted of crimes based on the illegally obtained evidence. Fat chance.

The measure of congressional cynicism was taken when the House adopted floor amendments retaining the exclusionary rule on searches by agents of the Internal Revenue Service and the Bureau of Alcohol, Tobacco and Firearms, but rejected an amendment imposing the rule's application on agents of the Immigration and Naturalization Service.

A decade ago Kevin Phillips [a noted conservative writer] suggested the Republican "New Right" contained the inherent potential for what he unhesitatingly identified as "American fascism," the formation of an electoral majority by blatant appeals to anger, frustration, and prejudice. In spite of ceremonial lamentations about excesses of government power, congressional "conservatives" seem willing to jettison the principles of limited government, sacrificing individual rights as a sop to a perceived majority.

Nowhere is this unprincipled policy more evident than in the attack on the Fourth Amendment.

Part IV

Debating the Role
of Crime Victims

- *Candy Lightner's daughter was killed by a drunk driver.*
- *Nicole Brown Simpson was brutally murdered.*
- *Polly Klaas was kidnapped and murdered by a career criminal.*

- *7-year-old Megan Kanka was raped and murdered by a neighbor who was a twice-convicted sex offender.*

Individually, these four crimes share nothing in common. Collectively, though, they speak volumes about the emerging importance of crime victims in the ongoing crime debate.

- Candy Lightner went on to form Mother's Against Drunk Driving (MADD).
- Nicole Brown Simpson's murder catapulted domestic violence into the national limelight.
- Polly Klaas's murder led to the passage of "three strikes and you're out" legislation (Issue 9).
- Laws requiring convicted sex offenders to register with local police are commonly referred to as "Megan's law."

The victims' rights movement began in the 1960s. This movement was partially a result of the "law-and-order" debate, particularly its fiery rhetoric about harm done to crime victims. It was also a spin-off of the women's movement, which emphasized helping victims of rape and spousal abuse. Today the victims' rights movement involves a loose coalition of local, state and national organizations with wide-ranging interests. While diverse in origins, the victims' rights movement shares a common ideology seeking to demonstrate the triumph of good over evil. Thus, the movement resonates with a moral view of crime held by many average citizens (Weed, 1995).

Some of the specific programs that have been adopted over the years include victim compensation programs, victim/witness assistance programs, rape crisis centers, battered women's shelters, and victim impact statements. Currently, efforts are directed at adopting the Victims' Bill of Rights. The VRA, as it is often called, is modeled after provisions found in many state constitutions; it would add an amendment to the U.S. Constitution giving crime victims a number of specific rights.

Some, though, have asked some penetrating questions: mainly, are these efforts aimed at aiding or manipulating victims? While some efforts indeed focus on providing short-term and long-term aid directly to crime victims, other efforts seem to help the victim only by making the life of the defendant miserable. In the words of Samuel Walker (1982), "most of the rhetoric about victim's rights is demagoguery, playing upon the very real feelings of pain, fear, and outrage to advance dubious proposals." This section examines two topics very directly tied to the emerging importance of interest groups representing crime victims. As will become clear, it is not by accident that both issues have a feminine face.

Issue 5 poses the question, "Should States Lower the Legal Threshold for Drunk Driving?"

Issue 6 discusses the question, "Should Mandatory Arrest Policies in Domestic Violence Offenses Be Adopted?"

World Wide Web Resources

Web Guides

http://dir.yahoo.com/Society_and_Culture/Crime/Victims__Rights/

http://dir.yahoo.com/Society_and_Culture/Crime/Crimes/Drunk_Driving/

http://dir.yahoo.com/Society_and_Cult.ure/Crime/Crimes/Domestic_Violence/

Searching the Web

Basic search terms: **victim; victims rights; victimization; drunk driving; DWI; DUI; domestic violence; battered women**

Useful URLs

ABA Commission on Domestic Violence: References a variety of studies and statistics. http://www.abanet.org/domviol/cdv.html

Mothers Against Drunk Driving (MADD): More than just an organization of angry women.   http://www.madd.org/

National Organization for Victim Assistance: The largest umbrella organization offering assistance to victims.   http://www.try-nova.org/

National Organization of Women (NOW): Oldest and best known of the feminist organizations.   http://www.now.org/

National Victims' Constitutional Amendment Network: Advocacy group dedicated to passage of the Victims' Rights Amendment. http://www.nvcan.org/

Office for Victims of Crime, U.S. Department of Justice: Federal agency most directly responsible for issues related to victims of crime. http://www.ojp.usdoj.gov/ovc/

Fun sites

Abused Men Association: Provides help to males who are victims of domestic violence.   http://www.abusedmen.org/

Crime Victims for a Just Society: Promotes progressive solutions to the problems of crime and victims.   http://www.crimevictims.net/

Dignity of Victims Everywhere (DOVE): Nonprofit organization dedicated to the support and advocacy of victims of violent crime.   http://www.dove-wa.org/

National Center for the Victims of Crime: A nonprofit organization dedicated to reducing the consequences of crime on victims and society by promoting victims' rights and victim assistance.   http://www.nvc.org/

National Drunk Driving Defense Task Force: Lawyers who defend those accused of drunk driving.   http://topgundui.com/tforce.htm

Victim Services Domestic Violence Shelter Tour: Offers a tour of a domestic violence shelter.   http://www.dvsheltertour.org/

InfoTrac College Edition Resources

Background

Reference books provide background on family violence and victims of crimes.

Basic Searches

victims of crimes; family violence; drunk driving

Related Searches

abused men; abused women; conjugal violence; wife abuse; drinking and traffic accidents; drunkenness (criminal law); adult child abuse victims; rape victim services; rape victims

Issue 5

Should States Lower the Legal Threshold for Drunk Driving?

Candy Lightner's 13-year-old daughter was walking home from a friend's house when she was killed by a hit-and-run driver. He had been out of jail on bail for only two days for another hit-and-run drunk-driving crash. Indeed, he had three previous drunk driving accidents (and two convictions). This tragedy led to the founding of Mothers Against Drunk Driving (MADD) in 1980. Through the years its focus has expanded to include crime victims, not just those who have been injured by drunk drivers.

MADD has been at the forefront of state and federal efforts to "get tough with drunk drivers." The drinking age has been increased to 21, the level at which a driver is presumed to be intoxicated has been lowered, and penalties have been increased. In turn, drunk-driving fatalities have decreased (as have traffic deaths overall).

Why then does the problem persist? The answer lies in societal ambivalence toward drinking and driving. While the American public views drunk drivers as villains, consumption of alcoholic beverages constitutes a major social and economic activity. Should even tougher laws be passed?

Pro	Con
Drunk drivers kill and injure too many people each year.	Drunk-driving deaths have declined steadily over the last several years.
Even a small amount of alcohol consumed by a driver (so-called "social drinkers") can cause accidents, some fatal.	"Problem drinkers" who have consumed large amounts of alcohol should be the real target.
Police need to devote more attention to apprehending drunk drivers.	The police arrest over 1.5 million people for drunk driving each year, more than any other category.
Tougher sentences need to be imposed on drunk drivers; often mandatory jail sentences for first offenders should be imposed.	High penalties for drunk driving lead to fewer arrests, more plea bargaining, fewer convictions, and earlier release from jail.

The following two articles are both advocacy pieces. Note that both use somewhat similar studies but reach sharply different conclusions about their meaning and impact. Note also that both seek to minimize the other's argument by discrediting the organization.

The first article, "Yes: Lowering the Threshold Will Prevent Injuries and Deaths Due to Drunk Driving," needs no further introduction. The author is Katherine Prescott (president of Mother's Against Drunk Driving) who urges even stricter laws.

The second article, "No: Criminalizing Social Drinking Will Not Save Lives and Does Not Deal with Drunk Drivers," likewise needs no further introduction. The author, Richard Berman (general counsel, American Beverage Institute) sounds the call for greater enforcement of existing laws.

World Wide Web Exercises

1. Locate one interest group on either side of the drunk-driving debate and summarize their arguments. Here are several possibilities:

   American Beverage Institute: http://www.abionline.org/

   Businesses Against Drunk Driving (BADD):   http://www.baddpage.com/

   National College for DUI Defense, Inc.:   http://www.ncdd.com/

   National Commission Against Drunk Driving: http://www.ncadd.com/

2. The debate over drunk driving has largely focused on "get tough" legislation but there are additional ways of reducing drunk driving, prevention and education for

example. Search the Web for two or more organizations that discuss such approaches.

InfoTrac College Edition Exercises

1. Using the search term **drunk driving** locate one article that argues in favor of tougher laws against drunk driving and another article that opposes such actions. Are the arguments similar or different from those presented in the readings?

2. Using the search terms **drunk driving, laws; drunk driving, research;** and/or **drunk driving, analysis,** locate two or more academic articles that analyze the causes and prevention of drunk driving. Two journals of particular relevance are *Alcoholism and Drug Abuse Weekly* and *Contemporary Drug Problems.*

Yes: Lowering the Threshold Will Prevent Injuries and Deaths Due to Drunk Driving

Katherine P. Prescott

In 1995, an estimated 17,274 people were killed and more than one million were injured in traffic crashes that involved alcohol, representing the first increase in alcohol-related traffic deaths in a decade. Preliminary estimates show that as many people died last year in alcohol-related traffic crashes. But the tragic fact remains that these deaths and injuries were preventable.

Federal legislation sponsored by Rep. Nita Lowey of New York and Sen. Frank Lautenberg of New Jersey, both Democrats, and Sen. Mike De Wine of Ohio, a Republican, would require states to lower their blood-alcohol content, or BAC, limit from .10 to .08 for all drivers or risk losing a percentage of federal highway construction funds. If .08 percent BAC laws were adopted in all 50 states, an estimated 500 to 600 lives would be saved each year.

Mothers Against Drunk Driving, or MADD, supports the .08 percent BAC law in defining intoxicated driving, as do a variety of national health, safety and law-enforcement groups, including the American Medical Association, the National Safety Council and the International Association of Chiefs of Police. The .08 law is a vital part of the solution to the overall problem of drunk driving, which affects two in every five Americans and costs our country more than $45 billion annually. The majority of the American public supports lowering the illegal BAC limit to .08.

But rather than argue the merits of this lifesaving legislation that will make our roads safer, the American Beverage Institute, or ABI, now has decided to attack the messenger, MADD, while continuing to distort the message.

The ABI, representing restaurants such as the Hard Rock Cafe, Chili's, TGI Fridays, Red Lobster, Outback Steakhouse, Olive Garden and Pizzeria Uno, as well as Marriott Hotels, began its campaign by opposing the passage of state .08 percent BAC bills. The ABI seems to fear the passage of .08 percent BAC legislation based on the concern that these laws will affect alcohol sales. But research has proven otherwise. There is no evidence that per-capita consumption of alcohol was affected in any of the five states with .08 percent BAC laws examined in a recent analysis.

The *American Journal of Public Health* in September 1996 reported a study showing that the five states that adopted the .08 percent BAC limit experienced a 16 percent reduction in fatal crashes with a fatally injured driver whose BAC was .08 or higher, as well as an 18 percent reduction in such crashes with a fatally injured driver with a BAC level of .15 or higher. The study was conducted by Ralph Hingson, chairman of the Social and Behavioral Sciences Department at the Boston University School of Public Health. He is an expert in the study of alcohol issues, with more than 20 years of experience. His reputation in the health and research community is beyond reproach. It was only after he submitted this study to the *American Journal of Public Health* that MADD asked him to sit on its Board of Directors.

The ABI argues that MADD wants you arrested if you have a slice of pizza and a few beers. Social drinking would be impossible, it says.

Source: *Insight*. July 28, 1997 V13. Reprinted with permission.

According to the National Highway Traffic Safety Administration, a 170-pound male can drink four 12-ounce cans of beer, four 5-ounce glasses of wine or four mixed drinks within one hour on an empty stomach before reaching .08 percent BAC. A 137-pound female can drink two to three drinks of the same size on an empty stomach in one hour before reaching that same level, a level at which all driving skills are affected. This hardly is social drinking.

Scientific evidence clearly shows skills such as braking, steering, lane changing, judgment, divided attention and emergency response all are affected at .08 percent BAC level. A person's crash risk at .08 is 16 times greater than that of a sober driver. And if you think that's dangerous, consider your crash risk at .10 BAC: 32 times greater than that of a sober driver.

The ABI and the alcohol beverage industry have been chasing MADD around from state capitol to state capitol spreading untruths about .08 percent BAC laws. Despite the misguided effort of the ABI, 15 states have passed .08 percent BAC limit-while-driving laws with Republican Gov. Jim Edgar of Illinois signing onto the measure on July 2. Yet, in many other states, .08 percent BAC bills were defeated. In those states, the public strongly supported a .08 percent BAC limit, as did most legislators, but the ABI and the alcohol-beverage industry succeeded in convincing a handful of legislators to defeat .08 percent BAC legislation.

This is why federal leadership is needed. The Safe and Sober Streets Act of 1997 introduced by Rep. Lowey and Sen. Lautenberg would require all states to pass .08 percent BAC-limit laws for drivers above the age of 21.

Having exhausted its misinformation campaign, the ABI has begun to oppose federal legislation by arguing that states should not be required to pass .08 percent BAC laws. And there are those in Congress who say this is a states'-rights issue and should be left to the states to determine what their blood-alcohol limit should be.

In response, MADD urges these opponents to look at the reality of the political system on the state level. When a handful of opponents can thwart the wishes of the majority of citizens and legislators in a state, there clearly is a problem that requires strong federal leadership. The safety of the citizens of this country cannot become a pawn in the political game of special interest groups nor can it be held hostage by the alcohol and hospitality lobby.

The millions of victims killed and maimed in alcohol-related traffic crashes have paid the ultimate price from inaction on the state level and have the right to have their voices and those of their survivors heard. They have not paid with campaign contributions but with their lives, their limbs, their blood and their tears. The time has come for Congress to decide whose interests have greater value. Will the value of these lives be measured by the price of one more drink?

In a national survey released last year, 91 percent of Americans surveyed believed that federal involvement in assuring safe highways is important and 78 percent said that such a role is very important. MADD credits the growing number of sponsors to the Safe and Sober Streets Act of 1997 with showing the federal leadership needed to help prevent further senseless injuries and deaths due to drunk driving.

The ABI claims MADD's mission has been achieved, and we should declare victory and stop fighting to save lives and prevent injuries. MADD is appalled that the ABI could believe that more than one million deaths and injuries each year are inconsequential.

For years, MADD fought hard to save lives and succeeded. Alcohol-related traffic deaths slowly and steadily declined even as miles traveled increased steadily each year. Now, the trend is changing. Unless stronger laws are passed throughout this country and existing laws are adequately enforced, drunk drivers will continue to terrorize the nation's roads.

The .08 percent BAC laws are an effective weapon in the war against drunk driving. Some might say that saving 500 to 600 lives each year doesn't really affect society, but 500 to 600 deaths is equivalent to the typical loss of life from four jetliner crashes. Public outcry for preventive action surely would be tremendous if 500 to 600 people were killed in airline crashes in just one year. MADD firmly believes that a violent death in one mode of transportation is just as tragic and preventable as another. Drunk-driving deaths are no less tragic just because they occur one, two or three at a time.

The ABI argues that .08 percent BAC laws don't target the real problem and that MADD is not focusing on repeat driving-under-the-influence, or DUI, offenders with high BAC levels. But MADD and other highway safety organizations long have advocated progressive sanctions aimed at such offenders. Where was the ABI when these issues were being debated and passed in states across the nation? Most of the time, their paid lobbyists were opposing these measures.

MADD supports laws that have been proven, through expert research, to deter drunk drivers. Lowering the BAC level to .08 is not the silver bullet to the drunk-driving problem, but it is a vitally important and effective element in fighting drunk driving and the slaughter and heartbreak that it causes.

MADD argues that any person who kills while driving impaired is part of the real problem. In 1995, more than 3,700 people died in crashes where drivers had BAC levels below .10. That's 3,700 families in America that never again will experience the joy of their precious loved ones. We think that's a real problem—one that .08 percent BAC laws will help solve.

While MADD is concerned about the habitual drunk driver, the truth is that approximately 85 percent of all alcohol-related traffic fatalities are caused by first-time offenders or people who haven't offended in the past three years.

The ABI makes the outrageous assertion that because drunken drivers themselves account for more than half of the fatalities in alcohol-related traffic crashes, they are not victims. This is absurd. The family members and friends of people who died while drinking and driving indeed are victims of this preventable and tragic crime. Their lives also are shattered and forever altered by the death of a loved one. They too have lost a precious family member. The ABI's discount of these grieving victims of the drunk-driving problem further demonstrates its total lack of compassion. But then, saving lives obviously is not the ABI's goal—selling alcohol is.

Instead of keeping people safe, it seems the ABI would rather sell more alcoholic beverages to people who already are impaired. It is time for the alcohol industry and the ABI to become part of the solution instead of being part of the problem. We urge them to cease their misinformation campaign and join MADD in our true goal of keeping people coming home to their families every day. Making .08 percent BAC the law of the land would help us reach our goal.

No: Criminalizing Social Drinking Will Not Save Lives and Does Not Deal With Drunk Drivers

Richard Berman

Say you and your neighbors are fed up with a few speeders who continue to race through your neighborhood. While most drivers obey the posted 25 mph speed limit, a couple of reckless fools consistently drive 50 mph or more, especially on weekend nights. Two solutions are proposed at the next neighborhood meeting: Either demand better police enforcement of the posted limit or drop the limit from 25 mph to 20 mph. Which would you choose?

That is the essence of the traffic safety debate now being played out in Congress about the drunk-driving problem. In an effort to reduce drunk-driving deaths, two Democrats, Rep. Nita Lowey of New York and Sen. Frank Lautenberg of New Jersey, proposed redefining the problem to include responsible social drinking—the legislative equivalent of dropping the speed limit to catch people who ignore current limits.

With the backing of Mothers Against Drunk Driving, or MADD, the lawmakers want to lower the blood-alcohol content, or BAC, limit from .10 percent BAC to .08 percent BAC. If they succeed, a 120-pound woman will be considered legally drunk if she drinks two 6-ounce glasses of wine during a two-hour period, according to National Highway Traffic Safety Administration, or NHTSA, data. If apprehended, this woman will face arrest, fines, jail, higher insurance rates and license revocation for behavior that is not part of the drunk-driving problem.

Meanwhile, the real problem of product abusers who drive goes unabated. According to

the Department of Transportation, or DOT, the average blood-alcohol content of fatally injured drunk drivers comes in at an incredible .18 percent—more than twice the level of drinking targeted by the legislation Congress is considering. Even MADD's national president recently lamented that the problem is down to a hardened core of alcoholics who do not respond to public appeals. So why target currently legal drinkers?

Ironically, proposals to redefine drunkenness actually will hurt the fight against drunk driving. By diluting the definition of a drunk driver to include social drinkers, lawmakers automatically will increase the pool of drunks by more than 50 percent without increasing the resources to fight it. This will have a debilitating effect on the already underfunded law-enforcement efforts to stop truly drunk drivers.

But the worst part about the proposal to lower the BAC threshold is that it won't work.

In the 14 years since the first of 15 states lowered their BAC thresholds to .08, not one government study has been able to show that lower BAC levels save lives. In fact, the only study in existence to make such a bold claim is a highly disputed four-page report written by anti-alcohol researcher Ralph Hingson (who, incidentally, sits on MADD's board of directors).

The study, which compares five .08 BAC states with five nearby .10 BAC states, concludes that 500 to 600 lives could be saved each year if all 50 states adopted a .08 BAC arrest threshold.

Independent analysis of the Hingson research by Data Nexus Inc. found that the conclusion of that study is not supported by the evidence.

Hingson's results, they found, depend upon which states were chosen to be compared with the .08-percent-law states. In other words, if you change the comparison states, the study falls apart.

The DOT did its own, much larger, study of the same five .08 percent states and couldn't verify Hingson's conclusion.

So if, as government data prove, alcohol abusers with high BAC levels cause most drunk-driving deaths and no credible research has shown that .08 percent BAC laws save lives, why does MADD insist on criminalizing social drinkers? The answer is simple: self-preservation.

Having succeeded in its original mission to reduce drunk-driving deaths by educating the public and strengthening laws, MADD has declined to declare victory. Instead, it has taken on a new crusade, one which keeps it in business: the de facto criminalization of social drinking.

Rather than relentlessly pursuing drunk drivers, MADD has charged into the Prohibitionist ranks, changing its motto from "Don't Drive Drunk" to "Impairment Begins With the First Drink." And, lest anyone miss the message, MADD president-elect Karolyn Nunnallee appeared on NBC's Today Show (Oct. 12, 1996) to lay down her marker: "We will not tolerate drinking and driving—period."

Here is what that means in real life: If you have one or two beers with a slice of pizza prior to driving home, MADD wants you arrested. Social drinking at a tavern would be made nearly impossible for most customers, save for those with chauffeurs. Those who drink a julep or two at the racetrack had better plan on departing on horseback. It seems that this once reasonable organization hopes to launch America into a new era of solitary drinking.

This, of course, is being done for our own good.

Or is it? A look at the organization's tax records makes it clear that securing the public good may not be the only motivation for this profound mission switch. MADD has become a big business. . . . The tale of the tape is unmistakable: MADD enjoyed a cash flow of $45.5 million in 1994. . . . There are a lot of people depending on MADD to stay in business. [From 1991 to 1994 a mere .348 percent was spent on direct lobbying]. . . .

If MADD only were interested in keeping its shingle aloft, that would make little difference. Unfortunately, they have embraced vintage self-preservation tactics that many Americans will find disturbing, including overstating the threat and relying on misleading anecdotes.

MADD insists that drunk driving is on the rise again—by four percent between 1994 and 1995, according to its press releases. What it fails to point out is that all highway fatalities increased by that amount, as Americans drove 55 billion more miles in 1995 than the year before. (Alcohol-related fatalities as a percentage of all fatalities stayed the same.)

MADD tells us that alcohol standards for intoxication and arrest in many other industrialized nations are lower than in the United States but fails to mention that the alcohol-related fatality rates of these countries are higher than that of the United States.

MADD continually suggests that every person killed in drunk-driving accidents is a victim. There are victims in this area to be sure. And one is one too many. Yet, according to the DOT, drunk drivers themselves account for more than half of all alcohol-related fatalities, and drunk pedestrians who walk in front of cars represent another 11 percent.

In characterizing every suicide as a homicide, MADD deliberately is inflating people's fears that they, too, will become victims, logically expecting the heightened fear to transfer into heightened financial support.

Though disheartening, there is nothing unusual about the practice of exaggerating a threat to enhance the support of the organization claiming to fight it. . . .

Training and experience make those of us in the restaurant and bar industry acute observers of Americans' drinking habits. Our servers and bartenders are workday social scientists whose data field comes with names, faces and highly visible types of alcohol-related behavior both normal and abusive.

We see the mainly responsible customers who enjoy a few drinks over conversation or food, get up from the table and drive safely home. We see the few problem drinkers who—if we permitted—would tie on a hellbender, then stagger out to their cars to menace the same highways traveled by our friends, families and loyal customers. Most important, we recognize the difference between these two types of drinkers. So should the law. So should MADD.

But isn't the restaurant and bar industry resisting a lower arrest threshold for its own selfish reasons, to sell one more drink to obviously impaired patrons as MADD accuses?

Hardly. Ringing up a few extra highballs isn't worth the risk that drunk drivers pose to our shared communities, and it's bad business to boot. In fact, the downside costs of overserving (litigation, obnoxious drunks, police scrutiny) far outweigh the profit on humoring the occasional drunk with more product.

And in the 44 states with dramshop laws, businesses who push drinks at customers can be held liable for millions of dollars in damages when those customers cause traffic injuries to themselves and others. And restaurants or bars that gain a name as kennels for boozehounds forfeit the business of a broader client base even as they draw the gaze of police and licensing boards.

Our industry would like to pick up the torch that MADD has dropped and hold it to the feet of the drunk driver. Does MADD remember that fellow? He was at one time their prime target. The organization did heroic work in yanking him from the driver's seat.

Brian O'Neill, president of the Insurance Institute for Highway Safety and no apologist for drunks, says of the .08 BAC crusade, "What [politicians] ought to be doing is to provide more resources to vigorously enforce the laws on the books, and they'll save many more lives."

That's the goal of the restaurant industry. And it should be the goal of MADD, with whom we would gladly work to enforce—indeed, stiffen—laws against truly drunk drivers.

We in the industry are well positioned to spot and deter the alcohol abuser—or any customer who overindulges. We know when people have gone too far and we know when to cut them off. MADD's efforts to criminalize social drinking have gone too far. It's time to cut them off.

Issue 6

Should Mandatory Arrest Policies in Domestic Violence Offenses Be Adopted?

The trial of O. J. Simpson for murdering his ex-wife Nicole Brown Simpson has been credited with awakening the U.S. to the problems of domestic violence.

The domestic violence movement in the U.S. originated in the 1970s as a grass-roots crusade led primarily by women's advocates. At the national level, the National Organization of Women (NOW) was at the forefront of efforts to dramatically change how domestic violence incidents are handled by the criminal justice system. Historically, violence against the wife (or girlfriend) was viewed as a husband's prerogative (Barnes, 1998). Now police departments and prosecutors are under pressure to treat reports of domestic violence as serious matters. Moreover, by the 1990s significant federal legislation was passed—the Violence Against Women Act of 1994.

As domestic violence has become a hot-button issue, placing it in perspective has become difficult. Murders, for example, are highly publicized but very atypical. In 1996 just over 1,800 murders were attributable to intimates—down 36 percent since 1976. Perhaps the most recent statistics (Bureau of Justice Statistics, 1998) can best provide a much need overview. Violence is defined as murder, rape, sexual assault, robbery, aggravated assault, and simple assault. An intimate refers to current or former spouse, boyfriend, or girlfriend.

- About 1,000,000 incidents of intimate violence occur each year.
- In 85 percent of incidents of intimate violence a woman is the victim.
- Half of the incidents of intimate violence experienced by women were reported to the police.

At the forefront of the debate over domestic violence has been the question of police arrest policy.

Pro	Con
Domestic violence represents an epidemic in U.S. society.	The number of female victims of violent crimes dropped 24 percent in recent years.
Physical injuries are all too common in domestic violence situations.	Only one in ten women victimized by a violent intimate sought medical treatment.
Police should arrest and D.A. prosecute no matter the wishes of the victim.	Victim's views should be primary even if there is no arrest or prosecution.
All too often police fail to make an arrest for domestic violence, prosecutors fail to prosecute, and judges don't send defendants to incarceration.	Those who committed a violent crime against an intimate represent about 25 percent of convicted violence offenders in local jails and seven percent in state prisons.

The first article, "Domestic Violence Can Be Cured," highlights the progressive steps taken in Tulsa, Oklahoma, to stop family violence. The author, Felicia Collins Correia (executive director of Domestic Violence Intervention Services, Tulsa, Oklahoma), argues that private, nonprofit groups have prompted extensive changes in the police response to domestic violence.

The second article, "Does Arrest Deter Domestic Violence?," reports that the effectiveness of arresting abusive spouses is still being questioned. The authors, Janell Schmidt (director of the Milwaukee office of the Crime Control Institute) and Lawrence Sherman (University of Maryland sociologist), find that arrests may result in increased cases of violence.

World Wide Web Exercises

1. Arrest is but one response to domestic violence. Others include prevention, treatment, and providing shelter for victims. Locate two or more Web sites that deal with domestic violence and examine responses other than arrest.

2. Using the search engine of your choice, locate several Web sites that focus on domestic violence. To what extent are these Web sites focused almost exclusively on this topic, or do they discuss other related issues? What are these other issues? What is the common thread that ties these issues together?

InfoTrac College Edition Exercises

1. Using the search term **family violence, laws,** find one article that argues for tougher laws against domestic violence and another article that supports other approaches. To what extent are the arguments similar to or different from those presented in the readings?

2. Using the search term **family violence, research,** locate two or more articles in academic journals that analyze laws that crack down on domestic violence. Do the results tend to support one side or the other in the debate?

Domestic Violence Can Be Cured

Felicia Collins Correia

Imagine this scenario: You are a woman walking on a street in your community this month. [You are assaulted.] You file a report with the police again, although you really don't know why you bother. They know who has been perpetrating these assaults on you, but do little more than talk to him to tell him to refrain from repeating the attacks. The police officers know he will do it again, yet seem apathetic. One cop informs you that, even if they were to arrest him, he would make bond and the crime would be plea-bargained down to community service. They suggest you walk on the other side of the street to avoid him next time.

There are a number of disturbing aspects in this hypothetical situation. For one, it appears that you no longer are safe from violent crime. More alarming is the response of the police force and judiciary. This criminal is free to continue assaulting you without any fear of facing jail time. On top of all of this, you feel powerless.

You may be inclined to dismiss this vignette as something that never could happen in the U.S. Unfortunately for millions of battered American women, the situation is not at all hypothetical. This is their reality:

- Every nine seconds, a woman is abused by her husband or intimate partner.

- That translates to almost 4,000,000 [abused] females each year.

Source: *USA Today* (Magazine), November, 1997 v126. Full text ©1997 Society for the Advancement of Education. Reprinted by permission.

- Women are victims of domestic violence more often than of burglary, muggings, or other physical crimes combined.

- Forty-two percent of murdered women are killed by their intimate male partners.

Injuries received by victims of domestic violence are at least as serious as those suffered in 90 percent of violent felonies. . . . Yet, in most states, battering still is considered a misdemeanor punishable only by small fines and/or a short time in prison. That presumes, of course, the batterer actually is arrested and charged with the crime.

For all of the latest political posturing about getting "tough on crime," many in the law enforcement and legal communities across the nation do not respond to this type of assault as a crime. Contrary to popular belief, domestic abuse is not a family matter. It is a crime and, as such, a public matter that should involve protection for the victims and justice for the batterers. In order to attack the epidemic of family violence effectively, a concerted response from various segments of society is necessary. These include lawmakers, the police, the judiciary, medical providers, educators, employers, and the general public. As public awareness of domestic violence has increased due to growing media coverage, the time is ripe to work toward "systems" changes. It is no small task, but can be done. . . .

While the strides made in the domestic violence movement have been laudable (shelters, counseling, batterer treatment, the Violence Against Women Act of 1994), there is room for improvement.

Politicians who tout the importance of family values must recognize the need for proper legislation regarding violence. How can they promise a return to family values if they can't promise their citizens protection and justice in the face of domestic abuse?

Traditionally, the state coalitions primarily have targeted the "top" of the system—i.e., state and national legislatures—to pass laws that apply to all citizens. While it is crucial to secure these laws, they mean nothing if not enforced in every town and city. Instead of relying on the top-down strategy favored by the state coalitions, local domestic violence groups should employ a bottom-up one, working together with local government, law enforcement, legal, judiciary, medical, and educational organizations to effect changes in their handling of domestic violence. . . .

One City's Fight

In Tulsa, Oklahoma, cited as an "average city" by *American Demographics* magazine, some progressive steps have been taken. The agency that has effected these changes is Domestic Violence Intervention Services, Inc. Like many other programs across the country, DVIS started as a telephone crisis line in 1975 and began sheltering women and their children in safe homes throughout the city in 1976. Since then, the private, nonprofit agency has expanded its services greatly. In addition to a 24-hour crisis line and a confidential shelter for battered women and their children, DVIS offers outpatient counseling for abusers, victims, and children; court advocacy; a transitional living program; and community education programs. . . .

In September, 1992, DVIS staff began tracking the number of women murdered in Tulsa. They only could determine if a murder was related to domestic violence through newspaper accounts, since the law enforcement community did not report domestic violence homicides accurately. By March, 1993, 12 deaths in the Tulsa area were found to have been related to domestic violence. DVIS researched each case to determine the victims' involvement with the various protection systems prior to their deaths.

At the same time, some officers in the police department reportedly were responding negatively to victims of domestic abuse and failing to make arrests even when signs of abuse were visible. Police administrators requested documentation to support these complaints. The outcome was the Police Response Report Form, which would be distributed to all DVIS clients who had interactions with a police officer. All interactions, positive or negative, were noted on these report forms. The chief of police supported the use of the form and assured that internal investigations would be initiated whenever necessary.

What happened next set the stage for the sweeping changes in the system's response to domestic violence. In a span of nine days in the spring of 1993, two Tulsa women were murdered—one by her abusive spouse; the other, a 39-year-old mother of four, hours after being released from a local hospital, where she had been treated for injures sustained from an earlier attack at the hands of her ex-husband. The first victim, a 35-year-old mother of three, was gunned down in the parking garage of a downtown building, where she worked as a human resources specialist.

In response to these murders, I publicly stated that the system failed these two women and called for the "creation of a review board to investigate domestic-related slayings and to hold the system accountable." Public outcry over the murders was mounting, and a member of the City Council requested that a special task force be appointed to review the system of protection for battered women. Members included the chief of police, the Tulsa County district attorney, the executive director of DVIS, the police commissioner, and a district judge who had worked on the protective order docket in recent years. The four major hurdles this group faced were police sensitivity to the response reports DVIS was maintaining; law enforcement officials not wanting task force members to "point fingers" regarding the recent murders; the D.A.'s contention that his constituents would prefer law enforcement dollars be spent on what they perceived as "more dangerous" crimes; and the belief that nothing could prevent a homicide if the batterer is determined to kill.

After meeting once a week for eight weeks, the task force delivered a report to the City Council that included a recommendation for a permanent city-wide effort to expand the safety net for domestic violence victims. Essentially, it called for a "system overhaul" that would encompass the formation of a domestic violence police unit; a review of the police probable cause policy; recommendation of adopting mandatory arrest of batterers; expansion of DVIS's court advocacy program; the training of all assistant district attorneys by Sarah Buel, a Massachusetts attorney and prosecutor who advocates full prosecution of abusers without victims' testimony; domestic violence training for all city prosecutors and 750 Tulsa police officers within six months; the district attorney, police chief, and DVIS executive director attending a domestic violence conference in San Diego and reviewing that city's system of protection for battered women and prosecution of abusers; and establishing a permanent Family Violence Council to be staffed by the mayor's office and chaired by one of the county commissioners.

The Tulsa Family Violence Council (FVC) was launched in January, 1994, with committees formed to address specifically public education, health and hospitals, data collection, the judiciary, and children who witness abuse. These committees continue to meet on a monthly basis, while a steering committee, made up of committee chairs, outside representatives, and the mayor's staff, meets quarterly. In addition, the entire council of 70 representatives meets semiannually.

Changes in the police response to domestic violence have been extensive and exemplary. A special unit of eight detectives follows up on all domestic violence cases handled by field officers. The unit's primary goal is to generate arrests and get the batterers into the judicial system at an early stage. These detectives interview the victim and witnesses and collect physical evidence. The responsibility for filing an affidavit to seek an arrest warrant no longer is the victim's; the detectives prepare the affidavits from their investigation. They then can testify in court with the evidence gathered, eliminating the need for the victim's testimony. This is significant because victims often change their minds about testifying against their abusers out of fear of retribution. Tulsa's court system has put into place a domestic violence court with one judge who hears all permanent protective order requests and rules on violations. . . .

When asking yourself if battering really does affect each of us, consider this statistic: Children raised in violent homes are 74 percent more likely to commit assault. As First Lady Hillary Clinton said in her address to the Fourth World Conference on Women, held in China, "What we are realizing around the world is that . . . if women are free from violence, their families will flourish. And when families flourish, communities and nations will flourish. . . . " Treating domestic violence as a crime, and its victims with dignity and justice, can go a long way toward ensuring a healthier, more productive nation.

Does Arrest Deter Domestic Violence?

Janell D. Schmidt and Lawrence W. Sherman

During the mid-1980s, widespread concern about the incidence and prevalence of domestic violence led many big-city police departments to radically change the way they policed a crime that affects millions of women each year. The often maligned "arrest as a last resort" tradition was replaced with written policies and state laws requiring arrest as the sole police recourse. Nationally, this enthusiastic shift generated a 70 percent increase from 1984 to 1989 in arrests for minor assaults, including domestic. Yet the movement to arrest batterers may be doing more harm than good. Research in six cities testing the "arrest works best" premise in deterring future assaults has produced complex and conflicting results. Police and policymakers are now faced with the dilemma that arrest may help some victims at the expense of others, and that arrest may assist the victim in the short term but facilitate further violence in the long term.

The revolution in policing misdemeanor cases of domestic violence can be attributed in part to the 1984 publication of the Minneapolis Domestic Violence Experiment, the first controlled, randomized test of the effectiveness of arrest for any offense. Results from this endeavor found that arresting abusers cut in half the risk of future assaults against the same victim over a six-month follow-up period. Alternative police responses tested were the traditional "send the suspect away for eight hours" or "advise the couple to get help for their problems." The efficacy of each treatment was measured by interviews with victims and official records tracking the offense and arrest history of each suspect. Because arrest worked better than separating or advising couples, the authors recommended that states change laws prohibiting police from making warrantless arrests in misdemeanor domestic violence cases . . . But absent further research results, their recommendation to law enforcement was "to adopt arrest as the preferred policy for dealing with such cases, unless there were clearly stated reasons to do something else."

Although the authors opposed mandating arrest until further studies were completed, within eight years, legislatures in 15 states . . . and the District of Columbia moved to enact laws requiring police to arrest in all probable-cause incidents of domestic violence. . . .

It is not clear, however, how well these policies and laws have been followed or whether they have controlled repetitive acts of domestic assault. Observations of the Phoenix, Minneapolis, and Milwaukee police departments' compliance found that only Milwaukee officers consistently adhered to the policy. . . .

What is known about the impact of police arrest policies relative to domestic assault is that the vast bulk of cases brought to police attention involve lower-income and minority-group households. One reason may be a higher rate of domestic disputes among these groups; another may be a lack of alternatives short of police intervention that offer immediate relief. Although arresting thousands of unemployed, minority males each year may assist the goals of victim advocates and provide a brief respite for the victim, the skepticism of many police and criminologists relative

Source: *American Behavioral Scientist,* May–June, 1993 v36. Reprinted by permission of Sage Publications.

to the deterrent power of arrest still remains. The key question of whether other police alternatives could prove more powerful, or whether the police could be effective at all, led the National Institute of Justice to fund replication studies in six major urban cities.

Beginning in 1986 and early 1987, police in Omaha (Nebraska), Milwaukee (Wisconsin), Charlotte (North Carolina), Metro-Dade County (Miami, Florida), Colorado Springs (Colorado), and Atlanta (Georgia) began research to replicate the Minneapolis findings. . . . The different results from different measures in these cities suggests that arrest has a different effect on suspects from different kinds of households. . . .

How carefully should policymakers and advocates tread through this maze of diverse findings? Applying these results to crime control strategies is complicated by the dilemmas and choices they present. Urban legislators and police chiefs in at least 35 states can choose between continuing the status quo and not mandating arrest, a choice that will continue to harm some victims. They can also legislate arrest, a choice that may harm victims presently served by a lack of policy. Choosing between the lesser of two evils is best guided by the following summary of the facts and dilemmas gleaned from the domestic violence research published to date . . .

1. Arrest reduces domestic violence in some cities but increases it in others. . . .

2. Arrest reduces domestic violence among employed people but increases it among unemployed people. Mandatory arrest policies may thus protect working-class women but cause greater harm to those who are poor. . . .

3. Arrest reduces domestic violence in the short run but can increase it in the long run. . . .

4. Police can predict which couples are most likely to suffer future violence, but our society values privacy too highly to encourage preventive action. . . .

To some, the choice between two wrongs invokes despair and inaction. Yet policing domestic violence may not be hopeless. Careful review of the policy implications, combined with the freedom to test alternative policies, can lead to more effective solutions. Use of the best information . . . guides the following five policy recommendations:

1. Repeal mandatory arrest laws. The most compelling implications of these findings is to challenge the wisdom of mandatory arrest. States and cities that have enacted such laws should repeal them, especially if they have substantial ghetto poverty populations with high unemployment rates. These are the settings in which mandatory arrest policies are most likely to backfire. . . .

2. Substitute structured police discretion. Instead of mandating arrest in cases of misdemeanor domestic violence, state legislatures should mandate that each police agency develop its own list of approved options to be exercised at the discretion of the officer. Legislatures might also mandate one day of training each year to assure that discretion is fully informed by the latest research available. The options could include allowing victims to decide whether the assailant should be arrested, transporting victims to shelters, or taking the suspect to an alcohol detoxification center.

3. Allow warrantless arrests. Whereas mandatory arrest has become the major issue in some states, warrantless arrest remains an issue in others. Sixteen jurisdictions have adopted mandatory arrest laws, but at last report nine others have still not given officers full arrest powers in misdemeanor domestic violence cases that they did not witness: Alabama, California, Michigan, Mississippi, Montana, Nebraska, New York, Vermont, and West Virginia. The success of arrest in some cities suggests that every state should add this option to the police tool kit. Deciding when to use it can then become a matter of police policy based on continuing research and clinical experience rather than the massive effort required to change state law.

4. Encourage issuance of arrest warrants for absent offenders. The landmark Omaha experiment suggests that more domestic violence could be prevented by this policy than by any offender-present policy. The kinds of people who flee the scene might be more deterrable than those who stay. A prosecutor willing to issue warrants and a police agency willing to serve them can capitalize on that greater deterrability. If the Omaha warrant

experiment can be replicated in other cities—a very big if—then the warrant policy might actually deter more violence than do arrests of suspects who are still present. . . .

5. Special units and policies should focus on chronically violent couples. Because a limited number of couples produce most of the domestic violence incidents in any city, it makes little sense for police to treat all violent couples alike. It makes even less sense to frame the whole policy debate around responses to incidents when most of the problem is those chronic couples. . . .

The opposition to mandatory arrest laws presented here may frustrate or even anger many tireless advocates who have relentlessly grasped arrest as the preferred police response to incidents of domestic violence. To them, the suggestion that other institutions, such as battered women shelters, treatment programs for victims and offenders, schools, and welfare agencies, may better serve victims is perhaps blasphemy. But they need not become too alarmed. However sensible that approach may be, the climate in many communities today is for law enforcement officials to get tough on crime. Regardless of the results of any scientific studies, the police will remain the primary institution coping with domestic violence among the poor and unemployed. This country's current fiscal crisis dooms any substantial investment in developing new programs in both the law enforcement and social service fields. The troublesome fact remains, however, that the punishment sought by advocates and community policymakers may encourage more crime.

Part V

Debating the Fairness of Courts

Anthony Porter came within two days of being executed for a murder he didn't commit. Only his IQ of 51 gained him a temporary stay of execution. Three months later he walked out of prison, exonerated. Porter had been convicted in 1982 of a double murder in Chicago's Washington Park. Concerned that key evidence had been overlooked, Northwestern University journalism professor David Protess, working with five students and a private investigator, turned up information that the crime could not have occurred as the police alleged. Indeed, as Porter left prison after 16 years on death row the police were arresting a suspect who confessed to the murder.

During the late 1990s other cases like Porter's made headlines. How typical are wrongful convictions? Organizations opposing the death penalty cite at least 75 instances of wrongfully convicted defendants on death row since the death penalty was reinstated in 1976. Indeed, some groups calculate that for every seven guilty persons on death row, there is one innocent person. (Not surprisingly, death penalty advocates dispute these numbers and also offer contrasting interpretations about the fairness of the process).

The possibility of wrongful convictions figures prominently in the debate over the death penalty (see Issue 10). But the release of innocent suspects from death row also highlights the importance of fairness in the court process. More so than other private or governmental institutions, courts are expected to be fair and just. Alas, defining justice proves to be difficult.

All too often in contemporary society, "justice" has become equated with winning. Consider, for example, reactions following a hotly contested murder trial. One side loudly applauds the verdict, stating that she knew justice would prevail in the end. Just as loudly the other side denounces the verdict as a miscarriage of justice, predicting vindication on appeal. What is most striking is that in similar cases, where the verdict was the opposite, the same references to "justice" were made. Separating rhetoric from reality within this sea of battling clichés is difficult at best.

Academics, likewise, have found it hard to define justice. Recall that competing philosophies approach this topic from sharply contrasting perspectives. The crime control model views the possibility of error as small, and therefore emphasizes speed and finality in the court process. The due process model, on the other hand, sees a much greater possibility of errors occurring in the legal system and therefore stresses checks and balances in the judicial process.

Although defining justice remains an elusive endeavor, it is important, nonetheless, to examine some of its multiple faces. This section, therefore, considers two contrasting issues relating to the fairness of the courts.

Issue 7 focuses on prosecution. Two types of unfairness can occur in deciding whom to prosecute. One is overprosecution—the prosecutor singles out a defendant or class of defendants for undue scrutiny. The other type of unfairness is the systematic underprosecution of a defendant or class of defendants. We will examine the latter in the context of rape prosecutions, probing whether the justice system improperly takes into account irrelevant past conduct of the rape victim.

Issue 8 examines how jurors should react if they think that the law is improper or the process unfair. "Jury nullification" refers to jury decisions to acquit guilty defendants. There is sharp debate over whether this practice should be encouraged (or discouraged) and whether in the end it produces better (or worse) justice.

World Wide Web Resources

Web Guides

http://dir.yahoo.com/Government/U_S_Government/Judicial_Branch/State_Courts/
http://dir.yahoo.com/Government/U_S_Government/Judicial_Branch/Federal_Courts/
http://dir.yahoo.com/Society_and_Culture/Crime/Crimes/Sex_Crimes/

Searching the Web

courts, rape, sexual assault, jury nullification

Useful URLs

Federal Judiciary Homepage: Official web site of the federal courts with links to other federal courts.   http://www.uscourts.gov/

National Center for State Courts: Nonprofit organization dedicated to improving the courts.   http://www.ncsc.dni.us/

National Coalition Against Sexual Assault: Feminist organization seeking to end sexual violence through advocacy, education, and public policy.   http://ncasa.org/

Rape, Abuse & Incest National Network (RAINN): National organization stressing rape counseling centers supported partially through concerts.
http://www.rainn.org

Fun Sites

Fully Informed Jury Association: Nonprofit organization dedicated to jury nullification.   http://www.fija.org/

Innocence Project: Co-chaired by Barry Scheck and Peter Neufeld, the Innocence Project uses DNA evidence to clear the falsely accused.
http://www.criminaljustice.org/public/cardozo.htm

Jury Rights Project: Nonprofit organization focusing on the 6th Amendment. http://home.utah-inter.net/don-tiggre/jrp.homepage.htm

Justice for Sale: PBS Web site examining how judicial campaign contributions corrupt justice.   http://www.pbs.org/wgbh/pages/frontline/shows/justice/

Sexual Assault Information Page: A good source of facts and figures. http://www.cs.utk.edu/~bartley/saInfoPage.html

The Injustice Line: Contains stories about alleged case of governmental injustice. http://home.earthlink.net/~ynot/index.html

InfoTrac College Edition Resources

Background

Encyclopedias and reference books provide background on courts, rape, and jury.

Basic Searches

courts, rape, jury; jury nullification

Related Searches

Courts—criminal courts; judges; federal courts; state courts; justice, administration of

Rape—acquaintance rape; gang rape; rape victim services; rape victims; rapists; trials (rape)

Jury Nullification—instructions to juries; jury members; jury selection; jury sequestration; right to trial by jury; verdicts

Issue 7

Are Sexual Assaults Against Women Underprosecuted?

- *"He raped me and I was yelling no," the victim, a 30-year-old single mother, tearfully testified.*

- *"How do you defend yourself from someone who says the word rape over and over again?" the defendant plaintively asked.*

These two contrasting statements summarize the typical dilemma jurors face in assessing whether sexual intercourse was forced or consensual. What is atypical is the highly publicized nature of the trial. The setting was Palm Beach, Florida, one of the nation's richest and most exclusive communities. The defendant was William Kennedy Smith, a member of the Kennedy clan. The subsequent verdict of not guilty evoked an unusually negative reaction. Advocates for rape victims called the verdict chilling. The National Organization of Women expressed outrage that rape victims were blamed for being raped. Jurors interviewed later, though, contended their not-guilty verdict was primarily based on the lack of credibility of the accuser.

Sexual assault is the most visible gender-based crime issue, discussed later in the section debating equal justice under law. Along with domestic violence (Issue 6), it is the topic that feminists have most identified as involving bias throughout the criminal justice system.

The first article, "The Response to Rape: Detours on the Road to Equal Justice," forcefully concludes that the justice system creates serious barriers to women who are sexually assaulted. This report of the U.S. Senate Judiciary Committee argues that prejudice is found throughout the process, from the time the police first investigate to when jurors deliberate.

In contrast, the article "The Influence of Blame and Believability Factors on the Processing of Simple Versus Aggravated Rape Cases" reports that the outcomes of aggravated and simple rape cases are surprisingly similar. The authors (Julie Horney and Cassia Spohn of the University of Nebraska, Omaha) find that there is little evidence that victim characteristics affect case outcomes.

Pro	Con
More than 876,000 rapes are committed each year, more than twice what other recent surveys have found (Violence Against Women Survey).	Rape rates have declined by over 50 percent in recent years (National Crime Victimization Survey).
Women don't lie about rape. The FBI reports that false accusations account for only two percent of all reported sexual assaults.	Rape is a charge that is easy to make but difficult to prove.
A delay in reporting this crime is an all too unfortunate psychological reaction, and doesn't undermine the credibility of the witness.	A delay in reporting the crime is a legitimate concern for law enforcement personnel and jurors. Moreover, this delay prevents collecting important physical evidence.

World Wide Web Exercises

1. Estimates on how many rapes occur each year vary, and are often part of the debate itself. First access the official governmental statistics on the topic. The Web address is http://www.ojp.usdoj.gov/bjs/cvict.htm. Next locate two or more advocacy Web sites that provide statistical information on rape (sexual assault). Do the estimates differ? Do interpretations of the extent of rape vary with the ideological position of the group? To what extent do contrasting statistical estimates reflect competing definitions of rape?

2. The drug Rohypnol is sometimes referred to as the date rape drug because some allege it can be secretly placed in a drink and the next morning the victim will not recall the rape. To some, this is a significant problem. To others it borders on being an urban myth. Using the search term **date rape drug** or **rohypnol** locate several articles and analyze the topic in terms of the concept of "moral panic" discussed in the earlier reading.

InfoTrac College Edition Exercises

1. Using the search term **rape,** find at least one article on each side of the issue. Do these articles provide similar or different arguments?

2. Using the search term **rape** find one or more articles in scholarly journals that analyze the topic. Do the findings tend to support the pro or con position on this issue?

The Response to Rape: Detours on the Road to Equal Justice

U.S. Senate Judiciary Committee

Try to imagine a legal system in which robberies of retail stores are treated seriously, but robberies of homes are not considered "real" crimes. Try to imagine a legal system predicated on the notion that robbery victims are likely to lie about whether the crime really occurred, or that renders the financial history of a robbery victim a central issue at trial. This is a fictional world for the victims of robbery. For the survivors of rape and family violence, it is all too real—it is the criminal justice system of the United States, today, in 1993.

Over a year ago, the Judiciary Committee issued a Report that surveyed state rape laws. It documented how "traditional State law sources of protection have often proven to be difficult avenues of redress for some of the most serious crimes against women." We found that, despite some reforms, serious legal barriers remained where women sought the prosecution of an attacker. . . .

These barriers of law, however, pale before the barriers of prejudice faced by women who are raped. Prejudice takes many practical forms in a rape prosecution—policemen refuse to take a report; prosecutors encourage defendants to plead to minor offenses; judges rule against victims in evidentiary matters; and juries, despite instructions to the contrary, continue to lay the blame on the survivor. At every step of the way, the criminal justice system poses significant hurdles for rape survivors.

Source: U.S. Senate Judiciary Committee, 1993.

A. Barriers of Practice: The Toll

Ours is a system which responds to victims of rape with suspicion rather than compassion. The figures we release today demonstrate the scope of the failures of practice. They reveal that the detours on the road to a rape conviction are far greater than the detours on the road to a conviction for other violent crimes. We found:

- More than half of those arrested for rape will not be convicted, making it 30 percent more likely that a robber is convicted than a rapist;

- Over half of all rape prosecutions result in either a dismissal or an acquittal, almost double the number for murder and almost 30 percent higher than for robbery;

- Almost one quarter of convicted rapists never go to prison, almost another quarter receive sentences to local jails housing minor offenders. This means that almost half of all convicted rapists can expect to receive a sentence of less than a year.

B. Barriers of Practice: The Survivors

The figures tell only part of the story, though. Not every arrest leads to a prosecution in the case of car theft; not every prosecution leads to a conviction or even a jail sentence in a whole host of criminal cases. But a consistent pattern that diverges from the norm does reveal that, overall, rape is different.

Accounts of individual cases are illustrative. In 1993, we would like to believe that our criminal justice system is getting better. The reality is that from the survivor's perspective, the system remains woefully inadequate. In fact, despite decades of legal reform and increased attention to rape, studies indicate that there has been no significant increase in the percentage of rape complaints that result in a conviction, or in arrest rates for rape.

One would hope that legal reforms would yield new attitudes as well as new policies. Yet today, we still encounter stories of individual rape cases that horrify. Consider the recent Pennsylvania case in which a young woman was raped in the dorm room of an acquaintance. While the victim testified that she said "no" throughout the incident, the judge ruled that because the dorm room door, although locked, could have been opened from the inside, the victim was technically able to leave the room. The judge ruled that her repeated "no" was not enough to support a rape conviction. Or, consider the South Carolina case in which a man tied up, blindfolded and raped his wife. After being shown a videotape of the incident made by the husband with the woman pleading, "please don't tie me up again, I'll do anything you want me to," a jury acquitted the defendant, concluding that the videotape depicted a "sex game" rather than a rape. . . .

C. Barriers of Practice: A Survey

Are these cases aberrations? After a survey of rape crisis centers throughout 12 states, we found that, unfortunately, cases like these happen on a daily basis. The old prejudices remain at work. . . . For example, in our survey, we found cases of police officers who refused to take reports from rape victims, prosecutors who offered plea bargains that resulted in the release of dangerous attackers, and judges who sentenced convicted rapists so they were back on the street in months, often to rape again. These cases reflect a fundamental misunderstanding of the nature of rape—a failure summed up by a report to committee staff of a county prosecutor's comments to rape crisis counselors that he had never seen a case of "real" rape. We heard stories like these:

- An 18-year-old woman is stranded on the highway because of car trouble. A man stops to help and grabs her, trying to get her clothes off. She fights the man off, and he runs. The police officer who responds to the scene initially refuses to help her from the scene of the attack, downplaying her allegations with: "I heard the guy was a little more interested in getting on you than with helping you fix your tire." The officer fails to make a report or investigate the allegation, although the woman has given a description of the attacker. Eventually, as a result of this mishandling, the officer is suspended for six days.

- A young woman reports to the police that she was kidnapped and raped by a former boyfriend. He had beaten her in the past, leading to his arrest on at least one occasion. The prosecutor resists bringing rape charges due to the victim's prior relationship with her assailant, and offers the man a plea to reduced charges—a misdemeanor assault for which the attacker receives a six-month suspended sentence and 18 months probation. Less than a year later, the attacker brutally rapes and almost kills another woman . . .

- Two women agree to go out for a drink with a man. He says he wants to stop at his house first. Once there, he pulls out a gun and rapes both women, threatening to kill them. The attacker is charged with aggravated sexual assault, but based on the police reports alone, the prosecutor concludes that the case is too difficult to win because the victims had voluntarily decided to accompany the attacker. The prosecutor accepts a plea to a fourth-degree felony—without consulting the survivors—and the attacker is given two years probation.

Unfortunately, these reports represent only the tip of the iceberg. Independent gender bias studies conducted across the nation conclude almost uniformly that prejudice pervades the system, citing cases similar to the ones we have described. As the Judiciary Committee stated in its report last year, "[s]tudy after study commissioned by the highest courts of the States—from Florida to New York, California to New Jersey, Nevada to Minnesota—

has concluded that crimes disproportionately affecting women are often treated less seriously than comparable crimes against men." Quoting an expert in the field, we stated then what our survey has again confirmed: "[C]ollectively these reports provide overwhelming evidence that gender bias permeates the court system and that women are most often its victims."

D. Barriers of Practice: What Do These Stories Tell Us?

These stories portray, all too graphically, how the attitudes of those within the system affect how it works. . . . Time and again, day after day, victims of rape are victims of our beliefs about rape. We would not tolerate this with any other crime.

These stories also help us pinpoint why the system fails. Most violence against women challenges deeply embedded assumptions our society holds about violence. Our stereotype of violence is an attack by a stranger that results in public outcry and vindication by state authorities. But the reality of violence against women is far different.

These crimes are most often committed by someone the victim knows, not by strangers. These are crimes that, many times, take place in a home or at a job, as well as in parking garages and on lonely roads. These are crimes that for the most part go unreported, their victims silenced by a belief that they are to blame.

It is where the stereotypes we hold about violence diverge from the reality of individual cases, that the system is most vulnerable to failure. Our stereotypes tell us that families are not violent; therefore, when a husband assaults his wife, we tend to ask, why did the survivor stay? Our stereotypes tell us that people do not assault someone they know; when we see that a victim of rape is charging her husband or date, we ask, why did she begin or pursue such a relationship? Our stereo-

types about violence undeniably shape our response to rape. In the words of one rape survivor, "Rape is the only felony that places the onus on the survivor. If an assailant held you at knifepoint, asked you for your wallet, and you complied, there is no question that a crime was committed. You would not be asked if you had consented. You would not be asked if you tried to resist. Only survivors of rape are asked these questions." These are the wrong questions. But, they are the questions persistently posed to rape survivors by the criminal justice system.

In fact, rape is not the only crime that suffers from a failure to meet our stereotypes of violence; and rape survivors are not the only ones who are not treated as crime victims. Other crimes that challenge the same stereotypes pose a significant challenge to our ideas of equal justice. For example, one study indicates that as many as 90 percent of all family-violence defendants are never prosecuted, and one third of the cases that would be considered felonies if committed by strangers are filed as misdemeanors when committed by nonstrangers. Similarly, child sex abuse cases suffer from some of the same difficulties. . . .

E. Conclusion

In the end, our challenge is as much one of imagination as legislation—it is a challenge to test our assumptions. We must demand to know why prior sexual history is relevant in a rape case, when prior financial history is irrelevant in a robbery case. We must ask why we doubt that a rape occurred if we know that the victim had something to drink earlier in the evening. We must ask why the clothes a rape victim wears has anything to do with whether she was forced to have sex. We must ask why our criminal justice system continues to disbelieve the survivor.

The Influence of Blame and Believability Factors on the Processing of Simple Versus Aggravated Rape Cases

Julie Horney and Cassia Spohn

The legal processing of sexual assault cases has been the focus of considerable research in recent years. Most of this research has explored the claims of feminist or conflict theorists who have asserted that outcomes of rape cases reflect decision makers' biases about acceptable and unacceptable behavior by women or their stereotypes about genuine rape victims. The empirical studies have thus concentrated on the role of victim characteristics in influencing case outcomes.

Researchers have shown that the processing of sexual assault cases is influenced by victim behavior that can be characterized as risk-taking behavior—such as hitchhiking or drinking, by evidence of victim "misconduct," by the victim's reputation, and by the victim's occupation [or] education. . . .

Some researchers also have found that the relationship between the victim and the accused has a strong effect on the outcome of sexual assault cases; rapes involving strangers are taken more seriously than rapes involving acquaintances. Studies have shown that police investigate reports of rape by a stranger more thoroughly than reports of rape by a friend or acquaintance and are more likely to unfound reports of rape by an acquaintance. The prior relationship between the victim and the defendant also has been shown to affect the prosecutor's charging decision and the likelihood that the defendant will be convicted.

Many have argued that such results signal widespread distrust of alleged victims of rape, and

indicate that women who are seen as behaving in gender-inappropriate ways are punished by being given less than the full protection of the law. Estrich (1987:29), however, maintains that the handling of rape complaints has always depended on the kind of rape that is alleged. She asserts that rather than being characterized by indiscriminate sexism, the processing of rape cases historically has reflected

> a far more sophisticated discrimination in the distrust of women victims: all women and all rapes are not treated equally. As the doctrines of rape law were developed in the older cases, distinctions were drawn, explicitly and implicitly, between the aggravated, jump-from-the-bushes stranger rapes and the simple cases of unarmed rape by friends, neighbors, and acquaintances. It was primarily in the latter cases that distrust of women victims was actually incorporated into the definition of the crime and the rules of proof.

Estrich (1987:28) suggests that the provisions of traditional rape law represented "a set of clear presumptions applied against the woman who complains of simple rape." . . . [S]he defines simple rape as a rape by a lone acquaintance with no weapon and no injury to the victim. An aggravated rape, in contrast, involves either an attack by a stranger, multiple assailants, the use of a weapon, or injury of the victim. Estrich asserts that, because of negative presumptions about victims of simple rape, these incidents are less likely than aggravated rape cases to result in conviction. . . .

Source: *Criminology* 34 (1996): 135–162. Reprinted by permission of the American Society of Criminology.

The Current Study

Our data come from a random sample of reports entered in the daily complaint logs of the Detroit Police Department's Sex Crimes Unit in 1989. For this analysis we considered the 662 cases with initial charges of first- or third-degree criminal sexual conduct, and in which the complainant was female and at least 16 years old . . . [82 percent of the cases in this Detroit sample . . . were black-on-black offenses]. . . .

Outcome Variables

. . . We first analyze whether a suspect is identified. . . . We next examine an ordered scale of the extent of case processing once a suspect has been identified. . . .

Independent Variables

The blame and believability factors included whether the victim physically resisted the offender and how promptly the complainant reported the incident to the police. We also included a variable for the victim's "moral character." The police file was reviewed to determine whether any of the following information about the complainant was mentioned: prior sexual activity with someone other than the defendant, pattern of alcohol use, pattern of drug use, work history in a "disreputable" situation (e.g., topless dancing or massage parlor), alleged prostitution, or criminal record. . . . In order to measure "risk taking" by the complainant, the data coders noted any indication in the police file of the following victim behaviors at the time of the incident: walking alone late at night, hitchhiking, agreeing to accompany the offender to his residence, inviting the offender to her residence, in a bar alone, using alcohol, or using drugs. . . .

Case characteristics included two variables measuring the strength of evidence in the case. We reasoned that the odds of successful prosecution would improve if there was a witness to the incident or physical evidence (semen, fingerprints, bloodstains, hair, or skin samples) that could be used at trial. In addition we considered whether the attack took place in the victim's home.

Finally, we determined whether the case would be categorized as an aggravated or a simple rape. Cases in which the complainant and defendant were strangers, in which there were multiple offenders, in which a weapon was used, or in which the victim was injured, were classified as aggravated rapes . . . ; cases without any of those characteristics were classified as simple rapes. . . .

Results

. . . Overall, the two kinds of cases are noteworthy more for their similarities than for their differences. The distinction between aggravated and simple rape is most important in determining case outcome at the first stage, that is, in determining whether a suspect is identified. Although it is perhaps belaboring the obvious to note that police work is greatly simplified when a complainant is able to name the alleged offender, the tremendous impact this has on initiating criminal justice processing cannot be overstated. . . . Once a suspect was identified, there was no significant difference between aggravated and simple rape cases in the depth of processing by the system. The majority of aggravated and simple rape cases were closed by the police.

. . . [A]ggravated rape cases were more likely than simple rape cases to have occurred in the victim's home and to have physical evidence of the crime. There were no significant differences between the two kinds of cases in whether the victim physically resisted the offender, whether there was a witness to the incident, how long the victim waited to report the incident to the police, the victim's moral character, or risk taking by the victim. There were also no differences in the age or race of the victim or the age, race, or prior record of the offender. . . .

Discussion

Our results indicate that the characteristics and outcomes of aggravated and simple rape cases processed by the criminal justice system in Detroit are surprisingly similar. Simple rape cases were more likely to have occurred in the victim's home, but less likely to have physical evidence of the crime. The two kinds of cases did not differ significantly with regard to any of the other case characteristics we measured, nor did they differ for any of the victim or offender characteristics.

Whether a suspect was identified did depend on the type of case. Not surprisingly, suspects were more likely to be identified in simple rape cases—those cases in which the victim and offender are acquainted. Having a name or address for a suspect is tremendously important in the initiation of any criminal prosecution and is probably more critical in determining whether a case goes forward than any evaluation of case worthiness that the police might make at that stage.

In the stages that followed identification of a suspect, we found that aggravated rape cases were no more likely than simple rape cases to move forward in the criminal justice system. The two kinds of cases were equally likely to be closed by the police rather than being referred to the prosecutor, to be rejected rather than accepted by the prosecutor, to be dismissed rather than fully prosecuted, and to result in not guilty rather than guilty determinations. . . . Case outcomes did not differ when we considered the more traditional distinction between stranger and acquaintance cases or when we created groups even more disparate in terms of the intimacy of the relationship. Thus, we find no evidence in this sample of Detroit cases for Estrich's (1987) claim that aggravated rape cases are taken more seriously by criminal justice officials.

Likewise, we find no support for the hypothesis that victim characteristics influence case outcomes differently in aggravated and simple rape cases. . . . The victim characteristics we studied not only did not interact significantly with type of case, but also had little influence on case processing in either kind of case. The only victim characteristic that was significantly related to outcome was physical resistance. Those cases in which the complainant physically resisted the offender were more likely to result in identification of a suspect. We can only speculate on the meaning of this relationship, but our guess is that physical resistance

is somehow related to the availability of identifying evidence that makes apprehension of a suspect possible. It is also possible, however, that police work harder to locate a suspect in these cases because they view the complainant as more deserving, or that complainants who have physically resisted an attack are more likely to pursue the case or work harder to help the police make an arrest.

In contrast to the findings of earlier research . . . none of the "blame and believability" characteristics was significantly related to case outcomes. The only one of these variables that even approached . . . significance was the number of case-file items that could be viewed as calling the victim's morals into question. The "morals" information that we found most frequently in the police files was evidence relating to prior sexual relations, evidence of a pattern of drug use, and evidence of a criminal record. Although the Michigan rape shield law makes it much more difficult than in the past to use a victim's prior sexual relations to prove that she consented or to impeach her credibility, there are no such restrictions on evidence relating to drug abuse or criminal history. Such factors . . . might be expected to lead police and prosecutors to take cases less seriously or to discourage victims from pursuing prosecution.

Our findings are subject to different interpretations. The findings may represent encouraging news about rape law reform and about changing attitudes toward rape victims and rape cases. We found no evidence that information about a victim's risk-taking affected outcomes. Thus, walking alone late at night, hitchhiking, and accompanying a man to his home apparently did not lead a victim to be blamed for precipitating a rape. We also found that physical resistance by a victim was not a necessary element for a case to proceed through the system once a suspect was identified.

The lack of support for the hypothesis that aggravated rape cases are treated more seriously than simple rape cases could also reflect real changes that have occurred in the processing of rape cases in the past 20 years. In 1975 Michigan enacted rape reform legislation that was considered by many to be a model for other states. . . . The results on case outcomes for aggravated and simple rape cases are consistent with . . . speculation that attitudes toward the "borderline" cases have changed. Because we are not able to isolate official decision making from decision making by rape victims, we cannot clearly address official attitudes, but the results suggest that distrust of victims in simple rape cases may have lessened.

The similarities in outcomes for aggravated and simple rape cases may represent acknowledgment by officials that an assault does not have to involve a stranger who holds a gun to the victim's head or a knife to her throat in order to be a "real" rape. The results of our study indicate that, at least in one jurisdiction, cases involving an acquaintance without a weapon, who does not seriously injure the victim, are being processed in the criminal justice system, and that some are leading to convictions. The conviction rate was even comparable for cases in which the victim and offender had a previous sexual relationship. If similar results were to be found in other jurisdictions, victims of simple rape could be offered greater encouragement in reporting their cases to the police and in pursuing prosecution. . . .

One other interpretation of our findings must be considered. It is possible that the type of rape case—whether aggravated or simple—has less impact on criminal justice processing than previously believed. Our somewhat surprising results led us back to the literature on the processing of rape cases. We discovered that although a few frequently cited studies have found the relationship between offender and victim to be a significant predictor of case outcome, there is hardly conclusive empirical support for the apparently widespread belief that cases involving strangers are consistently taken more seriously than those involving acquaintances.

Issue 8

Should Jurors Engage in Jury Nullification?

- *Jurors in a dry county find the local bootlegger not guilty.*

- *A prosecutor refuses to file charges because jurors will not convict in possession-of-marijuana cases.*

- *The subway vigilante Bernhard Goetz is acquitted of serious charges in the shooting of four black youths.*

- *In a verdict many find stunning, O. J. Simpson is acquitted of murdering his wife.*

- *Four Los Angles police officers are acquitted of the charges in the beating of Rodney King.*

- *Dr. Jack Kevorkian is acquitted of violating Michigan's assisted suicide law.*

These cases are often cited as examples of jury nullification. Raising the question "Was justice served in these cases?" highlights the difficulty of talking about this topic. Individually, each of these cases provokes disagreement over the correctness of the result. Collectively, these cases reveal competing definitions of the meaning of justice.

Jury nullification refers to the idea that juries have the right to refuse to apply the law in criminal cases despite facts that leave no reasonable doubt that the law was violated. In the United States, a trial involves a fundamental division of labor between judge and jury; the judge is the sole determiner of the law and jurors are the sole judge of the facts of the case. Under this formulation jurors are free to acquit if they find the evidence presented by the prosecution to be weak or unbelievable. They are not, however, allowed to vote not guilty because they do not like the law in question.

Jury research conclusively shows that juries introduce popular standards of justice into trials (Neubauer, 1999). By introducing community standards, lay jurors shape the law in ways that professionals sometimes find disagreeable. Thus, for centuries some American legal thinkers have denounced juries as enemies of an ordered legal system. More recently, though, others have championed the cause of jury nullification from a variety of perspectives, ranging from protesters (who point to injustices in specific cases) to anarchists (who have no use for modern-day government). Alas, even with a scorecard, it is hard to tell who the players are.

In outline form, the debate over jury nullification proceeds roughly along the following lines.

Pro	Con
Jury nullification restrains a lawless government.	Jury nullification undermines the rule of law.
The right to trial by jury creates the right to jury nullification.	Jurors have no constitutional right to vote their conscience.
Jurors should be told that they have a right to disregard the judge's instructions on the law.	Telling jurors that they have a "right" to disregard the judge will only produce untold mischief.
Jury nullification is freedom's shield.	Jury nullification is the anarchist's sword.

The article "Black Jurors: Right to Acquit?" argues that the huge numbers of black men in jail for drug crimes is the product of a white justice system. The author, Paul Butler (George Washington Law School) concludes that African-American jurors often have the moral justification to acquit guilty black defendants when the crime is victimless or nonviolent.

The article "Jury Nullification: A Perversion of Justice?" argues that jury nullification is rare. Nonetheless the author, Andrew Leipold, concludes that this is a dangerous power in the hands of unaccountable people.

World Wide Web Exercises

Locate two or more Web sites that discuss jury nullification. Analyze these pages using the following questions: What types of cases are featured? How easy or difficult is it to find out information about the group? Do the arguments fall along classic ideological divisions summarized in the due process versus crime control model? Do these groups reflect a fully-fledged social movement, or do they appear to represent just a few isolated people?

Select a trial that received national attention and resulted in the jury voting for acquittal. Locate two or more articles that represent different views of the correctness of the verdict. Is the verdict best understood as the result of the actions of reasonable jurors, polarized ideological positions, or jury nullification?

InfoTrac College Edition Exercises

Using the search term **jury nullification** select two or more articles that present differing views on the topic of jury nullification. Are the arguments similar to, or different from, those provided in the two readings?

Using the search term **jury** or **verdict** select two or more academic articles that analyze jury decision-making. Do the results of these studies tend to support one side or the other in the debate? Overall, does research suggest that jury nullification is a major issue, or do a few isolated cases tend to blow it out of proportion?

Black Jurors: Right to Acquit? (Jury Nullification)

Paul Butler

In 1990 I was a Special Assistant United States Attorney in the District of Columbia. I prosecuted people accused of misdemeanor crimes, mainly the drug and gun cases that overwhelm the local courts of most American cities. As a federal prosecutor, I represented the United States of America and used that power to put people, mainly African-American men, in prison. I am also an African-American man. . . . During that time, I made two discoveries that profoundly changed the way I viewed my work as a prosecutor and my responsibilities as a black person.

There is an increasing perception that some African-American jurors vote to acquit black defendants for racial reasons, sometimes explained as the juror's desire not to send another black man to jail. There is considerable disagreement over whether it is appropriate for a black juror to do so. I now believe that, for pragmatic and political reasons, the black community is better off when some nonviolent lawbreakers remain in the community rather than go to prison. The decision as to what kind of conduct by African Americans ought to be punished is better made by African Americans, based on their understanding of the costs and benefits to their community, than by the traditional criminal justice process, which is controlled by white lawmakers and white law enforcers. . . .

Why would a black juror vote to let a guilty person go free? Assuming the juror is a rational, self-interested actor, she must believe that she is better off with the defendant out of prison than in

prison. But how could any rational person believe that about a criminal?

Imagine a country in which a third of the young male citizens are under the supervision of the criminal justice system—either awaiting trial, in prison, or on probation or parole. Imagine a country in which two-thirds of the men can anticipate being arrested before they reach age thirty. Imagine a country in which there are more young men in prison than in college.

The country imagined above is a police state. When we think of a police state, we think of a society whose fundamental problem lies not with the citizens of the state but rather with the form of government, and with the powerful elites in whose interest the state exists. Similarly, racial critics of American criminal justice locate the problem not with the black prisoners but with the state and its actors and beneficiaries.

The black community also bears very real costs by having so many African Americans, particularly males, incarcerated or otherwise involved in the criminal justice system. These costs are both social and economic, and they include the large percentage of black children who live in female-headed, single-parent households; a perceived dearth of men "eligible" for marriage; the lack of male role models for black children, especially boys; the absence of wealth in the black community; and the large unemployment rate among black men.

According to a recent *USA Today*/CNN/Gallup poll, 66 percent of blacks believe that the criminal justice system is racist and only 32 percent believe it is not racist. . . . African-American jurors who

---

Source: *Harper's Magazine,* December, 1995 vol 29:11. Reprinted by permission of the author.

endorse these critiques are in a unique position to act on their beliefs when they sit in judgment of a black defendant. As jurors, they have the power to convict the accused person or to set him free. May the responsible exercise of that power include voting to free a black defendant who the juror believes is guilty? The answer is "yes" based on the legal doctrine known as jury nullification.

Jury nullification occurs when a jury acquits a defendant who it believes is guilty of the crime with which he is charged. In finding the defendant not guilty, the jury ignores the facts of the case and/or the judge's instructions regarding the law. Instead, the jury votes its conscience.

The prerogative of juries to nullify has been part of English and American law for centuries. There are well-known cases from the Revolutionary War era when American patriots were charged with political crimes by the British crown and acquitted by American juries. Black slaves who escaped to the North and were prosecuted for violation of the Fugitive Slave Law were freed by Northern juries with abolitionist sentiments. Some Southern juries refused to punish white violence against African Americans, especially black men accused of crimes against white women.

The Supreme Court has officially disapproved of jury nullification but has conceded that it has no power to prohibit jurors from engaging in it. . . . The criticism suggests that when twelve members of a jury vote their conscience instead of the law, they corrupt the rule of law and undermine the democratic principles that made the law.

There is no question that jury nullification is subversive of the rule of law. Nonetheless, most legal historians agree that it was morally appropriate in the cases of the white American revolutionaries and the runaway slaves. The issue, then, is whether African Americans today have the moral right to engage in this same subversion.

Most moral justifications of the obligation to obey the law are based on theories of "fair play." Citizens benefit from the rule of law; that is why it is just that they are burdened with the requirement to follow it. Yet most blacks are aware of countless historical examples in which African Americans were not afforded the benefit of the rule of law: think, for example, of the existence of slavery in a republic purportedly dedicated to the proposition that all men are created equal, or the law's support of state-sponsored segregation even after the Fourteenth Amendment guaranteed blacks equal protection. That the rule of law ultimately corrected some of the large holes in the American fabric is evidence more of its malleability than of its goodness; the rule of law previously had justified the holes.

If the rule of law is a myth, or at least not valid for African Americans, the argument that jury nullification undermines it loses force. The black juror is simply another actor in the system, using her power to fashion a particular outcome. The juror's act of nullification—like the act of the citizen who dials 911 to report Ricky but not Bob, or the police officer who arrests Lisa but not Mary, or the prosecutor who charges Kwame but not Brad . . . —exposes the indeterminacy of law but does not in itself create it.

A similar argument can be made regarding the criticism that jury nullification is anti-democratic. This is precisely why many African Americans endorse it; it is perhaps the only legal power black people have to escape the tyranny of the majority. Black people have had to beg white decision-makers for most of the rights they have: the right not to be slaves, the right to vote, the right to attend an integrated school. Now black people are begging white people to preserve programs that help black children to eat and black businesses to survive. Jury nullification affords African Americans the power to determine justice for themselves, in individual cases, regardless of whether white people agree or even understand. At this point, African Americans should ask themselves whether the operation of the criminal law system in the United States advances the interests of black people. If it does not, the doctrine of jury nullification affords African-American jurors the opportunity to exercise the authority of the law over some African-American criminal defendants. In essence, black people can "opt out" of American criminal law.

How far should they go—completely to anarchy, or is there someplace between here and there that is safer than both? I propose the following:

African-American jurors should . . . exercise their power in the best interests of the black community. In every case, the juror should be guided by her view of what is "just." (I have more faith, I should add, in the average black juror's idea of justice than I do in the idea that is embodied in the "rule of law.") In cases involving violent *malum in se* (inherently bad) crimes, such as murder, rape, and assault, jurors should consider the case strictly on the evidence presented, and if they believe the accused person is guilty, they should so vote. In cases involving non-violent, *malum prohibitum* (legally proscribed) offenses, including "victimless" crimes such as narcotics possession, there should be a presumption in favor of nullification. Finally, for nonviolent, *malum in se* crimes, such as theft or perjury, there need be no presumption in favor of nullification, but it ought to be an option the juror considers. A juror might vote for acquittal, for example, when a poor woman steals from Tiffany's but not when the same woman steals from her next-door neighbor.

How would a juror decide individual cases under my proposal? Easy cases would include a defendant who has possessed crack cocaine and an abusive husband who kills his wife. The former should be acquitted and the latter should go to prison.

Difficult scenarios would include the drug dealer who operates in the ghetto and the thief who burglarizes the home of a rich white family. Under my proposal, nullification is presumed in the first case because drug distribution is a nonviolent *malum prohibitum* offense. Is nullification morally justifiable here? It depends. There is no question that encouraging people to engage in self-destructive behavior is evil; the question the juror should ask herself is whether the remedy is less evil. (The juror should also remember that the criminal law does not punish those ghetto drug dealers who cause the most injury: liquor store owners.)

As for the burglar who steals from the rich white family, the case is troubling, first of all, because the conduct is so clearly "wrong." Since it is a non-violent *malum in se* crime, there is no presumption in favor of nullification, but it is an option for consideration. Here again, the facts of the case are relevant. For example, if the offense was committed to support a drug habit, I think there is a moral case to be made for nullification, at least until such time as access to drug-rehabilitation services is available to all. . . .

I concede that the justice my proposal achieves is rough. It is as susceptible to human foibles as the jury system. But I am sufficiently optimistic that my proposal will be only an intermediate plan, a stopping point between the status quo and real justice. To get to that better, middle ground, I hope that this essay will encourage African Americans to use responsibly the power they already have.

Jury Nullification: A Perversion of Justice?

Andrew D. Leipold

There has been a lot of discussion about jury nullification lately. When juries acquitted O.J. Simpson (in his criminal trial) and the Los Angeles police officers who beat Rodney King, there were loud and sharp claims in newspapers and coffee shops that these verdicts were based on racial prejudice, class bias, an irrational desire to punish the police, or naivete about police practices, not on the evidence presented. . . .

Paul Butler of George Washington University Law School, has helped fuel the debate. . . . These events and discussions have led some people to the brink of despair about juries: "It seems like guilt or innocence doesn't matter anymore," they think. "Today, trials are about politics and about power; the only thing that matters is who is on the jury."

It would be easy to draw this conclusion from watching the nightly news—easy, but wrong. The truth is that juries rarely acquit against the evidence, at least in serious cases. Most jurors are quite sensible and recognize that, if they acquit a factually guilty defendant, they may be turning a dangerous person loose, perhaps into their own neighborhoods. Juries may be merciful, but they are not stupid. More to the point, most garden-variety street crimes don't raise any issues that might lead a jury to nullify. Most crime is intraracial, so any ethnic kinship a jury might feel for the defendant is blunted by the greater sympathy for the victim. Most crimes also have no political overtones or present obvious examples of police misconduct or prosecutorial overreaching. Perhaps most im-

portantly, the majority of criminal cases never go before a jury. Most criminal charges end in a guilty plea prior to trial, often as a result of an agreement between the prosecutor and defendant. While it is true that prosecutors sometimes offer an attractive plea bargain because they are worried about what a jury will do (what lawyers euphemistically refer to as the "risks of litigation"), instances of nullification are rare enough that most plea agreements probably don't change much.

While the instances of jury nullification are small, the problems created by the existence of the nullification doctrine are very large. . . .

I think that the main reason we bar prosecutors from making an appeal from an acquittal is to protect the jury's power to nullify. We are so anxious to preserve the jury's discretion to nullify in the occasional case that we put up with other, probably more numerous, acquittals that are the product of bad legal rulings at trial. This, I would argue, is the real cost of jury nullification—not the convictions that are lost when the jury deliberately acquits against the evidence, but those lost when the jury wants to convict, but erroneously is prevented by the trial court from doing so.

The Right that Isn't

The notion that juries can acquit a defendant for any reason at all is older than our nation. By the late 17th century, English judges had decided that jurors must be left to their own devices and consciences when rendering verdicts, and the idea traveled with the colonists to America. The concept of a supremely powerful jury found a welcome home

Source: *USA Today* (Magazine), September, 1997 v126. Reprinted by permnission.

here. It gave the colonists the power to convict those who misbehaved, while still nullifying the charges against those who broke what many colonists felt were oppressive laws. At the time, the jury's right to "find the law"—to decide for itself what the criminal law should be—was quite logical. Judges often were untrained in the law, making them no better than jurors at interpreting and applying the often-complex common law. As a result, there was a great deal of writing in the decades around the Revolutionary War that seemed to support a "right" of the jury to acquit someone against the evidence.

Yet, if the framers of the Constitution and the Bill of Rights thought that nullification was an important part of the right to trial by jury, they were awfully quiet about it. There is very little in the debates surrounding the drafting or ratification to suggest that they even thought about the issue, much less intended to incorporate it in the Constitution. While the Supreme Court, in construing the constitutional right to a jury, has been curiously closed-mouthed about the topic, the one time the Court spoke clearly, it decisively stated that a jury's power to nullify does not mean that a defendant has the right to be tried before a jury with that power. In the 1895 decision of *Sparf and Hansen v. United States,* the Court laid the groundwork for the rule that still prevails in most of the country—judges are not required to tell juries that they have the power to acquit against the evidence nor are they required to let lawyers argue to the jury in favor of nullification. The message is clear—even if courts can't stop juries from nullifying, they are under no legal obligation to help juries exercise the power.

Just because something is not protected constitutionally does not make it a bad idea. In many cases, I think that jury nullification is an excellent concept. If I were on the jury of the man accused of helping his wife commit suicide and I believed he did it out of love for the victim, I would vote to acquit in a heartbeat. Prosecutors are not infallible. At times, they make bad judgments; occasionally, they are mean-spirited; and sometimes, they get so used to the unending stream of bad people and violent acts they miss the human and moral

dimension of actions that normally are crimes. So, even if I had the power to prevent all juries from acquitting against the evidence, I probably would not use it.

Nevertheless, jury nullification is a dangerous power, and when any power is left in the hands of an unaccountable group, there is cause for worry. . . . First, we don't know how the power is used. Because juries almost never explain their verdicts, it is impossible to say how often nullification occurs. Our inability to determine when and why it does also means that we do not know how often juries use this power for good ends rather than evil ones. For every case where a jury acts morally and shows mercy, there may be another where a jury acquits because of hatred toward the victim or favoritism to the defendant. It takes strong faith in human nature to support a doctrine like jury nullification, knowing that the decision to set someone free can be made on a whim or based on prejudice.

In most cases, of course, a decision to nullify will be neither good nor evil; the morality and wisdom of the decision will depend on our individual views. Some will cheer when an abortion clinic protester is acquitted against the evidence, others will despair; some will think justice is done when a man who assaulted a homosexual couple is convicted only of the lowest possible charge (another form of nullification), others will see it as a hateful sign of the times; and many will be shocked when an accused rapist or wife beater is set free because the jury believed that the victim was asking for it. What we think doesn't matter, though. If we want juries with the unreviewable power to acquit when the charges are unfair, we must accept juries that have the power to make decisions others find distasteful and stupid.

Second, juries often don't have enough evidence to make a reasoned nullification decision. Even if we take a kinder view toward juries, there still are reasons to be troubled by the breadth of their discretion. If a jury is to make a reasoned nullification decision, there is certain information it needs to have. Let's say a jury has before it a simple drug possession case by a college-bound high school senior. The evidence looks strong, but the thought of ruining a promising future troubles the jurors. The young man had only a small amount of drugs, looks remorseful, and has a supportive family with him in court. Rather than send another teenager to jail, the jury decides to nullify.

If the jury's perception were accurate, perhaps it made the right call. The problem is what a jury sees might not be the full story. The jurors might not learn that the defendant has had scrapes with the law before, that he is a troublemaker at home and at school, and that, in fact, the police found a load of drugs in the car, which were not introduced at trial because the car was searched illegally. If the jury had known these things, its feelings of mercy quickly might have evaporated. However, there usually will be no evidence introduced of these other facts because they are irrelevant to the technical question of guilt or innocence. Stated differently, because the jury has no right to nullify, evidence that might inform the exercise of that power usually is not admitted at trial, nor are defense lawyers usually permitted to make overt appeals to the nullification power. Juries therefore make the nullification decision in the dark, letting some go free who are not worthy of mercy and convicting some who might be more deserving of it.

Third, encouraging nullification encourages lawlessness. The urge to nullify may tug at our hearts because it is so easy to imagine cases where we would do so ourselves if we were jurors. Consider a woman who is walking alone when she is surrounded by a gang of thugs. The terrified woman brandishes a gun and the gangsters flee, but as they do, she shoots one, causing great bodily harm. In many states, the woman could be prosecuted for assault with a deadly weapon be-cause once the thugs turned and ran, she no longer had the right to use deadly force in self-defense. Yet, many of us would not be troubled with such legal niceties and would cheerfully acquit if given the chance.

In more reflective moments, though, we should wonder why we let a jury make this decision. We have an elected legislature to pass laws and elected or appointed judges to interpret them. The wisdom of the people's representatives has been that when a person no longer is in danger, he or she may not use force in self-defense. That decision may be right or wrong, but it was arrived at through a legitimate, representative process. Why, then, should the jury be able to ignore that mandate because they sympathize with the woman and detest thugs? The jury is unelected, unaccountable, and has no obligation to think through the effect an acquittal will have on others. Perhaps it will be that thugs will accost fewer women; perhaps the effect will be to blur the line further between legitimate self-defense and vigilantism.

Reasonable people can disagree on the proper reach of the criminal laws. Nevertheless, the place for them to disagree is in public, where the reasons for expansions and contractions of the laws can be scrutinized and debated by those who will be affected by the verdicts juries reach. It is enough that we ask juries to decide whether the defendant before them is guilty of the crime charged. To expect them to make a reasoned decision on the wisdom of the law itself, with virtually none of the information that normally would be required in making such a decision, calls for more wisdom from most juries than fairly can be expected. . . .

Part VI

Debating Sentencing

The Polly Klaas kidnapping dominated the national news for months. The twelve-year-old had two friends over for a slumber party when a stranger broke into the house. Her friends were found shortly thereafter, bound and gagged but safe. A general description of a bearded intruder was all the police had to work on. Nine weeks later came the tragic news—Polly's body had been found; she had been raped and murdered shortly after her abduction.

The police arrest of Richard Allen Davis further inflamed an already angry public; Davis had a long police record and had recently been released from prison on parole. In short order, the public dialogue diagnosed the problem as a flawed criminal justice system and the prescribed remedy was "get tough on crime" legislation. Thus, the California legislature passed a "three strikes and you're out" law, which mandated mandatory life imprisonment for anyone convicted of three felonies (only one of which had to be a violent offense). Other states quickly followed.

In analyzing the often-heated debate over sentencing in the United States, it is helpful to revisit the three themes discussed in the "perspectives" section (pp. 8–34).

- The debate over sentencing reflects fundamental ideological disagreements. Adherents of the crime control model stress that tough sentences will deter criminal wrongdoers. More quietly, supporters of the due process model argue that rehabilitation is appropriate for most offenders.

- The debate over sentencing involves important political dimensions. Elected officials and interest groups latch onto tragedies to package their favorite policy proposals. Indeed, some wonder whether crime victims have become merely disposable media props.

- The debate over sentencing illustrates the importance of social construction of events. Political scientists Malcolm Feeley and Sam Kamin (1996), for example, conclude that the public reaction to the murder of Polly Klaas is a classic example of a moral panic. They note that there was little new in the three-strikes laws passed by legislatures—most states had passed similar measures (sometimes repeatedly) over the last two decades.

This section, "Debating Sentencing," explores two of the many controversies centering on what to do with those who have been convicted of a crime. Issue 9 asks the question, "Do Tough Sentences Reduce Crime?" As we shall see, some offer a ringing affirmative, arguing that crime is down because punishment is up. Others present the case that expensive prisons are a misguided response.

Issue 10 raises the highly emotional question, "Should the Death Penalty Be Abolished?" Although most people tend to have their minds made up, it is useful nonetheless to examine the three central issues that frame the debate: morality, deterrence, and the fairness of putting some to death.

World Wide Web Resources

Web Guides

http://dir.yahoo.com/Society_and_Culture/Crime/Correction_and_Rehabilitation/

http://dir.yahoo.com/Society_and_Culture/Crime/Correction_and_Rehabilitation/
Death_Penalty/

Searching the Web

sentencing, mandatory sentencing, criminal sentencing, truth in sentencing, death penalty, capital punishment, Polly Klaas

Useful URLs

Bureau of Justice Statistics: Criminal Sentencing Statistics.
http://www.ojp.usdoj.gov/bjs/sent.htm

Death Penalty Information Center: Leading opponent to the death penalty.
http://www.essential.org/dpic/

National Coalition to Abolish the Death Penalty: http://www.ncadp.org/

Pro Death Penalty.com: http://www.prodeathpenalty.com/

The Sentencing Project: http://www.sentencingproject.org/

Today's Headlines

http://fullcoverage.yahoo.com/Full_Coverage/US/Death_Penalty/

http://headlines.yahoo.com/Full_Coverage/US/Prisons/

Fun Sites

Death Row: Annual publication of who is on death row.
http://www.editionnine.deathrowbook.com/deathrow.htm

Families Against Mandatory Minimums (FAMM): A national organization of citizens working to repeal statutory mandatory minimum sentences. http://www.famm.org/

Murder Victims Memorial Site   http://www.murdervictims.com/

California Criminal Law Observer: The Three Strikes and You're Out Law http://www.silicon-valley.com/3strikes.html

InfoTrac College Edition Resources

Background

Encyclopedia and reference books on capital punishment and sentences (criminal procedure).

Basic Searches

capital punishment; sentences (criminal procedure)

Related Subjects

capital punishment for juvenile offenders; capital punishment for mentally handicapped; cruel and unusual punishment; electrocution; executions and executioners; hanging; stays of execution, proceedings, etc.

Issue 9

Do Tough Sentences Reduce Crime?

The emergence of crime as a dominant political issue has dramatically increased the prison population in the U.S. Get-tough legislation has resulted in yearly increases ranging from eight to 12 percent. Today, the prison population stands at over 1.333 million. This figure does not include the 690,000 persons being held in jails (which are typically maintained by local sheriffs' departments).

In the debate over sentencing, however, swelling prison populations play a secondary role to headline crimes. The public attention largely focuses on a few, very atypical crimes like the kidnapping and murder of Polly Klaas. Violent offenses constitute 17 percent of state courts' felony caseload. More typically, defendants have been convicted of drug offenses or property crimes (burglary and theft, primarily). In a typical year, state courts in the U.S. convict about 1 million defendants of felonies. The judge has a number of sentencing options besides prison.

The most common sentence for convicted felons is probation (the offender remains in the community without incarceration but subject to certain conditions like keeping a job and not breaking the law). Like the prison population, the probation population has experienced a meteoric increase in recent years. Today, almost 3.5 million are on probation.

The judge may also impose "intermediate sanctions," a phrase that includes a variety of punishments that are more restrictive than traditional probation. Halfway houses, community service, electronic monitoring, and drug rehabilitation are common examples of intermediate sanctions.

A judge may also impose a fine; that is, require the defendant to pay a sum of money to the government. Fines, though, are most often used in misdemeanors.

A judge may also order restitution, which is a requirement that the offender pay to the victim a sum of money to make good the loss.

The large and growing prison population demonstrates that tougher sentencing laws have indeed had an impact—legislatures must now spend billions to house those under correctional supervision. Whether these tough sentences reduce crime, though, is subject to debate.

Pro	Con
Violent offenders belong in prison.	Most offenders have not committed violent offenses.
Tough sentences deter other potential wrongdoers.	Many offenders commit impulse crimes that are not deterrable.
For drug offenders, claims that rehabilitation works are premature.	For drug offenders, rehabilitation often reduces future criminal conduct.
Money spent on prisons provides protection for all of society.	Large expenditures on prison divert tax money from more useful governmental services like education and highways.

The article "Prisons Are a Bargain, by Any Measure" argues that increased incarceration is the reason for the drop in crime. John J. Dilulio, Jr. concludes that the high costs of prison are cost-effective.

The article "Does Getting Tough on Crime Pay?" argues that the emphasis on sending more people to prison is off target. The panelists from the Urban Institute conclude that the pressure to build prisons wastes taxpayers' dollars.

World Wide Web Exercises

1. Use the search engine of your choice and enter the search term **Polly Klaas** to locate several articles and sites on this case. Analyze the information on the Web in terms of the concepts discussed in the introduction to this book.

2. Choose a search engine and use the search term **truth in sentencing** or **mandatory sentencing** to locate two or more sites that are in favor of tougher sentences. How do they use the plight of individual victims to support their argument? What kinds of crimes do they highlight? What type of research and statistics do they use to support their argument? Next, locate two or more sites that oppose get-tough laws. Compare and contrast the two sets of sites.

InfoTrac College Edition Exercises

1. Using the search term **sentences (criminal procedure), laws** locate one or more articles on each side of the issue. In what ways are the arguments similar to or different from those discussed in the book?

2. Using the search terms **sentences (criminal procedure)** or **sentences (criminal procedure), research** locate two or more articles in academic journals that analyze the impact of get-tough sentencing laws. Do the findings tend to support one side or the other in the debate over sentencing? Does research identify any unintended consequences that are important to the debate?

Prisons Are a Bargain, by Any Measure

John J. Dilulio, Jr.

All 30 Republican governors elected or re-elected in 1994 promised to get tough on crime. Most, like George Pataki of New York, are keeping their word. But several, like Tommy Thompson of Wisconsin, who has said he would build no more prisons, are quietly promoting plans to put more convicted criminals back on the streets.

Most experts applaud Governor Thompson's new-found "wisdom" and lament Governor Pataki's "hard-line" approach. As these experts love to repeat, "incarceration is not the answer."

If incarceration is not the answer, what, precisely, is the question? If the question is how to prevent at-risk youths from becoming stone-cold predators in the first place, then, of course incarceration is no solution.

But if the question is how to restrain known convicted criminals from murdering, raping, robbing, assaulting and stealing, then incarceration is a solution, and a highly cost-effective one.

On average, it costs about $25,000 a year to keep a convicted criminal in prison. For that money, society gets four benefits: Imprisonment punishes offenders and expresses society's moral disapproval. It teaches felons and would-be felons a lesson: Do crime, do time. Prisoners get drug treatment and education. And, as the columnist Ben Wattenberg has noted, "A thug in prison can't shoot your sister."

All four benefits count. Increased incarceration explains part of the drop in crime in New York and other cities. As some recent studies

show, prisons pay big dividends even if all they deliver is relief from the murder and mayhem that incarcerated felons would be committing if free.

In two Brookings Institution studies, in 1991 and 1995, the Harvard economist Anne Piehl and I found that prisoners in New Jersey and Wisconsin committed an average of 12 crimes a year when free, excluding all drug crimes. In other studies, the economist Steven D. Levitt of the National Bureau of Economic Research estimated that "incarcerating one additional prisoner reduces the number of crimes by approximately 13 per year."

The economists Thomas Marvell and Carlisle Moody of William and Mary College found that "a better estimate may be 21 crimes averted per additional prisoner." Patrick A. Langan, senior statistician at the Justice Department's Bureau of Justice Statistics, calculated that tripling the prison population from 1975 to 1989 may have reduced "violent crime by 10 to 15 percent below what it would have been," thereby preventing a "conservatively estimated 390,000 murders, rapes, robberies and aggravated assaults in 1989 alone."

Studies by the Bureau of Justice Statistics found that 94 percent of state prisoners in 1991 had committed a violent crime or been incarcerated or on probation before. Of these prisoners, 45 percent had committed their latest crimes while free on probation or parole. When "supervised" on the streets, they inflicted at least 218,000 violent crimes, including 13,200 murders and 11,600 rapes (more than half of them rapes against children).

Most Americans are more likely to be a victim of violent crime than to suffer injury in a car accident. As estimated in a forthcoming National Institute of Justice study, the violent crimes committed each year will cost victims and society more than $400 billion in medical bills, lost days from work, lost quality of life—and lost life.

Here's the revolving-door rub. Known felons whom the system has put back on the streets are responsible for about one in three violent crimes, and barely one violent crime in a hundred results in imprisonment. On any given day in 1994, about 690,000 people were on parole and 2.96 million were on probation. About 1.5 times as many convicted violent felons were on probation or parole as were in prison.

All told, research shows it costs society at least twice as much to let a prisoner loose than to lock him up. Compared with the human and financial toll of revolving-door justice, prisons are a real bargain.

Prison definitely pays, but there's one class of criminal that is an arguable exception: low-level, first-time drug offenders. Most drug felons in state prisons do not fit that description. Instead, they have long adult and juvenile records involving plenty of serious non-drug crimes. And most Federal drug traffickers are not black kids caught with a little crack cocaine or white executives arrested for a small stash of powder cocaine. The average amount of drugs involved in Federal cocaine-trafficking cases is 183 pounds, and the average amount involved in Federal marijuana trafficking cases is 3.5 tons.

Still, though the numbers of petty drug offenders may prove small, it makes no sense to lock away even one drug offender whose case could be adjudicated in special drug courts and handled less expensively through intensively supervised probation featuring no-nonsense drug treatment and community service. Thus, Governor Pataki needs to repeal undiscriminating Rockefeller-era drug laws as part of his campaign to keep violent and repeat criminals where they can't harm the rest of us.

Meanwhile, Governor Thompson should pursue whatever "alternative to incarceration" policies he fancies, subject to one condition: He should agree to make public in a timely fashion the complete histories of all criminals released from custody because of his "reforms." All elected leaders should reckon that those who break their promises to protect society from career criminals can count on voters to shorten their political careers.

Does Getting Tough on Crime Pay?

The Urban Institute

The U.S. prison population nearly tripled from 330,000 in 1980 to over one million in 1995. Mandatory prison sentences and other sentencing reforms that were intended to punish serious offenders and deter potential offenders account for this unprecedented growth. But did the reforms deliver?

Evidence suggests that these "get tough" reforms may not have achieved their goals, according to two leading criminologists, Urban Institute senior researcher William Sabol and American University professor James Lynch. . . .

Sabol and Lynch argued that the public support for the reforms was based on beliefs that punishments for serious crimes were too lenient; that the offenders targeted by the reforms were "dangerous" people for whom incarceration is the only effective punishment; and that imprisonment reduces crime by taking criminals off the streets and deterring potential criminals. The researchers suggested that these beliefs were wrong. Evidence of the reforms' effectiveness is mixed, and the reforms may have led to unintended negative consequences for communities.

Public Misperception

Lynch noted that the United States has never been as lenient as other industrialized countries in punishing such serious crimes as murder or rape. For that matter, its punishments for less serious crimes, such as theft and drugs, are far more severe. The

Source: *Urban Institute Update*, Issue No. 28—December, 1997. Reprinted by permission.

public's misperception stems from a common misuse of statistics.

"Take 'homicide,' for example," said Lynch. "You might see in a newspaper report that the average prison sentence for homicide is seven years. That sounds incredibly low to the average reader because the public has been taught to equate 'homicide' with 'murder.'"

This equation is false, Lynch explained. "Homicide" legally defines a whole class of crime, including manslaughter due to drunk driving and planned, premeditated murder. "If the correct statistic—that a convicted murderer can expect to spend 16 to 17 years behind bars—were reported, the public might not be as outraged."

Were Reforms on Target?

Sabol and Lynch looked at the profiles of prisoners affected by the get-tough approaches. They found that between 1979 and 1991, the number of violent offenders in prison had in fact doubled, but represented less of the total prison population, falling from 58 to 47 percent.

During that same time, imprisoned drug offenders rose eightfold in number and represented more of the prison population, climbing from 6.5 to 21.1 percent in 1991. Nearly 84 percent of the drug offenders in 1991 had never before been imprisoned for violent crimes, and half had no prior incarcerations.

"Reforms were on target for violent offenders," Lynch concluded, "but it seems that many of the imprisoned drug offenders were not the high-profile, violent offenders targeted by reforms."

Did Crime Rates Fall?

The overall crime rate has remained relatively stable, stated Sabol, even with more people behind bars. And drug crimes have not been reduced demonstrably, for two very important reasons. "First, the drug market is driven by demand—as long as there are buyers there will be sellers. And low-level drug dealers who end up in prison are easily replaced on the streets."

Second, the collapse of inner-city labor markets over the past 10 to 15 years has resulted in a 30 percent decline in real earnings for less skilled men. "There are fewer sources of legitimate income for a lot of men," Sabol explained. "In monetary benefits, drug-related crime actually does pay."

Unexpected Costs

If tough reforms do not fully meet their goals, as the evidence suggests, what else do they do? Sabol and Lynch examined the effects of get-tough approaches not just within prison walls, but also in the communities from which offenders came—and to which nearly all will return. "Most of the one million people off the streets now," Sabol told participants, "come from a relatively small number of inner-city communities."

A growing number of the men incarcerated have strong ties to their communities, either through marriage, employment, or education. "While these men are in prison, their communities may be less able to prevent criminal behavior."

Just as important, most offenders enter prison between the ages of 16 and 34—formative years for educational, employment, and social opportunities. By the time they are released, the window of opportunity to get a high school education, land a job, or start their own families might have closed. Whether incarceration during the beginning stages of adulthood contributes to the decline of inner-city communities is a question worthy of further research, an effort now under way at the Urban Institute.

The Community View

But are these men "dangerous" or "violent?" The terms could be relative . . ."A low-level drug dealer may look like an angel compared to a murderer," suggested Matt Bonham of *Newsweek*. "But are you saying that 'first-time, nonviolent drug offenders' are harmless? To community residents, they are dangerous, they're terrorizing neighborhoods, and getting them off the streets prevents crime."

"A community's attitude may be even more complicated," added Maria-Rosario Jackson of the Urban Institute. "On the one hand, it's true, people want the drug dealers off their streets. But, at the same time, they don't want all of the men removed from their neighborhoods—men who could be working and raising families, and being positive role models."

"Clearly, these offenders aren't all 'angels' who should never be incarcerated," said Lynch. "Violent and repeat offenders may pose too great a risk to serve their sentence within their community. But other options might make more sense for low-level drug offenders."

Alternatives?

John Calhoun of the National Crime Prevention Council asked whether there were any data to support alternatives to incarceration. "Not yet," responded Harrell. Professionals in the criminal justice system struggle with the same question. "Increasingly, judges are turning to tightly supervised placement in drug treatment programs as an alternative to incarceration. We've seen positive effects in the District of Columbia, but there's no definitive answer yet," she explained.

The Bottom Line

"What are the implications for policy? What will your new research do in light of the pressures to build prisons?" asked Jenny Gainsborough of the American Civil Liberties Union National Prison Project.

"Alternatives to prison are likely to be more effective if they are developed strategically, in conjunction with economic opportunities," responded Sabol.

"As to whether prison is a cost-effective way to reduce crime," he concluded, "the jury's still out."

Issue 10

Should the Death Penalty Be Abolished?

Following World War II, all Western democracies debated capital punishment and all, except the U.S., eliminated the practice. As part of this worldwide debate the U.S. imposed an informal moratorium on executions in the late 1960s. Then in 1972 the Supreme Court by a bare majority declared the practice unconstitutional, but four years later adopted a different approach. Following in outline form, are some of the most significant legal developments in the capital punishment debate.

Eighth Amendment	1791	• Excessive bail shall not be required, nor excessive fines imposed, nor cruel and unusual punishments inflicted.
Furman v. Georgia	1972	• State death penalty laws violate the eighth amendment.
Gregg v. Georgia	1976	• Death penalty does not constitute cruel and unusual punishment in all situations.
		• Bifurcated process required.
		• Law must specify aggravating and mitigating circumstances.
Coker v. Georgia	1977	• Rape is not a death-eligible offense.
Thompson v. Oklahoma	1988	• Defendants who were 15 or younger at the time of the commission of the offense may not be executed
		• States may set a higher age limit.
Penry v. Lynaugh	1989	• There is insufficient evidence of a national consensus against executing mentally retarded persons convicted of capital murder.

The public debate over the death penalty tends to be highly emotional focusing on the pain an evil person has inflicted on the victim's survivors. By contrast, the academic debate over abolition of the death penalty (while also sometimes emotional) centers on three deep-seated issues: morality, deterrence and fairness.

Pro	Con
The death penalty is immoral because the state should not take a life.	The death penalty is moral because the defendant has already taken a life.
The death penalty does not deter murderers. Many defendants convicted of murder don't calculate the odds of later being executed.	The death penalty deters crimes. Persons who might murder refrain from doing so because they know they might themselves die.
The death penalty is unfairly administered. • Racial minorities are more likely than whites to be executed. • Too many people on death row have been found to be innocent.	The fairness of the death penalty is unimportant. • Blacks are no more likely to be executed than whites. • The few innocents on death row have been released.

The article "ACLU Briefing Paper: The Death Penalty" argues that capital punishment doesn't deter murderers. Of special concern to the ACLU is racial discrimination in selecting who should die.

The article "So What if the Death Penalty Deters?" argues that capital punishment does indeed deter criminals. The author, Steven Goldberg (a writer for the *National Review*), refutes the abolitionist arguments.

World Wide Web Exercises

1. Using the search term **death penalty,** locate one Web site that favors the death penalty and another one that opposes the use of the death penalty. What contrasting views do these Web sites offer about the morality of the death penalty? How do these Web sites talk about issues like taking an innocent life?

2. Using the search term **death penalty,** locate one Web site that favors the death penalty and another one that opposes the use of the death penalty. What contrasting views do these Web sites offer about the deterrent effect of the death penalty? Examine closely statistical assertions; what type of documentation is provided? Moreover, do these Web sites offer different interpretations of research findings or do they rely on totally different types of research findings?

3. Using the search term **death penalty,** locate one Web site that favors the death penalty and another one that opposes the use of the death penalty. What contrasting views do these Web sites offer about the fairness of current death penalty laws? In particular, to what extent do arguments for or against the death penalty reflect positions about racial equality in the justice system (Part VII)?

InfoTrac College Edition Exercises

1. Using the search term **capital punishment** locate one or more articles on either side of the debate. Are the arguments similar to or different from those raised in the book?

2. Using the search term **capital punishment** locate two or more academic articles that discuss the fairness of the death penalty. How would different sides of the death penalty debate react to these findings? Do these findings tend to support one side or the other in the debate over abolition of the death penalty?

Briefing Paper: The Death Penalty

The American Civil Liberties Union

Since our nation's founding, the government—colonial, federal and state—has punished murder and, until recent years, rape with the ultimate sanction: death.

More than 13,000 people have been legally executed since colonial times, most of them in the early 20th century. By the 1930s, as many as 150 people were executed each year. However, public outrage and legal challenges caused the practice to wane. By 1967, capital punishment had virtually halted in the United States, pending the outcome of several court challenges. . . .

Thirty-nine states now have laws authorizing the death penalty, as does the military. A dozen states in the Middle West and Northeast have abolished capital punishment, two in the last century (Michigan in 1847, Minnesota in 1853). Alaska and Hawaii have never had the death penalty. Most executions have taken place in the states of the Deep South.

More than 3,500 people are on "death row" today. Virtually all are poor, a significant number are mentally retarded or otherwise mentally disabled, more than 40 percent are African American, and a disproportionate number are Native American, Latino and Asian.

The ACLU believes that, in all circumstances, the death penalty is unconstitutional under the Eighth Amendment, and that its discriminatory application violates the Fourteenth Amendment.

Here are the ACLU's answers to some questions frequently raised by the public about capital punishment.

Q: Doesn't the death penalty deter crime, especially murder?

A: No, there is no credible evidence that the death penalty deters crime. States that have death penalty laws do not have lower crime rates or murder rates than states without such laws. And states that have abolished capital punishment, or instituted it, show no significant changes in either crime or murder rates.

Claims that each execution deters a certain number of murders have been discredited by social science research. The death penalty has no deterrent effect on most murders because people commit murders largely in the heat of passion, and/or under the influence of alcohol or drugs, giving little thought to the possible consequences of their acts. The few murderers who plan their crimes beforehand—for example, professional executioners—intend and expect to avoid punishment altogether by not getting caught. Some self-destructive individuals may even hope they will be caught and executed.

Death penalty laws falsely convince the public that government has taken effective measures to combat crime and homicide. In reality, such laws do nothing to protect us or our communities from the acts of dangerous criminals.

Source: ACLU Briefing Paper: The Death Penalty,
http://aclu.org/library/DeathPenalty.pdf   Used by permission.

Q: Don't murderers deserve to die?

A: Certainly, in general, the punishment should fit the crime. But in civilized society, we reject the "eye for an eye" principle of literally doing to criminals what they do to their victims: The penalty for rape cannot be rape, or for arson, the burning down of the arsonist's house. We should not, therefore, punish the murderer with death. When the government metes out vengeance disguised as justice, it becomes complicit with killers in devaluing human life.

Q: If execution is unacceptable, what is the alternative?

A: Incapacitation. Convicted murderers can be sentenced to lengthy prison terms, including life, as they are in countries and states that have abolished the death penalty. Most state laws allow life sentences for murder that severely limit or eliminate the possibility of parole. At least ten states have life sentences without the possibility of parole for 20, 25, 30, or 40 years, and at least 18 states have life sentences with no possibility of parole.

A recent U. S. Justice Department study of public attitudes about crime and punishment found that a majority of Americans support alternatives to capital punishment: When people were presented the facts about several crimes for which death was a possible punishment, a majority chose lengthy prison sentences as alternatives to the death penalty.

Q: Isn't the death penalty necessary as just retribution for victims' families?

A: All of us would feel extreme anger and a desire for revenge if we lost a loved one to homicide; likewise, if the crime was rape or a brutal assault. However, satisfying the needs of victims cannot be what determines a just response by society to such crimes. Moreover, even within the same family, some relatives of murder victims approve of the death penalty, while others are against it. What the families of murder victims really need is financial and emotional support to help them recover from their loss and resume their lives.

Q: Have strict procedures eliminated discrimination in death sentencing?

A: No. A 1990 Government Accounting Office (GAO) report summarizing several capital punishment studies confirmed "a consistent pattern of evidence indicating racial disparities in charging, sentencing and the imposition of the death penalty. . . . " Eighty-two percent of the studies the GAO reviewed revealed that "those who murdered whites were more likely to be sentenced to death than those who murdered blacks." In addition, the GAO uncovered evidence (though less consistent) that a convict's race, as well as the race of the victim, also influences imposition of the death penalty.

A 1987 study of death sentencing in New Jersey found that prosecutors sought the death penalty in 50 percent of the cases involving a black defendant and a white victim, but in only 28 percent of the cases involving black defendants and black victims. A 1985 study found that, in California, six percent of those convicted of killing whites got the death penalty compared to three percent of those convicted of killing blacks. In Georgia, a landmark 1986 study found that, overall, those convicted of killing whites were four times more likely to be sentenced to death than convicted killers of non-whites.

African Americans are approximately 12 percent of the U. S. population, yet of the 3,859 persons executed for a range of crimes since 1930, more than 50 percent have been black. Other minorities are also death-sentenced disproportionate to their numbers in the population. This is not primarily because minorities commit more murders, but because they are more often sentenced to death when they do.

Poor people are also far more likely to be death-sentenced than those who can afford the high costs of private investigators, psychiatrists and expert criminal lawyers. Indeed, capital punishment is "a privilege of the poor," said Clinton Duffy, former warden at California's San Quentin Prison. Some observers have pointed out that the term "capital punishment" is ironic because "only those without capital get the punishment."

Q: Maybe it used to happen that innocent people were mistakenly executed, but hasn't that possibility been eliminated?

A: No. A study published in the *Stanford Law Review* documents 350 capital convictions in this century, in which it was later proven that the convict had not committed the crime. Of those, 25 convicts were executed while others spent decades of their lives in prison. Fifty-five of the 350 cases took place in the 1970s, and another 20 of them between 1980 and 1985.

Our criminal justice system cannot be made fail-safe because it is run by human beings, who are fallible. Execution of innocent persons is bound to occur.

Q: Only the worst criminals get sentenced to death, right?

A: Wrong. Although it is commonly thought that the death penalty is reserved for those who commit the most heinous crimes, in reality only a small percentage of death-sentenced inmates were convicted of unusually vicious crimes. The vast majority of individuals facing execution were convicted of crimes that are indistinguishable from crimes committed by others who are serving prison sentences, crimes such as murder committed in the course of an armed robbery. The only distinguishing factors seem to be race and poverty.

Who gets the death penalty is largely determined, not by the severity of the crime, but by: the race, sex and economic class of the criminal and victim; geography—some states have the death penalty, others do not; and vagaries in the legal process. The death penalty is like a lottery, in which fairness always loses.

Q: Does the law permit execution of juveniles and people who are mentally retarded or mentally ill?

A: Yes. In 1989, the Supreme Court upheld as constitutional the execution of 16 and 17 year-old (though not 15-year-old) juvenile murderers. The Court likewise upheld the constitutionality of executing mentally retarded people. Although juries are permitted to consider retardation as a mitigating factor, many people on death row today are mentally retarded. Regarding people who are mentally ill, the Court has held that the Eighth Amendment prohibits execution only if the illness prevents the person from comprehending the reasons for the death sentence or its implications.

Q: "Cruel and unusual punishment"—those are strong words, but aren't executions relatively swift and painless?

A: The history of capital punishment is replete with examples of botched executions. But no execution is painless, whether botched or not, and all executions are certainly cruel. . . .

Electrocution succeeded hanging in the early 20th century. When the switch is thrown, the body jerks, smoke frequently rises from the head, and there is a smell of burning flesh. Science has not determined how long an electrocuted individual retains consciousness. . . .

Capital punishment is a barbaric remnant of uncivilized society. It is immoral in principle, and unfair and discriminatory in practice. It assures the execution of some innocent people. As a remedy for crime, it has no purpose and no effect. Capital punishment ought to be abolished now.

So What If the Death Penalty Deters?

Steven Goldberg

Opponents of the death penalty have many reasons for their opposition—that innocent people may be executed, that the death penalty is: 'uncivilized,' that the state should not take lives. But what these arguments come down to is: Does the threat of the death penalty deter people from murderous behavior more than the threat of imprisonment for life? We do not yet know with anything even approaching certainty whether the death penalty does or does not deter. The question is clearly empirical; and it is likely that sophisticated statistical techniques will eventually permit us an answer.

Professor Isaac Ehrlich and his colleagues, utilizing his statistical techniques, argue that there can be little doubt about the ability of the death penalty to deter. Ehrlich concludes that each additional execution prevents about seven or eight people from committing murder. All statistical arguments on the death penalty are, however, excruciatingly complex. Some critics, for example, have argued that increased likelihood of execution leads juries to convict fewer people, thereby offsetting the deterrent effect. If anything, the empirical evidence is that the death penalty does deter. But this is inevitably open to dispute. As a result, firm conclusions that the death penalty either does or does not deter are unwarranted and usually determined by one's psychological and moral leanings.

In academic and media circles, psychological and moral resistance to the idea of the death penalty usually leads to the assertion that it does not deter. These people's conclusion may or may not be correct, but it does not follow from the arguments they deploy:

1. Since many murders result from emotional impulse (e.g., the angry husband who kills his wife), the death penalty could have at best only the slightest deterrent effect. If the death penalty deters, it is likely that it does so through society's saying that certain acts are so unacceptable that society will kill someone who commits them. The individual internalizes the association of the act and the penalty throughout his life, constantly increasing his resistance to committing the act. Note that there is no implication here that the potential murderer consciously weighs the alternatives and decides that the crime is worth life in prison, but not death. No serious theory of deterrence claims that such rational calculation of punishment (as opposed to no rational calculation, or calculation only of the probability of getting caught) plays a role.

   There is no *a priori* reason for assuming that this process is less relevant to emotional acts than rational acts; most husbands, when angry, slam doors, shout, or sulk. Neither the death penalty nor anything else deterred the husband who did murder his wife, so the question is not what deterred the person who did murder (nothing did), but what deterred the person who didn't. If the death penalty deters, it is, in all likelihood, primarily because it instills a psychological resistance to the act, not because it offers a rational argument against committing the act at the time that the

Source: *National Review,* June 30, 1989 v41. © 1989 by National Review, Inc., 215 Lexington Avenue, New York, NY 10016. Reprinted by permission.

decision is being made. In short, it is only legisla-tors who calculate (or at least should calculate) the deterrent effect of the death penalty. Potential murderers simply act; the deterrent effect of the death penalty, if there is one, acts upon them. If it acts with sufficient strength, it prevents their be-coming murderers. The legislator is the physicist studying the forces that move particles; the poten-tial murderers are the moving particles.

2. There is no evidence that the death penalty deters. This is simply untrue. Ehrlich's complex statistical techniques establish a real case that the death penalty deters. But here let us assume, for argu-ment's sake, that there was no such evidence. The more important point is that there is a crucial dif-ference between there being no evidence that two things are correlated and there being evidence that two things are not correlated. The latter means that we have good evidence that the two things are not related; the former means simply that we have no evidence on either side of the case.

Now, it is quite true that we must have some sort of evidence in order to even entertain the idea that two things are related. Our reason for not be-lieving that tall Italian men are smarter than short Italian men is not simply that we have no direct evidence, but also because we have no informal evidence suggesting that this is true—and so we do not bother to even investigate the possibility. It is the lack of relevant informal evidence that per-mits us to ignore the difference between not hav-ing evidence that the hypothesis is true and having evidence that the hypothesis is not true.

But, in the case of penalties, we have an enormous amount of both informal and formal evidence—from everyday experience of socializ-ing children and limiting adult behavior and from such "experiments" as increasing the fees for parking violations—that, as a general rule, the greater a punishment, the fewer people will be-have in the punished way. Thus, it is perfectly rea-sonable to expect that the death penalty would have a more dissuasive effect than would life im-prisonment.

Finally, nearly every popular article and a good many academic articles invoke the experi-ence of the British with public hanging of pick-pockets as proof that the death penalty does not deter. The argument sees the fact that pickpocket-ing continued long after the introduction of (pub-lic) hanging as demonstrating that the death penalty has no deterrent effect. It demonstrates no such thing, of course; at best, it demonstrates that not every pickpocket was dissuaded, a fact no one would doubt. Even if it could be shown that all practicing pickpockets continued to pick pockets at the same rate, this would still not address the more important question of whether some people who had not yet become pickpockets were dis-suaded from doing so by the death penalty. I have no idea whether they were, but neither do those who deny the death penalty's effect.

3. The death penalty will inevitably be imposed on some innocent people. This is, of course, true. But it is also true that, if the death penalty deters, the number of innocent people whose lives are saved will, in all likelihood, dwarf the number of people executed—and a fortiori, the number wrongfully executed. Moreover, even the opponent of the death penalty who emphasizes wrongful execu-tions is willing to sacrifice thousands of lives each year for the social advantages of motor vehicles. Realizing this, the opponent differentiates between the death penalty and the use of motor vehicles on the grounds that:

4. In the case of the death penalty, it is the state that takes a life. This seems to be an argument but is, in fact, merely a restatement of the basic ad-hoc moral objection to the death penalty. Therefore, it is fair to point out that those basing their opposi-tion to the death penalty on the fact that it is the state that takes a life are, if the death penalty de-ters, maintaining their belief by sacrificing the (in-nocent) people who will be murdered because the death penalty is not invoked.

5. The death penalty exchanges "real lives" (those of the executed) for "statistical lives" (those of the people who will not, if the death penalty deters and is invoked, be murdered). This argument is es-sentially a sentimental shrinking from reality. But even if one grants this dubious distinction, this de-fense is available only to the pure pacifist. The most justified military action makes exactly this

exchange when it sacrifices many of society's young men in order to avoid a greater loss of life.

6. If we do not know whether the death penalty deters, we should not use it. As we have seen, if the death penalty deters, it deters the murder of people who are, in addition to being innocent, in all likelihood more numerous than the murderers who are executed. Thus, if society does invoke the death penalty on the assumption that the death penalty deters and is incorrect in this assumption, it unnecessarily accepts the deaths of a relatively small number of (nearly always guilty) individuals. On the other hand, if society refuses to invoke the death penalty on the assumption that the death penalty does not deter and is incorrect in this assumption, then it unnecessarily accepts the deaths of a relatively large number of innocent people. Consideration of this casts doubt on the intuitively plausible claim that, for as long as it is not known whether the death penalty deters, it should not be used. Supporters of the death penalty might turn this argument on its head, viz.: if we do not know for certain that the death penalty does not deter, then we are obliged to use it to save an unknown number of innocent lives.

7. The death penalty is "uncivilized." If the death penalty deters, then, by definition, it results in a society in which there are fewer murders than there would be if the death penalty were not invoked. The opponent of the death penalty can, of course, render this fact irrelevant and immunize his argument by detaching it from deterrence altogether; he can assert that the death penalty is wrong even if it deters. He can, in other words, see the death penalty as analogous to torture for theft: the threat of torture would no doubt deter some people from theft, but would still be unjustified. This is what is implied in the rejection of the death penalty on the grounds that it is "uncivilized" or that it "increases the climate of violence." Ultimately, these defenses of opposition are as invulnerable to refutation as they are incapable of persuading anyone who does not already accept their assumption that the deterrence of murders would not justify the use of the death penalty. . . .

8. It is those who oppose the death penalty who act out of humane motives. . . .

One such view is that the opponent's opposition flows not from feelings of humanity, but from the fact that the opponent can picture the murderer being executed, while he cannot picture the statistical group of innocent people who will be murdered if the death penalty deters but is not employed. The picture of the execution is capable, as the murder of the statistically expected victims is not, of eliciting guilt and fear of aggression with which the opponent cannot deal. He rationalizes his avoidance of these with feelings of humanity, which bolster self-esteem and avoid awareness of his true motivation. . . .

Like opponents of the death penalty, I too hope that the death penalty does not deter. If this proves to be the case, we will avoid the terrible choice that deterrence forces upon us. Unlike the opponents of the death penalty, however, I do not fool myself into thinking that this hope speaks well of one's character. After all, it is a hope that is willing to sacrifice the possibility of saving innocent people in order to avoid personal psychological pain. This doesn't count as altruism where I come from.

Part VII

Debating "Equal Justice Under Law": Race and Gender

"The Law in all of its infinite majesty prohibits the rich as well as the poor from sleeping under bridges." This old French adage clearly expresses the relationship between crime and poverty—it is the poor, much more than the rich, who are its subjects. More recently, Lawrence Friedman (1993) has written that criminal justice "has always fallen more heavily on the underclass, on the deviants, on the 'outs.' Criminal justice was the strong arm of the stratification system."

Perhaps what is most striking about contemporary society is the willingness to protest when practices in the criminal justice system appear to violate fundamental notions of equal justice under law. Consider the following:

- Civil rights groups have called attention to racial profiling, a practice in which police allegedly target blacks for traffic violations.

- Women's rights groups call for the passage of anti-stalking legislation, arguing that women are not protected by legal authorities when males follow women, sometimes with violent consequences.

- Spokespersons for women and minorities have sounded the clarion call for the passage of federal hate crime laws that would protect minorities, women, gays, and lesbians from violent crimes directed at them.

To be sure not all the poor, women, or minorities violate the criminal law. The converse is equally true—some defendants in court are middle class, and a few are even wealthy. This diversity aside, however, those arrested by the police and prosecuted in court reflect a definite profile. Compared to the average citizen, those most likely to be involved in criminal proceedings reflect the following three characteristics:

- Defendants are overwhelmingly male. Males, for example, constitute 93 percent of state prison populations.

- Defendants are mostly underclass. Typical felony defendants possess few of the skills needed to compete successfully in an increasingly technological society. For example, 65 percent of state prison inmates are high-school dropouts, and were either unemployed or only partially employed before their arrest.

- Defendants are disproportionately racial minorities. People of color in the U.S. are imprisoned at a significantly higher rate than whites.

It is also worth mentioning that poverty is directly related to social problems other than crime. The poor, for example, are more likely to have health problems and are also more likely to die younger. As will become clearer in the next section, in the U.S. it is racial minorities who most often suffer from poverty. Moreover, poverty is more likely to beset single women with children, particularly minority women raising children. [In short, *Debating Crime* in the U.S. reflects an overlap of race, poverty and gender.]

Issue 11 examines race and justice, asking: "Does the justice system discriminate against racial minorities?"

Issue 12 probes the question of gender and justice, asking, "Is the justice system biased against women?"

World Wide Web Resources

Web Guides

http://dir.yahoo.com/Society_and_Culture/Issues_and_Causes/Race_Relations/

http://dir.yahoo.com/Society_and_Culture/Cultures_and_Groups/People_of_Color/Racial_Profiling/

http://dir.yahoo.com/Society_and_Culture/Gender/

http://dir.yahoo.com/Society_and_Culture/Cultures_and_Groups/Women/Law/

Searching the Web

race relations, racial profiling, hate crimes, gender, feminism

Useful URLs

American Civil Liberties Union (ACLU): Race and gender are primary concerns of the ACLU.   http://www.aclu.org

National Association for the Advancement of Colored People (NAACP): Oldest and largest civil rights organization in the United States.   http://www.naacp.org

National Council of La Raza: The nation's largest Hispanic organization—"Making a Difference for Hispanic Americans."   http://www.nclr.org/

National Organization of Women (NOW): The nation's largest feminist organization.   http://www.now.org/

Today's Headlines

http://fullcoverage.yahoo.com/Full_Coverage/US/Racial_Profiling/

Fun Sites

American Bar Association Commission on Women in the Profession: http://www.abanet.org/women/home.html

Gender and the Law: http://www.udayton.edu/~gender/

National Center for Women and Policing: http://www.feminist.org/police/ncwp.html

Native Web: Resources for indigenous cultures around the world.
http://www.nativeweb.org/

Women and Justice: http://www.mcgill.pvt.k12.al.us/jerryd/cm/gender.htm

InfoTrac College Edition Resources

Basic Searches

gender and justice; criminal justice, administration of; administration of justice, demographic aspects; racial discrimination

Related Searches

racial profiling

Race and Crime: Does the Criminal Justice System Discriminate Against Racial Minorities?

- *"The police framed Lemrick Nelson," the defense attorney argued to the jury.*

- *"Wealthy whites are treated better by the criminal justice system than poor blacks," commented a local resident.*

These two statements summarize the still-controversial trial of Lemrick Nelson, Jr. The setting was Crown Heights, an area of Brooklyn, New York, inhabited by poor blacks (many of Caribbean ancestry) and Hassidic Jews (a fundamentalist group). A runaway car, driven by a Jewish driver, hit two children, killing one. The black neighborhood became enraged when the ambulance took the Jewish driver to the hospital but not the black victims. Amidst cries of "Kill the Jew!" an angry mob formed. Minutes later, Yankel Rosenbaum (a Jewish scholar visiting from Australia) was stabbed to death. A year later the sole person brought to trial (Nelson, who was black) was acquitted in state court. (Subsequently, though, he was convicted in federal court of civil rights violations and he was sentenced to prison.)

The racial tensions apparent in the trials of Lemrick Nelson illustrate that in debating crime, all roads eventually lead to issues of race. Sometimes the path is direct, as in concerns that black defendants are sentenced more severely than others. For example, half of all prisoners in the U.S. are African American, despite the fact that blacks represent only 12 percent of the U.S. population. At other times the highway is indirect, as in concerns that the war on crime and the war on drugs has a black face. For many Americans, fear of crime is an expression of racial fears. In short, it is impossible to talk about many of the questions discussed in this book without also addressing the issue of race. Consider the following:

- Allegations of police brutality are most likely to surface in confrontations between white officers and minority suspects.

- During jury selection, the press often focuses on the demographic characteristics of the jurors.

• About 40 percent of the people currently on death row, and 53 percent of all people executed since 1930, are African American.

To be sure, the issue of race is most publicly associated with African Americans. Some scholars, though, prefer to emphasize the whole spectrum of the color of justice including red (American Indians/Native Americans), black (African Americans), brown (Latinos and Latinas, Hispanics), yellow (Asian Americans) and white (Euro-Americans, Caucasians) (Mann and Zatz, 1998).

That minorities are more likely to be arrested, convicted, and imprisoned is beyond dispute. What is greatly contested, though, is the reason for these patterns. Blacks and whites view the outcomes, processes, and impacts of the criminal justice system through completely different prisms. All too often discussions quickly degenerate into finger-pointing diatribes, reinforcing notions of "us" versus "them." In these discussions the terms "racism" and "racist society" are often bandied about. Such slogans are useful for calling attention to a problem, but tend to be so elastic and expansive that they lack analytical rigor. In turn, studies disagree whether discrimination persists, and if so, how much impact it has on the criminal justice system.

Pro	Con
Racial prejudice is a preconceived attitude that a racial group is inherently superior or inferior. One in four black citizens believe that half of the white American public share the racial views of the KKK, but only a small percentage of whites expressed such attitudes (Erikson and Tedin, 1995).	Groups openly advocating racial supremacy operate only on the fringes of society. For example, white supremacist groups like the KKK will hold an occasional protest rally and members of the white Aryan nation sometimes are implicated in crimes with a racial motive.
Overrepresentation of minorities reflects imbalances in the criminal justice system, particularly in prison populations. This disproportionality means that racial groups are represented in a much higher (or lower) percentage than in the general population.	Disproportionality is not proof of discrimination. Discrimination refers to illegitimate influences in arrest, prosecution, and sentencing, based on the characteristics of the offender. While race is the most often discussed illegitimate influence, studies emphasize that most disproportionality is due to economic status.

In contemporary America, the issue of racial prejudice focuses on the question of what constitutes fair treatment for blacks. The central question is to what extent the government should help minorities move into the economic mainstream. Whites typically oppose, and blacks typically support, such efforts. These differences have given rise to racial resentment (the new term for what earlier had been called "symbolic racism"). Whites hold an animosity toward blacks, based not on belief of biological inferiority but on the belief that blacks have not tried hard enough to achieve economic and social success (Kinder and Sanders, 1996). The following two articles probe the touchy topic of race, crime, and justice.

"No Equal Justice" argues that race and class distinctions are the dominant reality of the criminal justice system and corrective actions must be taken.

"Race, Crime, and the Administration of Justice" attempts to marshal the available data on the topic, arguing that race plays a role but not as great a role as some contend.

World Wide Web Exercises

1. Choose a search engine and use the search term **racial profiling** to locate two or more articles on the topic. How would the authors of the two articles featured in this section react to the issue of alleged racial profiling by the police?

2. Using the search term **"crack cocaine" and race,** locate two or more articles that discuss allegations that the penalties against possession and distribution of crack cocaine are racially biased.

InfoTrac College Edition Exercises

1. Using the search term **discrimination in criminal justice administration** find one article on each side of the debate. Are the views of the authors similar to, or different from, the readings presented in the book? Why do some argue that race is a dominant issue while others argue that it is irrelevant?

2. Using the search term **police, race relations** or **discrimination in criminal justice administration** find two articles in academic journals that analyze the racial divide on criminal justice issues. Do these findings tend to support one side or the other in the debate?

No Equal Justice: Race and Class in the American Criminal Justice System

David Cole

The most telling image from the most widely and closely watched criminal trial of our lifetime is itself an image of people watching television. On one half of the screen, black law students at Howard Law School cheer as they watch the live coverage of a Los Angeles jury acquitting O. J. Simpson of the double murder of his ex-wife and her friend. On the other half of the screen, white students at George Washington University Law School sit shocked in silence as they watch the same scene. The split-screen image captures in a moment the division between white and black Americans on the question of O. J. Simpson's guilt. And that division in turn reflects an even deeper divide on the issue of the fairness and legitimacy of American criminal justice. . . .

In some respects, the racially divided response to the verdict was understandable. For many black citizens, the acquittal was a sign of hope, or at least payback. For much of our history, the mere allegation that a black man had murdered two white people would have been sufficient grounds for his lynching. Until very recently, the jury rendering judgment on O. J. Simpson would likely have been all white; Simpson's jury, by contrast, consisted of nine blacks, two whites, and an Hispanic. And the prosecution was poisoned by the racism of the central witness, Detective Mark Fuhrman, who had, among other things, called blacks "niggers" on tape and then lied about it on the stand. To many blacks, the jury's "not guilty"

verdict demonstrated that the system is not *always* rigged against the black defendant, and that was worth cheering.

The white law students' shock was also understandable. The evidence against Simpson was overwhelming. . . . To many whites, it appeared that a predominantly black jury had voted for one of their own, and had simply ignored the overwhelming evidence that Simpson was a brutal double murderer.

But there is a deep irony in these reactions. [I]t took an atypical case, one in which minority race and lower socioeconomic class did *not* coincide, in which the defense outperformed the prosecution, and in which the jury was predominantly black, for white people to pay attention to the role that race and class play in criminal justice. Yet the issues of race and class are present in every criminal case, and in the vast majority of cases they play out no more fairly. Of course, they generally work in the opposite direction: the prosecution outspends and outperforms the defense, the jury is predominantly white, and the defendant is poor and a member of a racial minority. In an odd way, then, the Simpson case brought to the foreground issues that lurk beneath the entire system of criminal justice. The system's legitimacy turns on equality before the law, but the system's reality could not be further from that ideal. As Justice Hugo Black wrote over forty years ago: "There can be no equal justice where the kind of trial a man gets depends on the amount of money he has." He might well have added, "or the color of his skin." Where race and class affect outcomes, we cannot maintain that the criminal law is just.

Source: © 1999. *No Equal Justice: Race and Class in the American Criminal Justice System,* by David Cole. Reprinted by permission of The New York Press.

Equality, however, is a difficult and elusive goal. In our nation, it has been the cause of a civil war, powerful political movements, and countless violent uprisings. Yet the gap between the rich and the poor is larger in the United States today than in any other Western industrialized nation, and has been steadily widening since 1968. In 1989, the wealthiest one percent of U.S. households owned nearly 40 percent of the nation's wealth. The wealthiest 20 percent owned more than 80 percent of the nation's wealth. That leaves precious little for the rest. The income and wealth gap correlates closely with race. Minorities' median net worth is less than seven percent that of whites. . . .

This inequality is in turn reflected in statistics on crime and the criminal justice system. The vast majority of those behind bars are poor; 40 percent of state prisoners can't even read; and 67 percent of prison inmates did not have full-time employment when they were arrested. The per capita incarceration rate among blacks is seven times that among whites. African Americans make up about 12 percent of the general population, but more than half of the prison population. They serve longer sentences, have higher arrest and conviction rates, face higher bail amounts, and are more often the victims of police use of deadly force than white citizens. In 1995, one in three young black men between the ages of twenty and twenty-nine was imprisoned or on parole or probation. If incarceration rates continue their current trends, one in four young black males born today will serve time in prison during his lifetime. . . Nationally, for every one black man who graduates from college, 100 are arrested.

In addition, poor and minority citizens are disproportionately victimized by crime. Poorer and less educated persons are the victims of violent crime at significantly higher rates than wealthy and more educated persons . . . Homicide is the leading cause of death among young black men. Because we live in segregated communities, most crime is intraracial; the more black crime there is, the more black victims there are. But at the same time, the more law enforcement resources we direct toward protecting the black community from crime, the more often black citizens, especially those living in the inner city, will find their friends, relatives, and neighbors behind bars.

This book argues that while our criminal justice system is explicitly based on the premise and promise of equality before the law, the administration of criminal law—whether by the officer on the beat, the legislature, or the Supreme Court—is in fact predicated on the exploitation of inequality. My claim is not simply that we have ignored inequality's effects within the criminal justice system, nor that we have tried but failed to achieve equality there. Rather, I contend that *our criminal justice system affirmatively depends on inequality*. . . .

White Americans are not likely to want to believe this claim. The principle that all are equal before the law is perhaps the most basic in American law; it is that maxim, after all, that stands etched atop the Supreme Court's magnificent edifice. . . .

If there is a common theme in criminal justice policy in America, it is that we consistently seek to avoid difficult trade-offs by exploiting inequality. Politicians impose the most serious criminal sanctions on conduct in which they and their constituents are least likely to engage. Thus, a predominantly white Congress has mandated prison sentences for the possession and distribution of crack cocaine one hundred times more severe than the penalties for powder cocaine. African Americans comprise more than 90 percent of those found guilty of crack cocaine crimes, but only 20 percent of those found guilty of powder cocaine crimes. By contrast, when white youth began smoking marijuana in large numbers in the 1960s and 1970s, state legislatures responded by reducing penalties and in some states effectively decriminalizing marijuana possession. More broadly, it is unimaginable that our country's heavy reliance on incarceration would be tolerated if the black/white incarceration rates were reversed, and whites were incarcerated at seven times the rate that blacks are. The white majority can "afford" the costs associated with mass incarceration because the incarcerated mass is disproportionately nonwhite.

Similarly, police officers routinely use methods of investigation and interrogation against members of racial minorities and the poor that would be deemed unacceptable if applied to more privileged members of the community. "Consent" searches, pretextual traffic stops, and "quality of life" policing are all disproportionately used against black citizens. Courts assign attorneys to defend the poor in serious criminal trials whom the wealthy would not hire to represent them in traffic court. And jury commissioners and lawyers have long engaged in discriminatory practices that result in disproportionately white juries.

These double standards are not, of course, explicit; on the face of it, the criminal law is color-blind and class-blind. But in a sense, this only makes the problem worse. The rhetoric of the criminal justice system sends the message that our society carefully protects everyone's constitutional rights, but in practice the rules assure that law enforcement prerogatives will generally prevail over the rights of minorities and the poor. By affording criminal suspects substantial constitutional protections in theory, the Supreme Court validates the results of the criminal justice system as fair. That formal fairness obscures the systemic concerns that ought to be raised by the fact that the prison population is overwhelmingly poor and disproportionately black.

I am not suggesting that the disproportionate results of the criminal justice system are wholly attributable to racism, nor that the double standards are intentionally designed to harm members of minority groups and the poor. Intent and motive are notoriously difficult to fathom, particularly where there are multiple actors and decision makers . . . In fact, I think it more likely that the double standards have developed because they are convenient mechanisms for avoiding hard questions about competing interests, and it is human nature to avoid hard questions. But whatever the reasons, we have established two systems of criminal justice: one for the privileged, and another for the less privileged. Some of the distinctions are based on race, others on class, but in no true sense can it be said that all are equal before the criminal law. . . .

Much of this book will be dedicated to demonstrating how the double standards in criminal justice operate. Some readers will need more convincing than others on this score. By a detailed description of the problem, I hope to shake the confidence of those who believe the system is fair. . . .

Race, Crime, and the Administration of Justice: A Summary of the Available Facts

Christopher Stone

We each know about race, crime, and the administration of justice in many ways: from our own experience, through stories we hear, and from our various understandings of history. We may also retain a current statistic or two, especially if we have stumbled on one that reinforces what we already believe. But what does the subject of race, crime, and justice look like if approached empirically, and with reference to all of what we refer to today as racial groups?

At the most general level, we know that many people of color—Native Americans, Asian Americans, Hispanic Americans, black Americans—do not trust the justice system. For example, a study of Hispanic Texans in the mid-1980s found that fewer than 30 percent rated the job performance of their local police as good (Carter, 1985). In a 1995 Gallup poll, more than half of black Americans said the justice system was biased against them. Moreover, two-thirds of black Americans in that same Gallup poll said that police racism against blacks is common across the country, and a majority of white Americans (52 percent) agreed (*Gallup Poll Monthly,* 1995). Social scientists usually explain this broad distrust in two ways: historical experience and present-day practice. The historical experience with the justice system among Native Americans, Asian immigrants, black Americans, and Hispanic Americans is more than enough to provoke distrust, but is it being reinforced by current practice?

Source: *NIJ Journal,* No. 239, Washington, D.C.: U.S. Department of Justice, National Institute of Justice, 27–32.

- How does the pattern of crime and victimization keep us from living as one America?

- How do stereotypes work to cause people of some races and ethnic groups to be unfairly suspected of crime?

- How and when does the justice system itself treat defendants and offenders differently on the basis of race or ethnicity?

- Does a lack of diversity in the justice system add to the distrust?

Social science research has shed some light on each of these concerns, but our empirical knowledge is uneven. We know a lot about some of these issues, but there are great gaps in what we know through research. We know much less about discrimination in judicial decisions regarding Asian-American defendants, for example, than we do about "black and white" discrimination. . . . The lack of data and good research on the experience of Asian Americans and Native Americans in particular is a problem.

Patterns of Crime Victimization

Consider first the pattern of crime victimization. In general, whites have the lowest victimization rates, followed by Asians, followed by Native Americans, then Hispanics, then blacks. But the differences are dramatic. In 1995, for example, there were 5.1 homicide victims per 100,000 non-Hispanic white males. The rate for Asian-American males was more than one-and-a-half times higher, at 8.3 per 100,000. But the rate for Native-American males was 18, more than three times the white rate, and the rate for Hispanics was 25.1, almost five times the white rate. And the rate for blacks was 57.6, more than 10 times the white rate (BJS, 1994)....

Why the differences? The crudest analyses focus on the offenders, telling us that most crime is intraracial. More than 80 percent of homicides where we know the race of the killer are either white-on-white or black-on-black. Research among Vietnamese and Chinese in California has also shown that most crime there is intraracial (Song, 1992).

Does this mean that groups with high victimization rates also have high offending rates? Yes, but with three crucial caveats. First, it is essential to remember that most crime is committed by whites. Their offending rates may be low, but there are so many of them that they still manage to commit most of the crime.

Second, the chances that a young adult has ever committed a violent offense is roughly equal across races....

Third, community conditions seem to be the reason that crime falls so heavily on some groups. The more sophisticated analyses today focus on neighborhoods, and they show us that the differences in victimization and offending rates between groups may have more to do with neighborhood and community conditions than with race itself. Where people live in neighborhoods of concentrated disadvantage, victimization and offending rates are high. When researchers compare similar neighborhoods of different races, the racial differences seem to disappear (Sampson, Raudenbush, and Earls, 1997). The problem is that researchers cannot find white communities to compare to the most disadvantaged urban communities.

Stereotypes and Criminal Profiles

Most people of all races and ethnic groups are never convicted of a crime, but stereotypes can work to brand all members of some groups with suspicion. These stereotypes may have their roots in past biases, but they also can be reinforced through broadcast news and newspaper reports. One social scientist, for example, finds that Asians are overidentified with Asian gangs ("Asians Are Automatically Labeled Gang Members," 1994). A team of researchers at the University of California at Los Angeles has found that blacks and Hispanics are overrepresented in TV news depictions of violent crime, while whites are overrepresented in stories involving nonviolent crime (Gilliam et al, 1996).

These stereotypes are bad enough in the culture at large, but they also work their way into law enforcement through the use of criminal profiles, putting an undue burden on innocent members of these groups. A particularly clear example of this phenomenon is found in a study of Maryland State troopers and the searches they made of motorists on Interstate Highway 95 in 1995. On this particular stretch of highway, motorists were found to be speeding equally across races. Black motorists, for example, constituted 17 percent of the motorists and 17.5 percent of the speeders. But black motorists were the subject of 409 of the 533 searches made by the police looking for contraband (Russell, 1998).

Why were black motorists searched so often? The police might justify such practices on the ground that blacks are more likely to be carrying contraband. And the statistics show this to be true: the police found contraband in 33 percent of the searches of black motorists, and in 22 percent of the searches of white motorists. But the mischief in this practice is quickly exposed. Blacks had a 50 percent higher chance of being found with contraband, but were searched more than 400 percent more often. The result is that 274 innocent black motorists were searched, while only 76 innocent white motorists were searched. The profiles apparently used by the Maryland State troopers make 17 percent of the motorists pay 76 percent of the price of law enforcement strategy, solely because of their race.

Disparities in Conviction Rates

The combination of higher rates of crime and higher levels of police attention produce disproportionate numbers of arrests among some groups. Arrest rates for violent crimes among . . . blacks are about five times that for whites. Again, as with crime, the arrest rate for whites may be low, but there are so many whites that they account for 55 percent of all arrests for violent crime (FBI, 1996).

But then what happens? Here is the problem that has attracted more research than any other area under discussion today. Black Americans account for fewer than half of the arrests for violent crimes, but they account for just over half of the convictions and approximately 60 percent of the prison admissions. At the beginning of this decade, the chance that a black male born in the United States would go to prison in his lifetime . . . was more than 28.5 percent. The corresponding chance for an Hispanic male was 16 percent, and for a white male, 4.4 percent (Bonczar and Beck, 1997) . . .

How has this happened? Is this simply the result of fair-minded prosecutors and courts applying the law to disproportionate arrests, or is there bias at work at these later stages of the justice process?

Researchers have looked carefully for evidence of bias, reaching different conclusions. Some of the disparity we see when we visit these institutions is clearly explained by differences in arrest charges, and much more is explained by differences in the prior records of those convicted. There is no evidence of disparity that stretches across the justice system as a whole when we consider index crimes. But studies of individual jurisdictions and specific parts of the court process do find some evidence of race bias in a significant number of cases. . . . [B]lack defendants in some jurisdictions are more likely to receive prison sentences than are white defendants. . . .

Across race and ethnic groups, concerns about both of these kinds of bias are regularly reported: underenforcement of laws within a minority community and overpunishment when that community is seen as a threat to the majority. These two kinds of bias can balance each other in simple studies. . . .

Strengthening Diversity Within the Criminal Justice System

If these biases were eliminated from the justice system, would we still have a problem? If the police abandoned the use of offensive stereotypes, if the remnants of institutional bias were driven from the courts, would the justice system deserve and win respect across lines of race and ethnicity? Or is the sheer volume of black and Hispanic prisoners in America a problem in its own right? . . .

Respect for the justice system can be won or lost not just in its decisions, but in who is making them. Slow but real progress has been made in strengthening the diversity of law enforcement throughout the United States, but some signs indicate that this effort is losing momentum. A recent study . . . concluded that the number of minority law enforcement executives has declined in recent years, after earlier gains. A large percentage of minority officers remain in entry-level positions throughout their careers and the outlook for any change, the researchers concluded, is bleak (NIJ, 1994).

Declining Crime Rates: A Reason for Optimism

If there is a strong reason for optimism among all these data, it is in the steady decline in crime over the last several years in most large U.S. cities. Let me focus here on the often neglected yet dramatic decline in domestic homicide, where we again find a stark difference between blacks and whites. Twenty years ago, white men were rarely victims of domestic homicide. . . . Rates for black victims of domestic homicide were roughly seven times higher 20 years ago, and they have plummeted since. The rate for black male victims has dropped from more than 16 to fewer than three homicides per 100,000; and for black women the rate has fallen from more than 12 to fewer than five (Greenfield et al, 1998).

These declines leave us with two important lessons. First, they remind us of the power of neighborhood disadvantage, for as stark as the black/white differences are, they disappear when researchers control for housing conditions. Second, they remind us of the power these communities have to help themselves. There are some aspects of the drop in crime for which police can claim the credit, and there is plenty of crime reduction for everybody to claim some, but this drop, occurring over 20 years, exceeds the reach of any single program or administration. It is an example of cultural change and communities working to heal themselves.

In sum, these declines hold out the promise of a day when race will no longer be a proxy for suspicion, and crime no longer a proxy for concentrated community disadvantage.

Gender and Justice: Is the Justice System Biased Against Women?

- *The war on drugs is really a war against black women.*

- *Female attorneys are addressed in court as "dear" or "honey" while male lawyers are addressed as "Mister" or "counselor."*

- *The number of women imprisoned in the U.S. increased sixfold in less than 15 years.*

- *There is a general belief that there are two types of rape—real rapes and rapes provoked by the victim.*

These are but four examples of the often-controversial topic of gender and justice in the United States.

The women's rights movement emerged as an important social movement during the 1960s, both reflecting but also stimulating a major transformation of U.S. society. Nowhere is this more apparent than in the workplace. Today two out of three women work outside of the home. Moreover, the jobs they hold are vastly different than before. No longer are women confined to traditional female occupations (nurse, teacher, waitress, and secretary). Today, women hold positions in virtually every segment of private and public employment. Even traditionally all-male occupations within the justice system now reflect significant female employment; in big-city police departments 14 percent of sworn officers are female, and across the nation over 10 percent of the judges are female.

These changes, and the women's movement generally, have aroused considerable controversy. Social conservatives continue to emphasize that women should be primary caregivers for children, not primary breadwinners for the family. Political conservatives insist on eliminating abortion. Meanwhile, women's groups focus on a range of justice issues. On the civil side of the legal agenda, gender justice issues include deadbeat dads and sexual harassment in the workplace. On the criminal side, gender justice focuses on crimes like domestic violence and sexual assault (topics examined elsewhere in this book). Gender is also indirectly an issue in other areas as well. Women, more than men, favor gun control and oppose the death penalty. It is also worth mentioning that organizations formed and led by women have become the leaders in championing the rights of crime victims and seeking to eliminate drunk driving.

Thus, throughout this book, we will examine issues that directly or indirectly pose the question: is the justice system biased against women?

Pro	Con
The role of women in the justice system has been neglected for too long.	The focus on women is excessive, diverting attention from pressing issues.
The percentage of women arrested, convicted, and sentenced is rising rapidly.	Women constitute only a small percentage of criminals.
Female defendants present unique issues for the justice system.	Equal protection shouldn't mean "special treatment."
Employment in the justice system has resembled a males-only club for too long.	All too often diversity means quotas, and quotas result in lowering standards.
Gender bias permeates the entire system, particularly the courts.	Complaints of gender bias are greatly overstated.
Women found guilty of committing "male" crimes are sentenced more severely than men.	Overall, women are sentenced more leniently than men.

The following two articles explore general issues directly related to gender, justice and equality under the law.

"Sex on the Docket" reviews reports in over 34 states, which find pervasive, multi-dimensional gender bias in the judiciary. In turn, officials have sought to take corrective action.

"Women in Prison" examines the dramatic rise in the number of female offenders in the U.S. since the early 1980s. It argues that what is needed is a woman-oriented response to the unique needs and problems of females in prison.

World Wide Web Exercises

1. In the search engine of your choice, use the search term **women lawyers** or **women judges** and identify two or more sites. To what extent are the concerns similar to or different from those identified in the Kearney and Sellers article that follows?

2. In the search engine of your choice, use the search term **women prisoners** to identify two or more sites. To what extent are the concerns similar to or different from those identified in the article by Chesney-Lind?

InfoTrac College Edition Exercises

1. In PowerTrac, first search for **women.** Next search for **judges** (or **lawyers**). Combine the two search results with the logical operator **and.** Locate two or more academic articles. Do the findings support or refute the arguments raised by Kearney and Sellers?

2. Using the search term **women prisoners,** locate two articles that discuss the topic. Do their arguments and findings agree with those of Chesney-Lind, or are they different?

Sex on the Docket: Reports of State Task Forces on Gender Bias

Richard Kearney and Holly Sellers

The struggle of women for equality will remain incomplete as long as there is sex discrimination in judicial administration. . . . Women have fought many political and legal battles against bias in the United States, winning the right to vote, access to jobs and occupations formerly dominated by men, and legal prohibitions against sex-based discrimination. Remarkable progress has been made during the past 30 years on many fronts. But one of the most durable fortresses of patriarchy and bias against women is also perhaps the most important in terms of both symbol and substance. . . . So long as women do not receive fair and equal treatment under the law and in the halls of justice, their struggle remains bittersweet and incomplete.

However, since the early 1980s, 39 states, the District of Columbia, and nine of the 13 federal circuits have established task forces on gender bias in the judiciary . . . This article is based on an examination of the 34 final state reports and numerous related documents. . . . As a collection, the reports present a rich source of empirical and anecdotal data and afford a unique opportunity to examine gender bias in a once-neglected yet critically important public administration setting.

Origins of the Gender Bias Movement

Historically, women were excluded from making, interpreting, studying, and practicing the law. As

Source: *Public Administration Review*, Nov.–Dec., 1996 v56. Used by permission.

recently as the early 1970s, women comprised only 15 percent of attorneys and four percent of judges. Sexual bias in the practice and administration of the law and against women as lawyers, litigants, and court employees was pervasive. As women entered the legal profession in much greater numbers, they began sharing their experiences—both formally and informally—in conferences, workshops, professional meetings, and conversations. Empirical studies of gender bias began appearing in scholarly and legal research. Fragmented activities coalesced in 1980, when the NOW Legal Defense and Education Fund and the newly-formed National Association of Women Judges created the National Judicial Education Program to Promote Equality for Women and Men in the Courts (NJEP), with the purpose of educating the judiciary on gender bias. . . .

NJEP activities encountered a substantial amount of disbelief, denial, and resistance. It became apparent that the attack on gender bias would require concrete data and evidence from the states. . . . Despite significant state differences in task force composition, court organization and processes, partisan make-up, political culture, and other distinctions, the methodology, findings, and recommendations are strikingly similar. One is left with a clear conviction that gender bias, in the words of the New York Task Force on Women in the Courts, is "a pervasive problem with grave consequences," and that it permeates the decision making, operations, and environment of state court systems. . . . Taken together, the task force findings are compelling and convincing; any reasonable person would conclude that gender bias is a pervasive, multi-dimensional problem in the courts.

The Findings and Recommendations

There are two general categories of findings: 1) gender bias in the courtroom and under the law, and 2) gender bias in court administration and the legal profession.

In the Courtroom and Under the Law

Judges and attorneys treat women and men differently in the courtroom. A common form of gender bias documented by task forces has to do with terms of address. Male attorneys, for example, are typically addressed as "counselor" or "Mister," while female attorneys sometimes are called by first names or "young lady," or by terms of endearment such as "honey" or "dear."

Task forces found that judges, who are overwhelmingly male, tend to treat women attorneys and witnesses dismissively and with less tolerance than they do men. Aggressive behavior by a male attorney may be rewarded, while similar behavior by a woman may be chastised. Verbal sexual harassment of female attorneys by judges and especially by male attorneys is widely reported. Such harassment includes suggestive comments, touching, sexually offensive jokes, and sexual comments on women's physical traits and appearance. According to a female attorney in Texas, "I've been patted on the head, endured condescending inquiries about whether I was having a bad hair day, broken fingernail day or a run in my stockings when my mood was less than perky. I have had judges stroke my hair and caress my shoulders as we discuss the upcoming docket." A Vermont judge told an attorney that she was "too pregnant to prosecute."

Much of this biased behavior is unconscious, unrecognized by men, and not malicious, but it diminishes women's credibility as lawyers in the eyes of judges, jurors, peers, and their clients. In other instances, male lawyers simply consider their sexist words and actions behavior to be just another litigation tactic. But some reported behavior in the courtroom rises above boorishness and aggressive representation of clients to approach clear and intentional harassment. . . .

As has been found in other research on gender discrimination and sexual harassment, male and female perceptions of the existence and frequency of these events are highly divergent. What many men may consider flattery or gentle teasing may strike women as unnecessarily calling attention to their sex. Interestingly, several reports . . . include data and anecdotes from male attorneys who claim that their female counterparts often receive favorable treatment in the courtroom from male judges, particularly if they are young and attractive.

Men are also discriminated against under the law. For example, men continue to be found less suitable as custodians of their children than women in many states. Task force reports duly take note of such forms of gender bias against men.

But it is apparent that women are discriminated against under the law in many more venues. No-fault divorce has worked to the great financial advantage of men while contributing significantly to the feminization of poverty. . . .

Domestic violence was a major topic in nearly all of the reports, which conclude, not surprisingly, that women are overwhelmingly the victims. They also find that domestic violence, despite its devastating physical and emotional effects on women and children, is not treated as a crime in many judicial settings. . . .

Sexual assault victims are also treated badly enough to discourage them from reporting the event, particularly if the attacker is known by the victim. . . . Florida's task force found that there is a "general belief that there actually are two kinds of rapes—'real' rapes and rapes somehow prompted by the victim," depending on such factors as the victim's virtuosity and physical wounds. In a real sense, the victim herself is placed on trial. . . .

Juveniles are treated differentially by gender. Boys tend to receive more lenient treatment than girls, who, as observed in the Kentucky report, "are institutionalized more often and for longer periods of time than male juveniles." However, fewer facilities and counseling programs are available for girls.

In Court Administration and the Legal Profession

Gender bias in court personnel systems is rampant and multi-faceted. Acute occupational segregation is documented in most states. Rhode Island found that 95 percent of female court employees were in the lowest seven pay grades and none were in the top seven. Men dominate key administrative positions throughout the court system, while women are clustered in clerical jobs. . . .

The courts have been slow to adopt modern employee-benefit packages that meet the special needs of women as primary caregivers. Parental leave, flextime, child-care facilities, and part-time work opportunities are rare. . . .

Women in 1994 made up 43 percent of law school admissions. But, according to every report, women continue to be discriminated against in the legal profession from the moment they enter law school. In the classroom, female students are subjected to stereotyping, teasing, and a presumption by some professors and fellow students that women are not suited for practicing law. . . .

After concluding that gender bias is a serious problem in the state court systems, the task forces then issued recommendations to judges, court administrators, attorneys, law schools, legislators, and others for erasing it. The need for continuing education and training of judges, attorneys, and court personnel permeates the recommendations. . . . Most reports called for substantive changes in the law and reform in personnel procedures, along with further research and study.

Impacts of the Task Force Movement

Although implementation of task force recommendations is variable, in all the task-force states gender fairness has been elevated from a quiet issue to an important professional norm. The reports, with perhaps two or three exceptions, have not been shelved and forgotten. They have been widely disseminated to the news media, bar associations, law schools, and general public. Chief justices, bar associations, and court administrators offices have established implementation committees, which have responded with activities intended to root out gender bias and eliminate it. Many states have issued progress reports and conducted follow-up surveys.

. . . [H]andbooks have been written on how to avoid various types of gender bias. Judicial education programs have been introduced. . . . The goal is to institutionalize change by integrating gender-bias issues into all appropriate curriculum elements. Sexual-harassment policies have been adopted by the court systems . . . and gender-bias complaint procedures have been adopted or revised. . . . Family-friendly policies are increasingly available to court personnel and witnesses. There have been gender-fairness changes in codes of judicial conduct, canons of judicial ethics, and codes of professional responsibility. Gender-biased language has been eradicated from statutes and court documents. . . . New child custody laws are on the books . . . , domestic violence laws have been passed . . . and divorce reform is in place in Rhode Island. . . .

The most important single change attributed to the task force movement has to do with the climate within the judicial system. In most places, both men and women are more aware of gender bias in the courts and in the legal profession, and they are less tolerant of it. Blatant sexism and sexual harassment have diminished.

Needless to say, gender bias in its many forms has not been eradicated in the courts or in the legal profession. . . . But the gender bias task force movement, as documented in these reports, is remarkable in its scope, comprehensiveness, and impact. And it is unique in that it represents a serious self-examination on a sensitive issue by a conservative political institution and a powerful profession, heretofore known for their determined resistance to change.

Women in Prison: From Partial Justice to Vengeful Equity

Meda Chesney-Lind

The Forgotten Offender

Throughout most of our nation's history, women in prison have been correctional afterthoughts. Ignored because of their small numbers, female inmates tended to complain, not riot, making it even easier for institutions to overlook their unique needs. . . .

Something dramatic happened to this picture in the 1980s: During that decade, the number of women in U.S. prisons jumped dramatically. In 1980, there were just over 12,000 women in U.S. state and federal prisons. By 1997, that number had increased to almost 80,000. In about a decade and a half, the number of women incarcerated in the nation's prisons had increased sixfold.

This astonishing increase should not be seen simply as a reflection of the increase in male incarceration during the same period. Women's "share" of total imprisonment has more than doubled in the past three decades, from three percent in 1970 to 6.4 percent in 1997. . . .

What has caused this shift in the way that we respond to women's crime? What unique challenges have these women inmates produced? And what could we do better or differently, as we struggle to create a woman-oriented response to the current state of affairs?

Women's Criminal Activity

Is the dramatic increase in women's imprisonment a response to a women's crime problem spiraling

out of control? Empirical indicators give little evidence of this. For example, the total number of arrests of adult women, which might be seen as a measure of women's criminal activity, increased by 31.4 percent between 1987 and 1996, while the number of women in prison increased by 159 percent. . . .

What explains the increase? A recent study by the Bureau of Justice Statistics (BJS) indicates that growth in the number of violent offenders has been the major factor for male prison population growth, but for the female prison population, "drug offenders were the largest source of growth." One explanation, then, is that the "war on drugs" has become a largely unannounced war on women. In 1979, one in 10 women in prison was doing time for drugs. Today, drug offenders account for more than a third of the female prison population (37.4 percent). Finally, while the intent of "get tough" policies was to rid society of drug dealers and so-called drug kingpins, more than a third (35.9 percent) of the women serving time for drug offenses in state prisons are there on charges of possession.

Policies Impacting Women's Imprisonment

Many observers suspect that the increase in women's imprisonment is due to an array of policy changes within the criminal justice system, rather than a change in the seriousness of women's crime.

Certainly, as data on the characteristics of women in prison indicate, the passage of increased penalties for drug offenses has been a major

Source: *Corrections Today*, December, 1998 v60. Reprinted with permission of the American Correctional Association, Latham, MD.

factor. Also important has been the implementation of a variety of sentencing reform initiatives which, while devoted to reducing class and race disparities in male sentencing, pay little attention to gender.

The scant evidence we have suggests that sentencing reform has played a major role in the soaring increase of women in federal prisons. In 1988, before full implementation of sentencing guidelines, women comprised 6.5 percent of those in federal institutions; by 1992, that figure had jumped to eight percent. The number of women in federal prisons climbed by 97.4 percent in the space of three years. . . .

Other less obvious policy changes also have played a role in increasing women's imprisonment. For example, look at new technologies for determining drug use (e.g., urinalysis). Many women are being returned to prison for technical parole violations because they fail to pass random drug tests. . . .

Vengeful Equity?

What has happened in the last few decades signals a major change in the way the country is responding to women's offending. Without much fanfare and certainly with little public discussion or debate, the male model of incarceration has been increasingly accessed in response to the soaring number of women inmates.

Some might argue that this pattern is simply the product of a lack of reflection or imagination on the part of those charged with administering the nation's prison systems. They are, after all, used to running prisons built around the male model of inmate. However, an additional theme also is emerging in modern correctional response to women inmates: vengeful equity. This is the dark side of the equity or parity model of justice—one which emphasizes treating women offenders as though they were men, particularly when the outcome is punitive, in the name of equal justice.

Perhaps the starkest expression of this impulse has been the creation of chain gangs for women. While these have surfaced in several states, the most publicized example comes from Arizona. There, a sheriff pronounced himself an "equal op-portunity incarcerator" and encouraged women "now locked up with three or four others in dank, cramped disciplinary cells" to "volunteer" for a 15-woman chain gang. Defending his controversial move, he commented, "If women can fight for their country, and bless them for that, if they can walk a beat, if they can protect the people and arrest violators of the law, then they should have no problem with picking up trash in 120 degrees." Other examples of vengeful equity can be found in the creation of women's boot camps, and in the argument that women should be subjected to capital punishment at the same rate as men.

Female Offender Characteristics

But who are these women inmates, and does it make sense to treat women in prison as though they were men? BJS recently conducted a national survey of imprisoned women in the United States and found that women in prison have far higher rates of physical and sexual abuse than their male counterparts. Forty-three percent of the women surveyed "reported they had been abused at least once" before their current admission to prison; the comparable figure for men was 12.2 percent. . . .

A look at the offenses for which women are incarcerated quickly puts to rest the notion of hyper-violent, nontraditional women offenders. Nearly half of all women in prison are serving sentences for nonviolent offenses and have been convicted in the past of only nonviolent offenses. By 1996, about two-thirds of women in the nation's prisons were serving time either for drug offenses or property offenses.

Even when women commit violent offenses, gender plays an important role. Research indicates, for example, that of women convicted of murder or manslaughter, many had killed husbands or boyfriends who had repeatedly and violently abused them. . . .

As with previous studies of women in prison, the BJS survey found that two-thirds of the women had at least one child under 18, yet more than half had never received visits from their children. . . . Just under three-quarters of the women had children who had lived with them before going to prison, compared to slightly more than half (52.9 percent) of incarcerated men. . . .

The surge in women's imprisonment, particularly in the area of drug offenses, has disproportionately hit women of color in the United States. Specifically, while the number of women in state prisons for drug sales has increased by 433 percent between 1986 and 1991, this increase is far steeper for African-American women (828 percent) and Hispanic women (328 percent) than for Caucasian women (241 percent).

Women in prison, then, have different personal histories than their male counterparts and less serious offense backgrounds. In particular, women's long histories of victimization, coupled with the relative nonviolence of their crimes, suggests that extensive reliance on imprisonment could easily be rethought without compromising public safety.

What Could We Do Differently?

Inattention to gender difference, willful or otherwise, has meant that many modern women's prisons have encountered serious, and unanticipated, difficulties in managing this population. Jails and prisons are generally unprepared for the large number of pregnant women in their custody (some estimates put this at one in 10). The sexual harassment of women inmates also is an increasingly well-documented problem that is receiving both national and international attention. Finally, procedures that have been routine in corrections for decades (strip searches) are now being understood as problematic in women's prisons (particularly when dealing with victims of past sexual traumas). To put it simply, gender matters in corrections, and a woman in prison is not, and never will be, identical to her male counterpart.

Given the backgrounds of women in prison, many would argue that they could be better served in the community due to the decreased seriousness of their crimes and the treatable antecedents to their criminality. Since the expansion of the female prison population has been fueled primarily by increased rates of incarceration for drug offenses, not by commitments for crimes of violence, women in prison seem to be obvious candidates for alternative, in-community sentencing. To make this shift requires both planning and focus—something that has been absent in U.S. corrections with reference to women in prison. . . .

As a nation, we face a choice. We can continue to spend tax dollars on the costly incarceration of women guilty of petty drug and property crimes, or we can seek other solutions to the problems of drug-dependent women. Given the characteristics of the women in prison, it is clear that the decarceration of large numbers of women in prison would not jeopardize public safety. . . .

By moving dollars from women's imprisonment to women's services in the community, we not only will help women—we also will help their children. In the process, we are helping to break the cycle of poverty, desperation, crime and imprisonment that burdens so many of these women and their families.

Part VIII

Debating Prisons

In 1980, Judge William Justice of the U.S. District Court for the Eastern District of Texas issued a sweeping order. The case of *Ruiz v. Estelle* listed a host of problems in the Texas Department of Corrections, including overcrowding, excessive use of force by prison guards, and a lack of protection of prisoners from violence by other prisoners. Based on these violations of the U.S. Constitution, the judge ordered massive changes.

Ruiz v. Estelle proved to be the most far-reaching federal court decision of its kind. But it was hardly unique. Historically, conditions in state prisons were considered to be hands-off to the federal judiciary. But in 1964, the U.S. Supreme Court signaled an end to this policy. Thousands of prisoners filed suit. These prisoner lawsuits had a dramatic impact on contemporary corrections. All across the nation, states were forced to hire more guards, cook nutritional, balanced meals, and provide adequate medical care. The result was a dramatic increase in the cost of housing each prisoner. (In 1996, Congress passed the Prison Litigation Reform Act, which reduced the authority of federal courts to oversee state prisons.)

Prisoners' rights is one of two trends that have greatly shaped contemporary corrections in the United States. The other was the rapid increase in the number of prisoners. As late as the early 1970s, U.S. prisons incarcerated about 200,000 prisoners daily. Today the number is over 1.333 million (and increasing by approximately seven percent a year). In short, public insistence upon punitive policies added 1.1 million new prisoners to the inventory, forcing states to engage in expensive building programs to add new cells, hire additional guards, buy more food, and hire more nurses.

In combination, the legal recognition of prisoners' rights and public pressures to get tough on crooks meant that states had to spend billions more each year. This section examines two topics related to these major trends.

Issue 13 examines the debate that has arisen as a result of increased use of private corrections facilities by state and local governments. Faced with rapidly rising costs, some argue that private prisons save government money. Others are concerned that cutting corners will reduce quality.

Issue 14 focuses on the debate over the early release of prisoners through parole, and asks, Should parole be abolished? Even though prisons are filled to overflowing there are substantial political pressures to hold inmates in prison longer.

World Wide Web Resources

Web Guides

http://dir.yahoo.com/Society_and_Culture/Crime/Correction_and_Rehabilitation/

Searching the Web

prison, private prisons, parole

Useful URLs

American Civil Liberties Union: The ACLU is a leading champion of prisoner's rights.   http://aclu.org/issues/prisons/hmprisons.html

American Corrections Association: This organization maintains a useful Web site that covers corrections news and issues.
http://www.corrections.com/news/private/privatearchives.html

Bureau of Justice Statistics: Corrections Statistics.
http://www.ojp.usdoj.gov/bjs/correct.htm

National Institute of Corrections: Provides assistance to federal, state, and local corrections officials.   http://www.nicic.org/inst/

Prisoner Activist Resource Center: The Prison Issue Desk offers updates from this activist group.   http://www.prisonactivist.org/

Today's Headlines

http://headlines.yahoo.com/Full_Coverage/US/Prisons/

Fun Sites

Alcatraz Island: Offering a close-up look at the historic and infamous federal prison where isolation was a constant of island life.   http://www.nps.gov/alcatraz/

Doin' Time: A site dedicated to the history of Washington State Prison, built in 1887.   http://bigjohn.bmi.net/garyl/history/garys.html

Islands of Infamy: A tour of island prisons around the world.
http://library.thinkquest.org/21109/

InfoTrac College Edition Resources

Background
Encyclopedia articles and reference book excerpts on prisons.

Basic Searches

corrections, prisons, private prisons, parole

Related Searches

Corrections Corporation of America, prison administration, alternatives to imprisonment, prisoners, Prison Litigation Reform Act of 1996, work release of prisoners, correctional law

Should Prisons Be Privatized?

One August night, Walter Hazelwood and Richard Wilson climbed a fence topped with razor wire at the Houston Processing Center, assaulted a guard, stole his car and headed for Dallas. Local officials were shocked. They thought that the private prisons, owned and operated by Corrections Corporation of America (C.C.A.), only held illegal immigrants awaiting deportation. The two escapees hardly fit this profile; both were convicted sex offenders from Oregon. C.C.A. argued that they had no legal obligation to inform local law-enforcement officials that 240 sex offenders from Oregon had been shipped to the Texas detention center earlier that month. Moreover, the company took the position that they were not even required to report the escape to local authorities (Bates). This escape, and other incidents as well, raise a host of ethical, economic, and political questions about the rapid growth of private prisons in the U.S. To critics, this trend belies the old adage that crime doesn't pay.

Across the nation, state and local governments are increasingly contracting with private firms to deliver services that were once performed by public employees. Garbage collection is the most prominent example. Others include fire protection, emergency ambulance services, and sometimes law enforcement itself. The major reason for this trend is cost. The public and government officials perceive that private companies can provide services cheaper and better. Whether these promises have actually materialized is the subject of considerable discussion.

Many of the same arguments and problems surface in the debate over privatizing prisons. Faced with a rapid increase in the number of prisoners, coupled with mounting costs to house each inmate, local, state, and national government agencies have contracted with private companies to house prisoners. Today, two major corporations—Corrections Corporation of America and Wackenhut Corrections Corporation—dominate, with 132,572 beds in 186 facilities in the U.S., U.K., and Australia. But problems have surfaced. Allegations of brutality, lack of adequate security, and substandard conditions have resulted in several instances of governments voiding a contract and returning the facility to direct state control.

The arguments for and against private prisons run along the following lines.

Pro	Con
Punishment has already been determined by proper government officials.	Punishment is a public function and should not be assigned to the private sector.
Costs of detaining prisoners will be reduced.	Pledges to lower costs are deceptive, because hidden costs are rarely included.
The quality of care will increase.	Cutting corners will reduce quality.
Public prisons face the same problems as private ones.	Cost cutting will result in greater security problems.

The first article, "Frequently Asked Questions about Private Prisons," argues the case for prison privatization. The author, Adrian Moore (Director of Economic Studies, Reason Public Policy Institute), concludes that private prisons are superior to public ones.

The second article, "Assessing the Issue: The Pros and Cons of Prison Privatization," offers a broad-based assessment of the privatization debate. The author, Richard Culp (Professor at John Jay College), concludes that ideological issues rather than substantive arguments fuel the debate.

World Wide Web Exercises

1. Read the Web pages of two or more of the following organizations. Where do these organizations stand on the issue of private prisons?

Koch Crime Institute: Private organization with a report on private prisons. http://www.kci.org/publication/private_prison/prison.htm

Private Corrections Project: Web site of Professor Charles W. Thomas at the Center for Studies in Criminology & Law at the University of Florida. http://web.crim.ufl.edu/pcp/

Anti-Prison Privatization at Oregon (AFSCME): AFSCME's (American Federation of State, County, and Municipal Employees) leading Web site in the fight against prison privatization.   http://www.oregonafscme.com/corrections/private/

Corrections Corporation of America: World's largest private prison corporation. http://www.correctionscorp.com/

American Corrections Association: This organization maintains a useful Web site about news about privatization. http://www.corrections.com/news/private/privatearchives.html

2. Select the search engine of your choice and use the search phrase **prison litigation reform act.** Analyze the arguments for and against allowing prisoners to file lawsuits about conditions of confinement in terms of the due process and crime control models of criminal justice presented by Herbert Packer.

InfoTrac College Edition Exercises

1. Using the search term **private prisons,** locate one or more articles on each side of the issue. Do these articles provide arguments similar to or different from those articulated in the readings in this book?

2. Using the search term **private prisons,** locate two or more articles in academic journals. Do the reported findings tend to support one side or the other of the debate over prison privatization?

Frequently Asked Questions About Private Prisons

Adrian Moore

Do private prisons save money?

[T]here are 14 reputable studies, performed either by a university or government entity, comparing the cost of government run and private prisons. This research supports a conservative estimate that private facilities operate at about 10 to 15 percent lower cost than do government facilities. . . .

What kind of quality corrections do private prisons offer?

There is clear evidence that private facilities provide at least the level of service that government-run facilities do. . . . There are six reputable independent studies examining the quality of private adult correctional services in the US and the UK. Every one of the studies found quality in the private prisons to be at least as high as in government prisons.

Independent accreditation by the ACA is designed to show a facility meets nationally accepted standards for quality of operation, management, and maintenance. Of the 50 private facilities that have been operating long enough to achieve accreditation, 29 (58 percent) have done so. By comparison, of the nearly 5,000 government correctional facilities 416 (eight percent) are ACA accredited. . . .

Since the first modern private prison opened in 1985 there have been only a handful of contract terminations. Virtually every contract up for re-newal has been renewed. In the few cases of contract termination that have occurred, competition in the industry has assured that public officials were quickly able to hire a new firm to replace the old. . . .

No privately operated prison has ever been placed under a court order for problems with conditions. In fact, several states have had tremendous success in getting facilities out from under court orders by contracting with a private firm to run it, and making meeting the court-imposed standards a term of the contract.

Are private prisons ethical?

Some people are concerned that "prisons for profit" are ethically inappropriate; they believe that a firm with a financial motive should not be put in control of prisoners' lives. But to an inmate who has had his freedom taken away, it makes little difference who guards his cell, a government or a private employee. Contracting with a private firm to run a prison does not relieve government officials of the ethical and legal responsibility to ensure proper treatment. They may achieve this with a properly run correctional department or through a well-written and well-monitored contract with a private firm. And, as the evidence indicates, the private operating firm can often ensure better treatment.

Is it legal to put prisoners in private prisons?

Federal, state, and local officials have all recognized the need for legal authority to delegate correctional responsibilities to nongovernmental entities. It is possible to define imprisonment as a

Source: Reprinted with permission from *Reason Public Policy Institute*, © 1999 by the Reason Foundation.
http://rppi.org/prison/index.html

uniquely governmental function that cannot be delegated. However, this interpretation is rare. The responsibility for sentencing individuals to be confined is certainly a purely governmental function, but the mechanics of holding someone in confinement are not. . . .

Can private correctional officers use deadly force? What about riots?

There are concerns about private prisons' ability to bring to bear the force or manpower to quell a riot. There have been only a few riots in private prisons, and most were dealt with appropriately. . . . [P]ublic authorities have been more careful to assure that contracts require private prisons to maintain enough personnel, with sufficient training, to manage disturbances. Ultimately, though, both government and private prisons rely on help from outside law enforcement to quell large riots. The difference is that private prisons may be asked to defray some or all of the costs of such aid.

How can we be sure private prisons do not violate prisoners' rights?

Critics of private prisons legitimately wonder who will watch the watchmen. The government remains responsible for ensuring that prisoners' rights are protected even if they send them to a private prison. Exploiting or abusing prisoners can occur in both government and private prisons. We hear terrible stories all too frequently: of "gladiator" fights between inmates orchestrated by correctional officers, sexual assaults by correctional officers, and other individual and systematic abuses. Our goal should be to prevent this in any institutional setting. . . .

Prisoners have more legal options against private prison officials than against government officials. Private prisons are monitored by state inspectors, and the state is liable for abuses committed by employees of the private firm, so they have an incentive to monitor their conduct. Government correctional departments police themselves, with obvious conflict of interest. . . .

How can public officials control private prisons?

Contracts with private prisons give public officials a great deal of control. Elected officials control government prisons through budgets, legislative requirements, and their power to appoint heads of correctional departments. With a private prison, public officials have these same tools of control, and more. The contract process lets them control the price paid for services and determine who is going to run the prison. And legislation regarding correctional polices can be applied to private prisons as well. In addition, contracts provide for termination for failure to perform, while no such measure can be used with a government prison. Finally, contracts with private prisons introduce an additional level of accountability through the monitoring process. Government corrections departments are largely self-policing, while private prisons are continuously monitored by an outside agency to assure compliance with the law and the terms of the contract. . . .

Do private correctional officers receive lower-quality training than government correctional officers?

This is usually not the case. Many states require by law or in contracts that all staff be trained to the same level as government staff. Moreover, most contracts now stipulate adherence to ACA standards, which include training standards more stringent than those of many correctional departments. Many private firms set very high training standards. The largest firm in the industry requires 160 hours of training for its correctional officers, while the ACA standard requires only 120 hours. . . .

What if a private prison has a strike, goes bankrupt, or fails to meet contract terms?

. . . In more than 10 years of modern private prison operations, there has never been a strike at a private facility. Strikes do not occur at government prisons either, but correctional officers' unions do engage in "job actions." In every state save Hawaii, it is illegal for correctional officers to strike. It seems likely that those laws would apply to private correctional officers as well as government ones, with the government asserting a right to step in as it did with air traffic controllers. In any event, contracts should ensure that the firm is financially liable for costs incurred by the government if private correctional officers do strike. . . .

Will private prisons seek to increase incarceration and to keep inmates in prison longer?

Critics of private prisons raise the specter of an evil "prison-industrial complex," lobbying for "tough on crime" laws and creating more prisoners with longer sentences and little chance of parole.

There is little evidence of this kind of lobbying. Do private garbage collectors lobby against recycling? Do day-care centers lobby against birth control? In fact, unions representing government prison correctional officers give vastly larger sums to politicians than do private prison operating companies. In California alone, correctional officers gave $1 million to Pete Wilson when he ran for governor in 1990, and another $500,000 to his 1994 reelection campaign. In contrast, the two largest private prison firms' total political contribution nationwide in 1995–96 was less than $150,000.

Will there be access to information for the public with private prisons?

Watchdog groups, family members, and others are sometimes concerned about access to information about conduct within private prisons. Of course, this is not a problem unique to private operations. Recent scandals regarding the FBI crime lab and IRS file tampering show that abuse of information can occur in government agencies as well. Private prisons must disclose any information not of a proprietary nature if they are operating on government contract, and proprietary information is of little public interest. Again, contract terms can specify conditions for inspections or audits by outside groups or state agencies to ensure that relevant information is freely available to the public. . . .

How are private prisons regulated?

The contract provides the primary regulatory oversight of private prisons. It can stipulate conditions on crowding, handling escapes, prisoner complaints, incidents, and so on. Moreover, performance in private prisons is monitored by an outside party; the same cannot be said for government prisons. . . .

What prevents a private prison from making "lowball" initial bids and then raising prices later?

Good contracting practices and competition can easily prevent this kind of problem. The government has little incentive to give in to price increases that are not specified in the contract—especially when there are plenty of other firms willing to take over for the original price. The more competitive the market, the more recourse the government has in contract terms. It is incumbent upon public officials to look after the public interest by crafting contracts that provide incentives to lower costs, rather than raise them.

Have private prisons been "skimming the cream"—taking only low-security and less-expensive inmates?

Private prisons do not just hold minimum-security prisoners. There are currently three maximum-security, 16 all-level, and 53 medium-security private facilities, as well as many minimum-security private facilities. They are not just taking the easy inmates.

For example, contracts typically do not allow private firms to refuse to take sick prisoners. But the higher costs of ill inmates are passed on to the public in the form of reduced savings. Older inmates are also more expensive to care for, and the private prison industry is developing a niche specialty providing facilities just for elderly inmates. They charge more than for younger inmates but still cost considerably less than keeping the older inmates in government prisons. . . .

Is prison privatization unfair to government correctional employees?

Contracting with private prisons has not led to large-scale firing of government employees. Despite this fact, correctional employees' unions are the most vocal and organized opponents of privatization. Since they are usually well organized, well funded, and quite vocal, it is difficult for policy makers to put their concerns in perspective. . . .

Assessing the Issue: The Pros and Cons of Prison Privatization

Richard F. Culp

The upsurge in prison population and overcrowding coupled with the movement to reduce the size and scope of government opened the window of opportunity for correctional privatization. Private prisons have emerged as an expedient solution, helping to neutralize the opposing forces impinging on government to do more with less. . . .

Prison privatization evokes both support and opposition from two levels: ideological and substantive. Arguments from an ideological perspective tend to view private prisons as a secondary consequence of a larger social issue, and opposition (or support) stems from one's perspective on that issue rather than on the substantive merits of the prisons themselves. For example, . . . civil rights advocates are alarmed by the growth of the criminal justice system, particularly in its disproportionate effect upon people of color, and applaud measures which limit the coercive powers of the state. . . .

The important point is that ideological issues quite removed from the individual prison cells in public and private prisons are framing the overall debate over correctional privatization. We'll now turn to the major players who are lining up on both sides of the debate. First,

The Opponents

The American Civil Liberties Union's (ACLU) position on prison privatization is summarized by

Source: Richard F. Culp (1997, 1998). "Privatization of Prisons: The Public Policy Debate," http://www.geocities.com/CapitolHill/Lobby/6465/topic.html Used by permission.

Jenni Gainsborough, the public policy coordinator of the ACLU's National Prison Project:

> I'm completely opposed to the concept of private prisons. The most extreme sanction the state has against the individual, short obviously of the death penalty, is imprisonment, and that should not be turned over to an organization whose primary concern is the profit of its shareholders.

The ACLU voices an anti-privatization rhetoric containing the implicit assumption that prisoner rights will be compromised in the drive to make money. It is assumed that profit-making supersedes running a good program as the primary motivation of private operators. In practice the ACLU, and other activist organizations opposing prison privatization, target their opposition on three prison reform issues: 1) Prisoner's Rights Litigation; 2) The "Prison-Industrial Complex"; and 3) Prison Labor.

1. Prisoner's Rights Litigation.

One of the major advantages of private prisons cited by privatization advocates is the relative absence of prisoners rights litigation and court orders involving private prisons. As the National Center for Policy Analysis notes, "not a single private facility is operating under a consent decree or court order as a consequence of suits brought by prisoner plaintiffs. Yet about 75 percent of American jurisdictions now have major facilities or entire systems operating under judicial interventions."

The legal exposure that government-operated prisons contend with is relatively absent (so far) in private operations. This has translated into the possibility of greater management flexibility and lower administrative costs in the private sector. However, these two advantages may be eroding as evidenced by recent legal and legislative developments.

While a body of case law involving prisoners in private prisons is beginning to emerge, correctional privatization remains a relatively new phenomenon and the law is murky in this area, although the general guideline has been that prisoners in private facilities have exactly the same rights as public-facility inmates. Still, the ACLU's success in advancing prisoners' rights has been attained by challenging public agencies and facilities where substantial legal precedent has been established. In the private sector, the extent of private agency immunity from civil rights lawsuits is unclear, and this uncertainty concerns the ACLU. . . .

2. The Prison-Industrial Complex.

The near doubling of the U.S. jail and prison population in the past ten years has been disproportionately balanced on the backs of African Americans. A dubious milestone was reached during 1996 when, for the first time in U.S. history, the absolute number of black prisoners surpassed the number of whites incarcerated in prisons and jails. . . .

For the ACLU, and several other opponents of privatization, the problem of racial discrimination in incarceration is viewed in light of what has been termed "the prison-industrial complex. . . . ":

African Americans are grist for the fast-growing prison industry's money mill. Crime pays. It certainly does pay for those who profit from the expanding correctional-industrial complex. They include private prison operators, those who build and supply prison cells, the suppliers of food and medicine—and guards, who recently have realized a new level of clout. Companies vie for

everything from building contracts to the right to sell hair products to prisoners, while economically strapped towns see prisons as a source of jobs.

The dramatic increase in prisoners over the past ten years has spawned not only private prisons but a concomitant increase in marketing and sales of the entire panoply of products and services related to prison operations as well as employment in the correctional industry. This "prison-industrial complex," a play on Eisenhower's coinage of the term "military-industrial complex," has become a focus of criticism from the ACLU and other left-of-center organizations on the political spectrum. . . . These sources are short on specific information regarding prison privatization, but express the general view that prison privatization is a cog in the overall machinery of oppression of minorities and the poor and thus a suitable target of opposition. . . .

Regardless of the ideological take on the "prison-industrial complex," there is no doubt that the huge upsurge in prison population has generated considerable investment in all aspects of prison related business, and private prison speculation is no exception. For example, a recent article in *Fortune Magazine* (*Fortune,* September 29, 1997), entitled "Getting Rich with America's Fastest-Growing Companies," ranked Corrections Corporation of America, the largest private operator of prisons in the world, as the 67th fastest growing small company in the U.S., with the value of its stock appreciating some 746 percent over the past three years. To be sure, "crime does pay" as the ACLU rhetorically observes.

3. Prison Labor.

The privatization controversy reaches a new level of complexity when the issue of privatizing prison labor is considered. . . .

The issue is divisive within the community of privatization opponents, with several opponents (such as the ACLU) voicing ambivalence on the issue. On the one hand are correctional reformers who are pressing to provide prisoners with more meaningful, lucrative, and rehabilitative opportunities to actually "learn a trade" while behind bars. On the other hand are those who voice concern over exploitation of prisoners and over taking away jobs from law-abiding citizens. The notion of "private prisons" contracting out the labor of their inmates to other private companies adds even greater complexity to the dilemma. . . .

Understandably, The American Federation of State, County, and Municipal Employees, the largest union representing employees in the public sector, is concerned about the effect that privatization in all levels of government is having on its membership. AFSCME maintains a Web page entitled "Government For Sale," which presents arguments against contracting out of government services and case histories of negative privatization experiences. In the specific area of corrections, AFSCME includes a very brief report entitled "Private Prisons: Cutting Costs by Cutting Corners," which cites selected negative findings on private prisons from a Tennessee government sponsored comparison of public and private prisons . . . The report notes a higher rate of inmate injuries and staff use of force incidents in the private prison. The AFSCME report neglects to note the overall findings of the evaluation that the two public and one private prison were operating without significant difference in security, safety, and overall program quality. . . .

Aside from the potential loss of union membership through privatization of prisons, organized labor's opposition stems from the assumption that wages and benefits of correctional workers will be lower in the public than in the private sector, as profits take priority over working conditions. However, the current state of data on this key point is slim at best. In one of the only studies which compared such salaries (Logan, 1996 . . .), the average salary of staff in the private prison was actually higher than salaries at the state prison, although not significantly so. Likewise, the study reported a higher quality of management/staff relations in the private prison than in the state facility. . . .

The Proponents

The driving force behind correctional privatization is, quite simply, elected officials. The sheer cost of incarcerating a prison population that is growing by 7.8 percent per year . . . has meant that the share of the U. S. gross domestic product (GDP) devoted to the criminal justice system has more than doubled since 1965. Jerome Miller recounts the phenomenal growth in criminal justice spending since 1970:

> Federal, state, and local funding of the justice system literally exploded in the two decades leading up to the 1990s. Average direct federal, state, and local expenditures for police grew by 16 percent; courts by 58 percent; prosecution and legal services by 152 percent; public defense by 259 percent; and corrections by 154 percent. Federal spending for justice grew by 668 percent; county spending increased by 710.9 percent; state spending surged by 848 percent. By 1990, the country was spending $74 billion annually to catch and lock up offenders (Miller, 1994).

As prisons consume more and more scarce tax revenue, privatization is being advanced as a means to help curb a seemingly endless drain on government revenue.

A call for the privatization of various services currently operated by government agencies has worked its way into the official platforms of the Republican, Democratic, and Libertarian parties in the U.S. . . . These general policy statements do not specifically address the privatization of correctional services, but promote privatization as part of a larger agenda.

The 1996 Republican Platform is the most direct in advocating the use of privatization at all levels of government: "Republicans believe we can streamline government and make it more effective through competition and privatization.". . .

The Democratic Party shies away from using the term "privatization," preferring the phrases "reinventing government" and "partnerships with the private sector" to advance their privatization message . . . As the 1996 Democratic National Platform notes: "In the last four years, President Clinton . . . has cut the federal government by almost 240,000 positions, making the smallest federal government in 30 years. . . . "

Like the Democrats, the Libertarian Party, ostensibly the most ardent advocate of privatization, does not use the "p" word in the 1996 National Platform of the Libertarian Party, offering instead the following language: "We advocate the termination of government-created franchise privileges and governmental monopolies for such services as garbage collection, fire protection, electricity, natural gas, cable television, telephone, or water supplies. . . . "

Should Parole Be Abolished?

While on furlough from a Massachusetts prison, Willie Horton raped a woman and assaulted her husband in Maryland. This event soon became a political issue in the 1988 presidential election with George Bush blaming Michael Dukakis, the governor of Massachusetts at the time of the furlough, for the decision to let him out.

News stories like this one reinforce the public's assumptions that prison inmates cannot be reformed. Thus government officials find a sympathetic audience when they articulate demands that convicts (particularly those convicted of violent offenses) serve their entire sentence in prison.

Many "get tough" crime policies focus on the judicial branch of government. Thus legislators have enacted "three strike" laws (Issue 9) and the death penalty (Issue 10). Some policies, though, focus on corrections—an executive branch of government. Typically, those sentenced to prison serve part of their sentence and then are paroled (granted conditional release subject to supervision) to serve the remainder of their sentence. Moreover, the length of time when an inmate becomes eligible for parole can be shortened by good time—days off for good behavior in prison. In recent years many legislatures have limited good time, and in some jurisdictions abolished parole altogether. Most recently these efforts have taken the form of truth-in-sentencing laws that mandate that violent offenders serve a minimum of 85 percent of their sentence before being released from prison.

At some point, political demands that judges sentence offenders to longer prison terms, and that corrections officials keep them in prison longer, must face fiscal realities. In many jurisdictions, legislators are unable (or some say unwilling) to increase taxes to generate sufficient revenue to keep pace with rising prison populations. Indeed, some states have made the conscious decision to increase prison funding by decreasing spending on higher education.

Fiscal realities, therefore, more than ideological forces, push policy makers to search for less costly alternatives to incarceration, all of which involve rehabilitation. Among the most often mentioned alternatives are community-based corrections and prison rehabilitation programs. All agree that these programs are less costly. But are they effective? In 1974, R. Martinson reviewed numerous studies that evaluated the results of rehabilitation programs. This now-famous article, titled "What Works? Questions and Answers about Prison Reform," challenges the assumption that we really know how to cure criminal offenders. Martinson's summary was widely perceived to conclude that nothing works. (This apparent refutation of rehabilitation, in turn, fueled the "get tough" movement.)

Yet there is evidence that some rehabilitation programs are effective in reducing recidivism (a return to criminal behavior). But there is no agreement about acceptable rates of recidivism. Crime control advocates tend to discredit rehabilitation by insisting upon a high success rate. Supporters of the due process model counter that these are impossibly high standards; more reasonable yardsticks find that rehabilitation programs often yield acceptable rates of recidivism.

In a nutshell, here are the pros and cons of abolishing parole.

Pro	Con
Building more prisons is the only way to protect citizens.	Building "fortress America" will only bankrupt governments.
Prison rehabilitation programs are a waste of money.	Prison rehabilitation programs are reasonably effective.
Increase spending on prisons by decreasing expenditures for higher education.	Increase spending on higher education by decreasing expenditures on prisons.

The first article, "The Courage of Our Convictions," argues that abolishing parole will save lives and money. The author, George Allen (Governor of Virginia), berates liberals for not spending more on prisons.

The second article, "Work Release in Washington," reports on empirical evaluations of recidivism and costs. The authors, Susan Turner and Joan Petersilia (both researchers at RAND), conclude that few offenders committed some type of infraction while on work release.

World Wide Web Exercises

1. From the list below, select two or more organizations that represent different facets of the parole abolition argument. Analyze the arguments presented in terms of the due process versus crime control model of criminal justice articulated by Herbert Packer in an earlier reading in this book.

National Center for Policy Analysis: Favors abolition of parole. http://www.ncpa.org/pi/crime/crime3.html

Justice Policy Institute: A private nonprofit organization whose mission is to reduce society's reliance on the use of incarceration as a solution to social problems. http://www.cjcj.org/

Sentencing Project: Independent source of factual analysis, data, and program information for the public, policy-makers, and criminal justice professionals. http://www.sentencingproject.org/

National Criminal Justice Association: Washington, D.C.-based special interest group that represents states on crime control and public safety matters and supports truth-in-sentencing legislation.   http://www.sso.org/ncja/

2. Using the search engine of your choice, enter the phrase **parole and abolition** to find at least one article on each side of the issue. Do these articles provide similar or different arguments to those raised in the readings?

InfoTrac College Edition Exercises

1. Using the search term **parole,** locate at least one article on each side of the issue. Analyze the types of arguments made using the concepts presented in the article in the appendix.

2. Using the search term **community-based corrections** locate two or more articles in academic journals that discuss work release programs. Are the results similar to or different from those reported in the Turner and Petersilia article on the State of Washington? Do the findings tend to support the pro or con position on this issue?

The Courage of Our Convictions: The Abolition of Parole Will Save Lives and Money

George Allen

On Father's Day 1986, Richmond Police Detective George Taylor stopped Wayne DeLong for a routine traffic violation. DeLong, recently released from prison after serving time for murder, shot and killed the policeman. . . .

Tragic as such stories are, what makes these two particularly disheartening is that both could have been easily prevented. Both killers, jailed earlier for violent crimes, spent only a fraction of their sentences in prison. We are now paying the dividends of a liberal justice system that refuses to take punishment seriously: Virginia has witnessed a 28 percent increase in criminal violence over the last five years. Three out of every four violent crimes—murder, armed robbery, rape, assault— are now committed by repeat offenders.

This is why my administration pushed through legislation, which took effect on January 1, 1995 that will impose penalties for rape, murder, and armed robbery more than twice the national average for those crimes. We have abolished parole, established the principle of truth-in-sentencing, and increased as much as fivefold the amount of time that violent offenders will actually spend in jail. Experience vindicates what common sense has always told us: The only foolproof crime-prevention technique is incarceration.

Our new system is attempting to unravel 30 years of paper-tiger laws based on the questionable philosophy that people can change, criminals

Source: *Policy Review,* Spring, 1995. Used by permission.

can be rehabilitated, and every violent criminal— even a murderer—deserves a second chance. The new law in Virginia will prevent thousands of crimes, save lives, save money, and restore trust in the criminal justice system. Despite this, we now face entrenched opposition from liberals in the General Assembly, who hope to thwart reform by withholding funds to build the minimal number of prison facilities needed to house Virginia's most violent inmates.

A few weeks after taking office in January 1994, I created the Commission on Parole Abolition and Sentencing Reform. . . .We were quickly able to show why a complete overhaul was necessary. Convicted felons were serving about one-third of their sentences on average, and many served only one-sixth. Violent criminals were no exception. First-degree murderers were given average sentences of 35 years, but spent an average of only 10 years behind bars. Rapists were being sentenced to nine years and serving four. Armed robbers received sentences averaging 14 years and served only about four.

Amazingly, a prior conviction for a violent crime did not affect this phenomenon. Even murderers, rapists, and armed robbers who had already served time for similar offenses were receiving the same sentences and serving the same amount of time as first offenders. . . .

The Plan

Only a multi-pronged approach can begin to turn these numbers around. Virginia's new law means, first of all, eliminating discretionary parole, in which a parole board can release an offender after he has served only part of his sentence. In Virginia, this policy clearly was being abused: offenders received 30 days of good time for every 30 days they served—effectively cutting their sentences in half as soon as they came in the door.

But this is not all. We need to eliminate "good time" as well. In order to encourage good behavior among inmates and allow correctional officers to maintain order, the commission proposed a system of earned-sentence credits. This system would allow inmates to earn a maximum of 54 days per year—a dramatic reduction from the average of 300 days they had been given in the past.

Long before our bill became law, we held town meetings across the state to solicit advice from citizens, and discussed the plan's details with prosecutors, victims rights groups, corrections experts, and criminologists. The need for more prison space became a primary concern. Even before I took office, Virginia was expected to double its prison population by the year 2005. The state was facing a shortfall of 7,100 prison beds by 1999. At the same time, opponents of the plan were already carping about too little spending on crime prevention and education and too much on building prisons.

Obviously, judges need some mechanism to guide their sentencing decisions. A system with no parole and no "good time" could not afford 70-year sentences for drug dealers or 150-year sentences for armed robbers. But how much do we increase the time served for violent offenders? Our commission found an answer by evaluating the relationship of recidivism to time served and age of release. The data showed that the longer an offender remained behind bars, the less likely he is to commit another crime after finishing his sentence. Similarly, the older the offender upon release, the less his propensity to commit more crime. In fact, after 37 years of age, the likelihood of violent crime drops dramatically.

Although preventing criminals from committing further acts of violence was the primary goal, the increases had to reflect the notion of retribution as well. We wanted Virginia to send a message to violent criminals: We will not tolerate violence, and if you commit a violent crime, you will stay in prison until you're too old to commit another one.

Virginia increased prison time for violent criminals as follows:

- 100 percent increase for first-time violent offenders.
- 125 percent for first-time murderers, rapists, and armed robbers.
- 300 percent for those with previous convictions for assault, burglary, or malicious wounding.
- 500 percent for those with previous convictions for murder, rape, or armed robbery. . . .

By abolishing a bankrupt parole system, and by drastically reforming the "good time" credit provisions, Virginia courtrooms are redefining what the truth-in-sentencing debate is really about. Under our system, every inmate convicted of a violent crime will serve a minimum of 85 percent of his or her sentence. Nationwide, criminals on average serve well below 50 percent of their sentences. There is simply no surer way for the state to protect its citizens from society's most dangerous members.

Saving Lives and Money

Had the law been in effect nine years ago, it would have saved the life of Detective Taylor. . . . The most conservative estimates show that more than 4,300 felony crimes would have been prevented between 1986 and 1993 if the current system had been in place. That number is based on actual convictions—real cases, not projections.

Over the next 10 years, the new law will prevent at least 119,000 felonies, including 26,000 violent crimes. Because of those averted violent crimes, an estimated 475 lives will be saved, 3,700 women will be spared from rape, and more than 11,300 aggravated assaults will not be committed. As a result, citizens will save more than $2.7 billion in direct costs. Back in September, when it became clear that the legislation would pass with overwhelming support, some vocal opponents claimed that abolishing parole was a declaration of war on young black males. They demanded that the Commonwealth spend more money on prevention programs, and charged that, by focusing on punishment, we were merely catering to "white fear." Their arguments fell on deaf ears.

The crime prevented as a result of the new law will benefit the African-American community—one-fifth of Virginia's population—more than any other group. Of the preventable murders that occurred between 1986 and 1993, about 65 percent involved black victims. For assaults during that same period, about 60 percent of the victims were black. Taylor and Webb were both African Americans.

Of all the crimes committed by recidivists during that same period, 60 percent would have been prevented if the current law had been in place. There is no other prevention program that can show even a fraction of this success. That is not to say that other prevention programs are not valid or important. However, it is clear that when it comes to violent offenders, incarceration is the most just and the most efficient.

Virginia has been spending an average of $658 million in taxpayers' money each year on handling recidivists. This is the cost of new investigations, new arrests, and new trials. The total cost of the prison construction needs for the next 10 years is about $750 million. The new law will force us to build more prisons—but not many more. Virginia would have doubled its prison population in the next 10 years anyway.

The difference is that under the old system, the ratio of violent criminals among the prison population to nonviolent has been 50:50. Marijuana dealers, embezzlers, and petty thieves have been serving time in the same $40,000-per-year hard cells as murderers, rapists, and armed robbers. Under the new guidelines, the inmate ratio will be 70 percent violent, 30 percent nonviolent. This is obviously a more cost-effective use of medium- and maximum-security prison space.

Try telling that, however, to the liberals in the General Assembly. I asked lawmakers in February for $402.6 million as a first installment in revamping our prison system. They voted to provide only $104.4 million. They are shortchanging prison construction, making it more likely that dangerous criminals will be released early—and be back in our neighborhoods. Increasing prison terms without increasing prison capacity is precisely the mistake that too many other states have already made.

Part of the problem with the current system of incarceration is its near inability to distinguish between dangerous criminals and the more routine, petty offenders. Under our plan, we are building low-cost work centers to house first-time and non-violent offenders. These work centers operate at about half the cost per inmate as a standard prison, and they ensure that the inmates get work opportunities while incarcerated. The average length of stay at a work center will be about 10 to 18 months. We can build these facilities quickly, freeing up bed space in the prisons for violent criminals. . . .

The principle that guided this effort, and should guide policymakers in all issues, is honesty. Easy-release rules prevent judges and juries from preempting the community's judgment about the proper punishment for illegal conduct. Under the new law, judges will not have to play guessing games when imposing sentences. Police officers will not have to see the same criminals out on the streets only a year after their last arrest. Criminals will know that they cannot beat the system. Crime victims and their families will finally see justice done. Virginia's citizens can now trust that their government is working to make this Commonwealth a safe place to live, to work, and to raise families.

Work Release in Washington: Effects on Recidivism and Corrections Costs

Susan Turner and Joan Petersilia

Each year, U.S. prisons release more than 400,000 criminal offenders back to their communities. Most of those released will not remain crime-free, and national statistics show that within three years of release, 40 percent will be returned to prison or jail (Bureau of Justice Statistics, 1995). Experts debate the reasons for such high recidivism rates, but nearly everyone agrees that the lack of adequate job training and work opportunities is critically important. Offenders often have few marketable skills and training and, as a result, have a difficult time securing legitimate employment. With no legitimate income, many resort to crime.

Corrections officials are well aware of the problem and since the early 1920s have attempted to remedy it through prison work-release programs. Work-release programs permit selected prisoners, nearing the end of their terms, to work in the community, returning to prison facilities or community residential facilities in nonworking hours. Such programs are thought to prepare inmates to return to the community in a relatively controlled environment, while at the same time learning how to work productively. Work release also allows inmates to earn income, to reimburse the state for part of their confinement costs, to build up savings for their eventual release, and to acquire more positive living habits.

During the 1970s, prison work-release programs expanded considerably, but enthusiasm for them has dimmed in recent years. Although 43

states now have statutes authorizing work release, only about one third of U.S. prisons report operating such programs, and fewer than three percent of U.S. inmates participate in them.

Part of the reason why work release programming has declined pertains to funding. Many work release programs begun in the 1970s were paid for by the federal government, using funds from the Law Enforcement Assistance Administration (LEAA). When the federal funds dried up, many of the programs were discontinued. And as the rehabilitation ideal—of which work release was very much a part—started to fade, the public embraced imprisonment as the only sure way to forestall crime. Programs that focused on rehabilitation, job training, and transitional services seemed hopelessly out of touch with a public mood that had turned punitive.

Moreover, a few highly publicized and sensational failures convinced the public that early-release programs, such as work release or furlough, threatened public safety. The most extreme example was Willie Horton, the Massachusetts inmate who absconded and committed serious and violent crimes while on furlough. . . . By widely advertising the incident during the 1988 presidential campaign, George Bush was able to portray his opponent, Michael Dukakis, as "soft on crime." Such negative publicity helped further erode community support for work release programs. . . .

Nevertheless, the state of Washington has continued to maintain its commitment to work release since the Department of Correction (DOC) first initiated the program in 1967. Currently, the DOC contracts with 15 residential work release

Source: *Prison Journal*, June, 1996 v76. Reprinted by permission of Sage Publications, Inc.

facilities, which house more than 350 offenders on any one day throughout the state. In the 1991–1993 biennium, approximately $115 million of the $312 million DOC budget was allocated to community corrections. About 38 percent (or $43 million) of the community corrections budget was for work release. . . .

Washington's work release program has benefited enormously from a particularly close working partnership with private industry, particularly Pioneer Human Services (PHS). PHS has been contracting with the DOC to operate work release facilities since its inception nearly 30 years ago, and they now operate four such facilities that house about 1,200 work releasees annually (or about one third of all Washington's work releasees). Over the years, PHS has grown to a full service organization, providing job training at a manufacturing facility they run, pre- and post-release employment in a food service business they founded, housing for special-need offenders, and electronic monitoring of state and federal offenders. . . .

It is not that Washington has been immune from the challenges faced by other states. Washington's prison population has jumped 71 percent since 1980, whereas the state's general population has grown just 13 percent. Citizens are frustrated with high levels of crime and violence, as is evidenced by the fact that they passed the nation's first three-strikes law, in part as a result of a felon committing a rape while on parole. Nevertheless, the state has weathered it, and their work release program continues to attract attention from observers who wonder how the program can continue to operate successfully in a time of punitive policies and politics. . . .

Prior Studies of Work Release Effectiveness

. . . Generally speaking, the evaluation evidence is mixed, but studies using stronger research designs generally find fewer effects. Those few studies with an adequate design have found that work release did not reduce recidivism or costs. . . .

In sum, there are some positive results of work release—mostly on employment rather than recidivism. Most prior research relies on quasi-experimental methods that have failed to control adequately for preexisting differences between study groups. Thus one cannot determine whether outcome differences are due to the effect of the intervention (i.e., work release) or characteristics on which work release and comparison offenders differ.

The Current Study

This research project was conducted between 1991 and 1994 and consisted of two separate studies.

Study 1: A Statewide Analysis of Work Release: Who Participates? Who Succeeds? At What Cost?

The first study analyzed a cohort of male prisoners (N = 2,452) released from Washington prisons in 1990. Data pertaining to their criminal and social background and their participation in, and performance on, work release were analyzed to provide a general description of how work release is implemented in Washington and how successfully inmates perform in the program. Detailed information on how inmates transitioned into, and exited from, work release and other corrections programs was used to estimate the costs of work release versus prison.

Study 2: A Randomized Experiment in Seattle: The Impact of Work Release on Recidivism and Corrections Costs

The second study was designed as a randomized experiment, where eligible offenders being released to Seattle work release facilities were randomly assigned to participate in work release or not. Program implementation and follow-up recidivism information were collected at six and twelve months following random assignment. . . .

Summary and Conclusions

We regard the results of this evaluation of Washington's work release program as mostly positive.

The program is successful on several fronts: Nearly one quarter of all prisoners released in Washington under current statutes successfully transitioned to the community through work release. While in the program, these inmates maintained employment, remained mostly drug-free, reconnected with family and friends, and paid for their room and board.

Generally speaking, the program achieved its most important goal, that of preparing inmates for final release and facilitating their adjustment to the community. The program does not cost the state any more than if inmates remain in prison, and the public safety risks are nearly nonexistent because program operators are quickly returning to prison any offender who misbehaves. Of the almost 1,100 work releasees tracked as part of this evaluation, less than five percent were associated with committing a new crime while on work release, and 99 percent of those crimes were less serious property offenses, such as forgery and petty theft. Moreover, offenders who participated in work release were somewhat less likely to be re-arrested, but the results were not statistically significant. One could reasonably conclude from these results that work release in Washington is a program "that works."

However, the work release program did not reduce offender recidivism rates or corrections costs. Critics of community corrections often argue that such programs should deliver all of the above services, while showing a reduction in recidivism and cost savings. Such expectations are unrealistic and naive. If we do not want to set work release and other community-based programs up for failure, we must assign to them goals we might reasonably expect them to fulfill.

Charles Logan, a corrections expert, has written on such matters for the Department of Justice and recommended that realistic goals for prison programs should be fairly narrow, achievable, and measurable within the policies and programs operated by the corrections department (Logan, 1993). In other words, prison programs should not assume the goals and functions of other social institutions such as schools and welfare agencies. He says that prison programs should be expected to, and held accountable for, keeping prisoners safe, in line (not committing crimes), healthy, and busy—and try and do it all without undue suffering and as efficiently as possible. If those outcome measures are adopted (and they were recently endorsed by the U.S. Government Accounting Office), Washington's work release program is certainly successful.

It is becoming more important that we adopt realistic measures for corrections that account for their daily activities and for the constraints under which they normally operate. Realistic, however, does not mean easy to achieve. Recall that most participants in Washington's work release program had lengthy criminal histories, serious substance abuse problems, and possessed little education and few job skills. Yet, when supervised in this work release program, they found jobs, paid rent, and refrained from crime.

Citizens often expect corrections officials to solve society's crime problem and have been continually frustrated by the inability of them to do so. The popular perception is that "nothing works" in corrections. But most corrections evaluations adopt recidivism as their primary outcome measure. Few corrections officials believe that what they do chiefly determines recidivism rates. As John Dilulio (1993) recently wrote, "Justice practitioners understand that they can rarely do for their clients what parents, teachers, friends, neighbors, clergy, or economic opportunities may have failed to do." By adopting more realistic outcome measures, we may help to bridge the wide gap between the public's expectations for the justice system and what most practitioners recognize as the system's actual capacity to control crime. And by documenting what corrections programs can accomplish, we can move toward integrating programs such as work release into a more balanced corrections strategy, where lower risk inmates are transitioned successfully into the community, thereby making room to incarcerate the truly violent.

Part IX

Debating Juvenile Justice

The April 20, 1999 massacre in Littleton, Colorado, was the most lethal school shooting in history. For a couple of hours two heavily armed social outcasts—Eric Harris and Dylan Klebold—walked through Columbine High School deciding who would live and who would die, killing 13 and wounding 23 others before taking their own lives. This massive tragedy quickly became the focal point in the nation's ongoing debate over gun control. But the tragedy at Columbine High also fueled a national debate over the future of the juvenile justice system.

Juvenile courts are a distinctly twentieth-century development. Through the nineteenth century, children accused of a crime were prosecuted in adult court and sentenced to prison with adults. The major economic and social changes associated with the industrial revolution prompted, however, a rethinking of the place of youth in the society. The result was the creation of specialized courts to deal with children. The historic mandate of juvenile court was to rescue children from a criminal life by providing the care and protection formerly afforded by the natural parents. The result was a hybrid system of justice. The compromises inherent in this approach are increasingly under scrutiny. Advocates of the due process model have diagnosed the problem as a lack of legal rights, and would extend adult due-process guarantees to juveniles. Backers of the crime control model counter that the problem is too much emphasis on rehabilitation, and urge imposing harsher punishments. Indeed, the disquiet runs so deep that some now openly wonder whether juvenile courts should be abolished altogether.

Beginning about 1975, state legislatures across the country began systematic changes to the juvenile justice system, mostly along the lines advocated by conservatives. By the mid-1990s, the issue of youth violence was at or near the top of the political agenda in every state of the union. Moreover, the U. S. House of Representatives was about to begin a debate over the reauthorization of the Juvenile Justice and Delinquency Prevention Act when news of the shootings in Littleton stunned the nation.

Current get-tough juvenile policy reforms are based on the assumption that juvenile crime—particularly violent juvenile crime—has been increasing. Indeed, over the past 200 years, it has been persistently believed that juveniles currently were committing more frequent and more serous crimes than juveniles in the "good old days" (30 or 40 years earlier) (Bernard, 1992). But does reality match this crime debate rhetoric? In terms of homicides, the answer appears to be yes—the number of juveniles arrested for murder tripled over the last two decades. But taken as a whole, juvenile crime has declined by one-third over the last twenty years (Bernard, 1999).

These contradictory realities are sufficient to fuel the increasingly heated rhetoric of debate over the next 100 years of the juvenile justice system. Of the numerous issues involved we will explore two:

Issue 15 examines sentencing in juvenile court, asking, "Should juvenile offenders be tried and punished as adults?"

Issue 16 explores rehabilitation programs, asking, "Are boot camps an effective means of dealing with juvenile crime?"

World Wide Web Resources

Web Guides

http://dir.yahoo.com/Society_and_Culture/Crime/Juvenile/

Searching the Web

juvenile justice

Useful URLs

Center on Juvenile and Criminal Justice: A private nonprofit organization whose mission is to reduce society's reliance on the use of incarceration as a solution to social problems.   http://www.cjcj.org/

Juvenile Justice Center: American Bar Association site.
http://www.abanet.org/crimjust/juvjus/home.html

National Center for Juvenile Justice: Research division of the National Council of Juvenile and Family Court Judges.   http://www.ncjj.org/

Office of Juvenile Justice and Delinquency Prevention: Agency within the U.S. Department of Justice.   http://ojjdp.ncjrs.org/

Today's Headlines

http://fullcoverage.yahoo.com/fc/US/School_Violence/

Fun Sites

Straight Ahead Ministries   http://www.webss.com/StraightAhead/

Citizens for Juvenile Justice: Strengthening Massachusetts juvenile justice through dialogue, education and advocacy.   http://www.cfjj.org/

Peer Justice and Empowerment: An implementation guide for teen court programs, from the Justice Information Center.   http://www.ncjrs.org/peerhome.htm

InfoTrac College Edition Resources

Background
Encyclopedia excerpts and reference books.

Basic Searches
juvenile delinquency, juvenile crime

Related Searches
juvenile justice, administration of; juvenile corrections; juvenile courts

Should Juvenile Offenders Be Tried and Punished As Adults?

- *In Mt. Morris, Michigan, a six-year-old shot and killed another first grader.*
- *In Conyers, Georgia, a 15-year-old stands accused of shooting six high school classmates in 1999.*

- *In Pearl, Mississippi, a jury finds 17-year-old Luke Woodham guilty of two counts of murder and seven counts of aggravated assault for a school shooting.*
- *In Arkansas an 11-year-old and a 13-year-old are charged with five counts of murder and ten counts of battery after opening fire on fellow students.*

The massacre at Columbine High is the most remembered of a series of violent crimes committed by juveniles. These and other highly publicized examples of teen violence have sparked an unprecedented re-examination of the nation's juvenile justice system. The call for getting tough is reflected in the following headlines:

- "Punishing Teen Criminals Like Criminals" (Sexton, 1996)
- "Treat Juveniles Like Adults" (Hunzeker, 1995)
- "Three Strikes for Kids" (Sorrentino, 1996)

These headlines reflect public pressures to shift the juvenile justice system away from its historic focus on rehabilitation to place more emphasis on retribution.

Alas, getting behind the public rhetoric of "getting tough" to focus on specifics is not always easy. In the context of the juvenile justice system, some of the specifics include:

- lowering the age at which a person is considered an adult in the eyes of the criminal justice system;
- transferring more violent and repeat juvenile offenders from juvenile court to be tried and sentenced as adults;
- sending some violent juvenile offenders to adult prisons; and
- imposing longer periods of custodial custody.

In many ways, the current debate over juvenile justice represents an extension of the decades-old debate over the adult justice system. Proponents of the due process model stress that prevention works. Advocates of the crime control model, on the other hand, reject rehabilitation in favor of detention (the term used in juvenile justice to refer to prison). In a nutshell, here are some of the major arguments in the debate:

Pro	Con
Violent juvenile crime is on the increase.	The juvenile crime rate is decreasing.
Shootings at Columbine and other schools dramatize the need for fundamental change in the juvenile justice system	School shootings are very atypical and should not be used as justification for a wholesale transformation of juvenile justice.
More public money should be spent on juvenile detention facilities.	More tax dollars should be spent on juvenile rehabilitation programs.

The article "Let's Hold Juveniles Responsible for Their Crimes" forcefully states the case for getting tough. The author, Darlene Kennedy (a tax attorney and a member of the National Advisory Committee of the African-American Leadership Group, Project 21), argues that sanctions, not prevention, are the answer.

The companion article, "Delinquents or Criminals?," places various policy options in political context. The authors, Jeffrey Butts and Adele Harrell (of The Urban Institute), stress that transferring juveniles to adult court may result in more lenient sentences.

World Wide Web Exercises

1. Using the search engine or search guide of your choice, identify two or more organizations which offer different viewpoints on getting tough with juvenile offenders. Analyze their perspectives in terms of the due process and crime control models of justice introduced earlier in the reading by Herbert Packer. Here are two possible sites:

American Civil Liberties Union: Fact sheet on the juvenile justice system. http://aclu.org/library/fctsht.html

National Center for Policy Analysis (NCPA): Fact sheet on juvenile crime. http://ncpa.org/hotlines/juvcrm/jchln.html

2. Select the search engine of your choice and use the search term **juvenile courts** to find two or more articles that present different viewpoints on trying juvenile offenders as adults. To what extent are the arguments similar to or different from those presented in the readings?

InfoTrac College Edition Exercises

1. Using the search term **juvenile courts, waiver of jurisdiction,** locate two or more articles that offer contrasting viewpoints on trying serious juvenile offenders as adults. To what extent are the arguments similar to or different from those presented in the readings?

2. Use the search term **juvenile courts, juvenile justice** or **juvenile delinquency** to locate two or more articles in academic journals that analyze actual practices and problems in juvenile justice. Analyze the contemporary debate over the juvenile justice system in terms of the concepts presented in the introduction to the book.

Let's Hold Juveniles Responsible for Their Crimes

Darlene Kennedy

The meek may be blessed, but they're not likely to inherit the earth anytime soon.

In May, President Clinton stood proudly before an audience of law enforcement, community leaders and others at Georgetown University in Washington, D.C. to announce preliminary Justice Department figures citing a seven percent drop in crime from 1995 to 1996. What he neglected to mention is that juvenile crime is rapidly on the rise and does not show signs of slowing down. A recent Justice Department study revealed that in 1995 14 percent of all violent crimes were committed by juveniles, up from 10 percent in 1980. Thugs too young even to vote now account for 15 percent of all forcible rapes, 20 percent of robberies, 13 percent of aggravated assaults and nine percent of murders.

In an era in which violent crime among our youth is more commonplace than jump rope and stickball, the time has come for young criminals to be stopped in their tracks. To that end, the Senate Judiciary Committee recently passed a juvenile crime bill to be voted on by the full Senate sometime in September or October. The House of Representatives has already passed a juvenile crime bill. Remarkably, 77 Democrats joined the 209 members of the Republican side voting in favor of this measure. Under the proposed law, hoodlums 14 and older who commit violent federal crimes including murder, rape, aggravated assault, armed robbery, and major drug offenses could be tried as adults. In extraordinary circumstances, the attorney general would have the discretion to charge 13-year-old (alleged) miscreants as adults as well.

The House should take a bow for addressing a serious problem forthrightly. President Clinton cannot. His smells-of-politics contribution to the debate has been to assert that " . . . a juvenile justice bill [which] doesn't limit children's access to guns is a bill that walks away from the problem." Which is to say that in order to stem the wretched tide of teenage thugs and gang members who murder, rape, and rob we must take guns from the hands of the law abiding—an argument that insults the intelligence of the American people. To lay blame for the acts of thousands of young criminals and the intolerably high crime rate they have created on guns and lawful gun ownership is absurd. The House was not addressing the relatively rare but well-publicized instances of children who accidentally, tragically, fire a pistol and injure or kill another.

First things first. Congress properly (and finally) responded to the problem of marauding sociopaths who make the terrorist teens depicted a quarter-century ago in "A Clockwork Orange" look like the Bowery Boys. We're talking about young venal minds who abuse the gift of free will by electing hate over love, and cruelty over compassion. Safety locks and background checks are the answers to serious but tangential problems, and will not stop these young criminals from their appointed rounds. Though the anti-gun crowd may be loathe to admit it, guns are not always the weapon of choice for young killers. In the first two weeks of May, the citizens of Baltimore were

Source: Darlene Kennedy (1997). *Let's Hold Juveniles Responsible for Their Crimes*. National Policy Analysis Paper #166; The National Center for Public Policy Research. Reprinted by permission.

witness to two children murdered in separate incidents at the hands of fellow adolescents. The alleged criminals in these cases, a girl and a boy, were both under the age of 15; both wielded knives, not the firearms that Clinton and his misguided acolytes claim to be the real menace to society.

To encourage state involvement in their effort, the House bill also includes $1.5 billion in state grants. To qualify for this funding, states must impose escalating sanctions on juvenile offenders for every delinquent or criminal act; establish a felony tracking system where juveniles' records would become public adult criminal records after a second offense; and finally, violent criminal acts committed by 15-year-olds would be treated as adult offenses.

Opponents argue the bill is ineffective if it doesn't include prevention programs. Will little Jane and Johnny really abstain from a life of crime if given basketballs and baseballs (and perhaps a few golf balls) as the late evening news anchors are signing off? Kids on the brink of choosing a life of crime *will not do so* on the promise of unlimited access to sports programs. What turns potential criminals around, quite often, is the same thing that prevents growing kids from advancing from mischievous pranks . . . the certainty that their crimes will not go unpunished. A juvenile who rapes, robs, or commits the ultimate sin of murder should no longer be treated as a child but must pay the piper for his transgressions. Soon, we will see if the President and Senate agree.

Delinquents or Criminals: Policy Options for Young Offenders

Jeffrey A. Butts and Adele V. Harrell

America's juvenile courts have changed considerably in the past 30 years. The purposes and procedures of juvenile courts have become very similar to adult criminal courts. No state retains an inviolable, legal distinction between the status of "juvenile" and "adult," and the age threshold for trial in adult court seems to fall every time a new incident of juvenile violence captures the nation's attention. When four Arkansas students and their teacher died in a schoolyard shooting in March 1998, many people demanded that the alleged perpetrators be tried as adults. One boy was 13 years old; the other was 11.

Such extreme violence by very young juveniles is rare, but the reaction to it reflects public opinion about the juvenile justice system. Youth who violate the law are no longer guaranteed special treatment simply because they are young. As yet, no state has formally abolished the juvenile court's exclusive jurisdiction over young offenders, but every state in the country has taken significant steps in that direction. It appears increasingly likely that the states will ultimately abolish the concept of delinquency and that all law violations by young people will one day be handled in criminal court. In other words, the day may come when a crime is a crime is a crime, regardless of the offender's age.

Of course, even if states abolish the practice of sending young offenders to a separate court, children and adolescents will continue to be cognitively, emotionally, and socially different from adults. Criminal court judges and prosecutors will undoubtedly want to use different procedures for handling very young defendants. Eventually, it will be necessary to design a new justice process for young offenders within the existing criminal courts system.

This *Crime Policy Report* suggests that the work to design a new youth justice system should start before states actually begin to abolish the legal concept of delinquency. A good starting point would be to identify the best practices of the many specialty courts now emerging throughout the country, and to begin blending them more thoroughly with the juvenile court process. Innovative, specialty courts such as drug courts, gun courts, and community-based courts are bringing new ideas and effective new programs to the justice system. Some specialty courts actually resemble the traditional juvenile court in their use of pre-trial diversion, individualized assessments and proactive case management.

Meaningful reforms in juvenile crime policy have been difficult to achieve. Lawmakers are torn between the views of youth advocates who defend a traditional juvenile court that no longer exists, and hardliners who want to send even more youths to an adult court system that is still not prepared to deal with them properly. Focusing the attention of policy makers on the need to build a new youth justice system with a diverse menu of options for young offenders might help calm the acrimonious debates about transferring young offenders to adult court. Public officials could return to the serious business of ensuring that the court system as a whole balances the interests of justice, public safety, and the individual rights of all defendants regardless of age.

Source: Jeffrey A. Butts and Adele V. Harrell (1998). *Delinquents or Criminals: Policy Options for Young Offenders,* The Urban Institute.

In 1995, U.S. juvenile courts handled more than 1.7 million cases involving delinquency charges. Nearly half (45 percent) were handled without formal court action. In cases involving youth under age 13, 73 percent of all delinquency referrals ended with the youth receiving no formal services or sanctions. . . .

The Battle Over the Juvenile Court

Two opposing groups have polarized recent policy debates about juvenile courts, those that wish to preserve the traditional juvenile court as envisioned by its nineteenth-century founders, and those who want to abolish it. State and federal policy makers have spent the last three decades trying to hold the middle ground. Unfortunately, the moderate approach to juvenile justice reform has produced a system that critics contend protects neither the public safety nor the rights of youth (Feld, 1998).

In trying to claim the middle ground, elected officials have "criminalized" the juvenile court (Singer, 1996). Particularly since the 1970s, state and federal lawmakers have enacted policies to increase the severity of punishment in juvenile court, reduce the informality and confidentiality of juvenile court proceedings, and transfer large numbers of juvenile offenders to adult court. The similarities of juvenile and adult courts are becoming greater than the differences between them. . . .

Moving Juveniles to Adult Court

Nearly every state in the country has been moving greater numbers of juvenile offenders into the criminal court using a variety of mechanisms known collectively as "transfer." When juveniles are "transferred" to adult court, they lose their legal status as minor children and become fully culpable for their behavior. Transfer is often used for juveniles charged with violent crimes, but many youth are transferred for lesser charges. . . .

Many policy makers believe that serious and violent juvenile offenders should be tried in criminal court in order to achieve more certain and more severe punishment. Does this, in fact, happen? Does the public get more punishment for its money when juveniles are tried as adults? Researchers who examine this question tend to find that the use of transfer does increase the *certainty* and *severity* of legal sanctions, but only for the most serious cases, perhaps 30 percent of transferred juveniles.

In about half of all transfers, the offenders receive sentences comparable to what they might have received from the juvenile court. Some (about one-fifth) actually receive more lenient treatment in criminal court. Some may be convicted of lesser offenses or the charges against them may be dismissed due to the greater evidentiary scrutiny in criminal court. The bottom line is that criminal court transfer does not ensure incarceration, and it does not always increase sentence lengths even in cases that do result in incarceration.

Despite inconsistent results, criminal court transfer remains very popular. The politics of the issue are somewhat reminiscent of the death penalty, even including a popular political slogan (e.g., "do an adult crime, do adult time"). As with capital punishment, criminal court transfer offers a drastic and permanent solution for an offender thought to be beyond redemption. It is the court's way of saying, "there are no more second chances for you." Permanent and drastic punishments are very appealing to a public confronted with high rates of violent crime. Unlike the death penalty, however, criminal court transfer is not permanent. It is merely a change of venue that exposes a young offender to more severe court outcomes but does not guarantee any particular outcome.

Advocating criminal court transfer has become the very definition of toughness for elected officials. Once state officials begin to enact transfer provisions, they are tempted to revisit the criteria repeatedly and slowly expand the use of transfer to more types of offenses. The State of Illinois, for example, began the use of automatic transfer in 1982, initially only for juveniles charged with violent crimes. By 1995, automatic transfer had been expanded to include drug violations committed within 1,000 feet of a school, felonies committed in "furtherance of gang activity," and drug offenses committed within 1,000 feet of public housing property.

Are Boot Camps an Effective Means of Dealing with Juvenile Crime?

The 1979 documentary "Scared Straight " follows 17 juvenile delinquents who are taken inside Rahway's maximum security prison where they are brought face to face with the "lifers." Using strong language and graphic descriptions of the brutality of prison life, these hardened convicts literally try to scare the kids into going straight. But did it work? A follow-up documentary twenty years later found that some of the original participants were indeed law-abiding citizens. But others had themselves become lifers.

Through the years, the concept behind "Scared Straight" has reappeared in different ways. Today, it is most likely to be termed "shock incarceration" or "juvenile boot camps." The driving force behind the idea, of course, is deterrence. Based on the crime control model, proponents argue that repeat juvenile delinquents need to be confronted with their moral failures. Thus, what some have labeled a "second last chance" will instill individual responsibility.

Contemporary programs tend to be more elaborate and sophisticated than the early brief encounter. To choose just one, the About Face residential program in Memphis, Tennessee, has four main components:

- Military training conducted by current and former navy and marine personnel

- Group and individual counseling

- Education using immersion techniques, computer-assisted learning, and individualized instruction

- Spiritual support that includes voluntary attendance at religious services

There is, however, no one single blueprint. Program evaluations find that details can be quite important.

Are contemporary juvenile boot camps like the one in Memphis any more effective than the 1979 program, "Scared Straight"? Evaluations have yielded mixed results. There is no evidence, for example, that they reduce recidivism. Moreover, these programs have been associated with several practical problems. In several locations, for example, prison guards have been accused of excess brutality. Moreover, fully fledged programs can be quite costly; indeed a number of programs have been terminated for cost reasons.

Despite a lack of clear demonstration that these programs are either effective or cost-efficient, approximately 50 juvenile boot camps exist in about 30 states. The debate runs roughly as follows.

Pro	Con
Juvenile boot camps reduce recidivism.	Juvenile boot camps do not reduce recidivism.
Shock incarceration is cost effective.	These programs are not cost effective.
A brief taste of prison life is the most important part of juvenile boot camps.	Educational and vocational training coupled with drug counseling or other treatments are most effective.
Removing juveniles from their crime environment is critically important.	Aftercare is the most critical (and most costly) part of juvenile boot camps.

The article "Colorado Has a New Brand of Tough Love" discusses Colorado's Youth Offender System (YOS), which suspends the adult sentences of convicted violent offenders between the ages of 14 and 18 if they agree to attend the boot-camp-like program for two to six years. The author, Gordon Witkin (a reporter for *U.S. News & World Report*), notes that only 12 youths have completed YOS since its 1994 inception.

The article "Juvenile Boot Camps: Lessons Learned" reports on the evaluation of three juvenile boot camps. The author, Eric Peterson (Office of Juvenile Justice and Delinquency Prevention (OJJDP), uses the phrase "lessons learned" to highlight why these programs don't always work as advocates hope.

World Wide Web Exercises

1. Choose a search engine and use the search term **juvenile boot camp** or **juvenile justice programs** to locate two or more articles that discuss the topic. Do these Web sites provide similar or different arguments to those presented in the readings? Do the Web sites that focus just on juvenile matters differ in significant ways from those that discuss other topics as well?

2. Using the search engine of your choice, enter the search term **juvenile justice** and locate two or more Web sites that discuss juvenile delinquency and/or juvenile crime. In discussing solutions, what is the relative balance of sites that place

emphasis on punitive approaches versus those that stress education, prevention or treatment?

InfoTrac College Edition Exercises

1. Using the search term **juvenile boot camps, juvenile corrections—innovations,** or **rehabilitation of juvenile offenders—innovations,** locate two or more articles on each side of the issue. Do these articles provide arguments similar to or different from those presented in the readings?

2. Using the search term **juvenile boot camps, juvenile corrections—innovations,** or **rehabilitation of juvenile offenders—innovations,** locate two or more articles in academic journals that analyze the effectiveness of boot camps. Do the findings tend to support the pro or the con position on this issue?

Colorado Has a New Brand of Tough Love: Helping Young Offenders Shape Up and Ship Out

Gordon Witkin

For most of the nation, Colorado conjures up images of snow-capped peaks and suntanned skiers. But in the summer of 1993, the gang graffiti and crackling gunfire in neighborhoods like Denver's Park Hill were as frightening as any urban nightmare.

In May 1993, an infant was hit in the face by a stray bullet while watching polar bears at the Denver Zoo. Weeks later, 6-year-old Broderick Bell was wounded in the crossfire of a gang fight. A store owner was killed and his wife beaten and kidnapped in a carjacking outside a supermarket. A young elementary-school teacher who'd just arrived in the area was gunned down in a robbery. All these crimes were believed to be linked to juveniles or young adults. And although there was no dramatic spike in Denver's crime rate in 1993, the randomness and ruthlessness of the crimes during the city's "summer of violence," says Mayor Wellington Webb, left ordinary citizens asking, "Are we losing control as a city?"

Webb put an unprecedented number of cops on the street, hired new officers, deployed teams to fight gangs and instituted an innovative juvenile-curfew program that melded enforcement with counseling. Colorado Gov. Roy Romer called a special legislative session on youth violence and the state's underfunded juvenile justice system. What emerged from the five-day marathon was a lowering of the age most juveniles could be charged as adults, from 15 to 14; a ban on handgun possession by youths; a juvenile boot camp, and a new, hybrid Youth Offender System to deal with juveniles who commit violent felonies. The legislature also moved to spend $45 million to build facilities with 430 new places for both short-term juvenile detention and longer sentences.

Alternative

Colorado's experimental Youth Offender System, a new middle tier between juvenile detention and adult prison, has attracted national attention. Juveniles between 14 and 18 who have been transferred to adult court and convicted of violent felonies can have their adult sentences suspended in favor of a two-year to six-year term in the YOS, which is both tough and nurturing.

A YOS term begins with a month or so of bruising, military-style, mini-boot camp to break down tough-guy attitudes and teach respect for adult authority. A look at these teens, many still with baby fat and acne, standing ramrod straight in banana-yellow jumpsuits while a drill instructor barks out orders, leaves little doubt who's in charge.

Next comes a program of personalized counseling and education that can last from eight months to almost five years. Traditional classroom subjects are mixed with computer literacy and a

Source: March 25, 1996 V120. © 1996, *U.S. News & World Report*. Visit www.usnews.com for additional information.

bit of vocational training in the hope that residents will earn high school equivalency diplomas and begin to think about careers.

Monitoring

That's followed by a prerelease phase that's now done in-house but may eventually be located in a series of halfway houses—three months of life-skills training and intensive planning for how the youth will make it on the outside. Following release, there's a final, six-to-12-month phase of intensive supervision involving frequent reporting, electronic monitoring, random urinalysis and community support programs. Youngsters who get in trouble can be yanked back inside, and if they wash out of YOS, they know their suspended sentences in adult prison are still out there waiting for them. "I had to tell myself, 'I'm walking a thin line here,'" says George, 19, a YOS participant. "If I play around too much, I realize now I can go to prison."

Since accepting its first kids in March 1994, the program has had some growing pains. While awaiting construction of its own $25 million, 300-bed facility in Pueblo, YOS is housed in cramped quarters in an adult facility, the Denver Reception and Diagnostic Center. Some juveniles have to be sent to private facilities for part of the program. Colorado judges initially were unsure who should go to YOS, and some started out imposing YOS sentences that were as long as the alternative adult sentences, which didn't give kids enough incentive to stick with the YOS regimen.

Critics such as Denver Juvenile Court Judge David Ramirez, who calls YOS a "shot in the dark," admit that something different is needed for violent teens but believe the money could be better spent within the existing juvenile justice system. "We've taken all the programs with merit and put them together," counters YOS Deputy Director Richard Swanson.

It's too early to evaluate the success of YOS. Only 12 kids have reached the community supervision phase so far; two have washed out, one for committing a new crime. The other 10 are in school or working, although five of them have been briefly yanked back into YOS for positive drug tests, curfew violations or reassociating with their former gangs.

Colorado's answer to growing juvenile violence also includes efforts to prevent youth crime. Denver is distributing $1 million yearly for prevention projects as part of a "Safe City" initiative. In 1994, the Colorado General Assembly appropriated $3.6 million—later hiked to $5 million annually—for a Youth Crime Prevention and Intervention Program, and Governor Romer more recently has pushed two public/private partnerships, an early childhood program known as Bright Beginnings and a "Responsible Fatherhood" initiative.

Tough Sell

Still, Colorado is spending a great deal more new money—$71.5 million for construction alone—on juvenile incarceration. "We have a lot more to do—we're not cutting it yet on the prevention side," Romer admits.

But Romer and key Colorado legislators say prevention is a tough sell. Its benefits are hard to measure and won't occur until after most of the politicians who approve crime-prevention programs have retired. YOS costs about $90 a day per resident, compared with about $79 daily for a maximum security adult prisoner. And in an atmosphere of anger, fear and limited dollars, sighs Romer, "people simply want to lock them up and throw away the key."

What's more, while many Coloradans want a solution to their juvenile-crime problem, few want any part of it in their neighborhoods. Denver is facing a juvenile-detention crisis because rampant "not in my back yard" syndrome has prevented the city from finding a suitable place for new facilities. With the population of the city's Gilliam Youth Services Center capped after litigation last year, Denver has been forced to release some incarcerated juveniles early. And almost no one believes that turning young criminals loose is the answer to the problem.

Teen Criminals and Justice

- The number of cases sent from juvenile to adult courts for trial increased 41 percent between 1989 and 1993, to 11,800.

- Juvenile courts order imprisonment for about one fourth of juveniles involved in violent crimes.

- The average stay in youth corrections facilities is about one year for crimes against persons, 248 days for drug offenses and 187 days for weapons crimes.

- More than 60,000 juveniles are in custody, many in overcrowded facilities. Almost all are boys.

Juvenile Boot Camps: Lessons Learned

Eric Peterson

In response to a significant increase in juvenile arrests and repeat offenses over the past decade, several States and many localities have established juvenile boot camps. The first juvenile boot camp programs, modeled after boot camps for adult offenders, emphasized military-style discipline and physical conditioning. OJJDP has supported the development of three juvenile boot camp demonstration sites. This Fact Sheet describes those demonstration projects, their evaluations, and lessons learned that will benefit future boot camp programs.

Pilot Programs

In 1992 OJJDP funded three juvenile boot camps designed to address the special needs and circumstances of adolescent offenders. The programs were conducted in Cleveland, Ohio; Denver, Colorado; and Mobile, Alabama.

Focusing on a target population of adjudicated, nonviolent offenders under the age of 18, the boot camp programs were designed as highly structured, three-month residential programs followed by six to nine months of community-based aftercare. During the aftercare period, youth were to pursue academic and vocational training or employment while under intensive, but progressively diminishing, supervision.

Evaluations

OJJDP undertook impact evaluations for all three sites that compared the recidivism rates for juveniles who participated in the pilot programs with those of control groups. The evaluations also compared the cost-effectiveness of juvenile boot camps with other dispositional alternatives. Reports of the three impact evaluations are available. The evaluations of the Mobile and Cleveland programs are interim reports that present data from the earliest cohorts. As neither program had stabilized when the data were collected, OJJDP is considering expanding the evaluation to include the remaining cohorts. The Denver program is no longer active.

Findings

Most juvenile boot camp participants completed the residential program and graduated to aftercare. Program completion rates were 96 percent in Cleveland, 87 percent in Mobile, and 76 percent in Denver.

At the two sites where educational gains were measured, substantial improvements in academic skills were noted. In Mobile, approximately three-quarters of the participants improved their performance in reading, spelling, language, and math

Source: Office of Juvenile Justice and Delinquency Prevention.

by one grade level or more. In Cleveland, the average juvenile boot camp participant improved reading, spelling, and math skills by approximately one grade level.

In addition, where employment records were available, a significant number of participants found jobs while in aftercare.

The pilot programs, however, did not demonstrate a reduction in recidivism. In Denver and Mobile, no statistically significant difference could be found between the recidivism rates of juvenile boot camp participants and those of the control groups (youth confined in State or county institutions, or released on probation). In Cleveland, pilot program participants evidenced a higher recidivism rate than juvenile offenders confined in traditional juvenile correctional facilities. It should be noted that none of the sites fully implemented OJJDP's model juvenile boot camp guidelines, and that some critical aftercare support services were not provided.

Lessons Learned

Several significant lessons have emerged from the pilot programs:

The appropriate population should be targeted. Boot camps should be designed as an intermediate intervention. At one site, youth who had been previously confined were significantly more likely to recidivate, while youth with the least serious offenses were also more likely to recidivate.

Facility location is important. Cost issues and community resistance were major obstacles to securing residential and aftercare facilities. To increase attendance and reduce problems, aftercare facilities should be located in gang-neutral areas accessible by public transportation.

Staff selection and training needs are critical. To reduce staff turnover, fill gaps in critical services, and ensure consistent programming, the screening, selection, and training of juvenile boot camp and aftercare staff must be sensitive to the programmatic and operational features of a juvenile boot camp. This is particularly important with regard to youth development issues.

Moreover, continuous treatment between the residential and aftercare phases should be integrated philosophically and programmatically, particularly through staffing.

Aftercare programs are challenging to implement. Successful aftercare programs require attention at the outset to develop a comprehensive model with the flexibility to respond to local needs and concerns. Aftercare programs are unlikely to succeed if their participants fail to receive the full range of services prescribed for them. Aftercare programs must be broad-based and flexible enough to meet the particular educational, employment, counseling, and support needs of each participant. The aftercare component should form dynamic linkages with other community services, especially youth service agencies, schools, and employers.

Coordination among agencies must be maintained. All three sites experienced difficulties in maintaining coordination among the participating agencies. Considerable attention should be paid to building and maintaining a consensus among participating organizations concerning the program's philosophy and procedures.

Effective evaluation begins with planning. To assess the program's successes and failures, quantifiable data should be collected about participation in treatment by juveniles in the boot camp and in the control group. Measures of program success should include a broad spectrum of outcomes. Recidivism measures should capture all subsequent delinquent activity, not simply the first new adjudication, and data on new offenses should include information on the origin and circumstances of the complaint to determine whether there is a monitoring effect, in which the intensity of the supervision causes an increase in recorded offending.

When boot camps are used as an alternative to confinement, savings can be achieved. Communities often implement juvenile boot camps, in part, to reduce costs. The experience of the pilot sites indicates that when boot camps are used as an alternative to traditional confinement, costs can be reduced considerably because of the significantly shorter residential stay. However, if boot camps are used as an alternative to probation, savings will not be realized.

Conclusion

Juvenile boot camps embrace a variety of objectives: reducing recidivism, improving academic performance, cutting the cost of treating juvenile offenders, and inculcating the values of self-discipline and hard work. In attempting to reach these objectives, OJJDP is collaborating with the Office of Justice Programs (OJP) to enhance program models, policies, and practices of juvenile boot camps. As a result, many of the lessons learned from OJJDP's three demonstration sites have been incorporated in the OJP Boot Camp Corrections Program.

Part x

Waging Holy War: Public Morals and Private Vices

Laws governing gambling, prostitution, pornography, alcohol, smoking and drugs are shaped by an uneasy tension between public morals and private vices. On the one hand, some segments of society publicly condemn some, or all, of these actions as undermining public morals. Religious leaders and moral entrepreneurs are quick to denounce gambling, prostitution, pornography, and the like, as undermining values in society, particularly among youth. At the same time a goodly number of citizens, old and sometimes young, engage in these vices. These offenses are typically called crimes without victims, because they involve a willing and private exchange of goods or services that are in strong demand. Thus, in the sense that the persons involved do not feel that they are being harmed, the crimes are "victimless." But conservatives are quick to challenge such notions, arguing that allowing vice offenses results in the deterioration of neighborhoods, which fosters more serious crimes.

The uneasy tension between public morals and private vices explains why the public is so divided over these matters. In fact, what is most distinctive about crimes of public morality is public ambivalence. A direct result of this ambivalence is the contradictory nature of the public laws. As one moves from state to state, for example, one finds a bewildering array of laws about gambling. Bingo is legal almost everywhere but betting on horses only in some states. Wagering on sporting events is pretty much illegal in every state but is a mainstay of the Nevada economy, and legally so.

Another consequence of public ambivalence about private vices is the creation of illegal markets. Given the willingness of some citizens to place a bet, or unwind with a marijuana cigarette, private entrepreneurs spring up to provide the forbidden fruits, making a profit along the way (a most American value). But these illegal markets in turn often produce other forms of criminality. The growth of organized crime in the U.S., for example, has been traced to Prohibition.

Demand for private vices, coupled with the illegal markets that satisfy the demand, give rise to another important aspect of the criminal justice system—corruption of public officials. Through the years, police officers, prosecutors, judges and prison guards have accepted economic gratuities (a polite word for bribes) from the businessmen and businesswomen who provide these forbidden services.

Vice crimes, of course, cover a wide range of activities, and for that reason public reactions differ. Religious groups vary, for example, in which activities they condemn, tolerate or accept. We will examine only two. Drugs and cyberporn, for very different reasons, are two issues that are a part of the national crime debate.

World Wide Web Resources

Guides

http://dir.yahoo.com/Health/Diseases_and_Conditions/Gambling_Addiction/

http://dir.yahoo.com/Society_and_Culture/Crime/Crimes/Sex_Crimes

http://dir.yahoo.com/Society_and_Culture/Sexuality/Pornography_Issues/

http://dir.yahoo.com/Society_and_Culture/Issues_and_Causes/Civil_Rights/
Censorship/Censorship_and_the_Net/Communications_Decency_Act/

http://dir.yahoo.com/Arts/Humanities/History/U_S_History/20th_Century/1920s/
Prohibition/

http://dir.yahoo.com/Health/Pharmacy/Drugs_and_Medications/Drug_Policy/
U_S_War_on_Drugs/

Searching the Web

war on drugs, gambling, prohibition, prostitution, pornography, communications decency act

Useful URLs

American Civil Liberties Union: Cyber-liberties.   http://www.aclu.org/issues/cyber/

Drug Library: Presented by the Drug Reform Coordination Network.
http://www.druglibrary.org/

Enough Is Enough: Lead proponent of the Communications Decency Act.
http://www.enough.org/

Office of Drug Control Policy: White House agency that spearheads the war on drugs.   http://www.whitehousedrugpolicy.gov/

Today's Headlines

http://fullcoverage.yahoo.com/Full_Coverage/AUNZ/Gambling_Issues/

http://fullcoverage.yahoo.com/Full_Coverage/Tech/Internet_Child_Pornography/

Fun Sites

Coalition Against Trafficking in Women: Feminist human rights organization that works internationally to oppose all forms of sexual exploitation.
http://www.uri.edu/artsci/wms/hughes/catw/

COYOTE: COYOTE stands for "Call Off Your Old Tired Ethics" and represents sex workers, particularly on the West Coast.   http://www.bayswan.org/COYOTE.html

Free Expression on the Internet: Reports, briefing papers, and press releases on the issue from Human Rights Watch.   http://www.hrw.org/advocacy/internet/

Prohibition 1920–1933: From Michigan State University.
http://www.msu.edu/course/mc/112/1920s/Prohibition/index.html

InfoTrac College Edition Resources

Basic Searches

crimes without victims, prostitution; gambling, telecommunications act of 1996;
narcotics, control of

Background

Encyclopedia articles and reference works on a variety of topics.

Issue 17

Should the U.S.
End the War on Drugs?

U.S. drug policy dates from the Harrison Narcotics Act of 1914, when the federal government for the first time outlawed marijuana, opium, and cocaine. "Wars on Drugs" have been waged intermittently ever since. Modern efforts date to the 1968 presidential election of Richard Nixon. In various ways, all subsequent presidents have waged a war on drugs.

There is little doubt that the war on drugs now parallels "soft on crime" as a third rail of American politics—touch it and you die. Public opinion polls stress that Americans are very concerned that their children will do drugs and become addicts. These public sentiments are reflected in the moral rhetoric employed in waging the war on drugs. (Recall that an earlier article argued that the war on drugs was best viewed as a moral panic.) Legalizing drugs, for example, has been equated to the moral equivalent of "genocide." Other fiery phrases, like the "scourge of illegal narcotics," are also often used.

The demonizing of drugs and drug users explains why there is little public opposition to anti-drug campaigns. Even asking questions about the War on Drugs is often labeled as illegitimate. In the words of former drug czar Lee Brown: "there is no need to debate the facts" and "we are not going to be distracted by silly arguments about why drugs should be legalized." (Brown, 1995). But behind the public war of words condemning drugs and drug users, there is a private questioning. Why, after almost forty years of fighting drugs, does it seem that the war on drugs is unwinnable? Equally troubling is the shifting agenda of what drugs are targeted for criminalization. Rarely has medical and scientific evidence about harmfulness played a major role in this debate. Rather, the specific drugs chosen for criminal sanctions are those associated with unpopular segments of society.

Even the terms used to debate the war on drugs are contentious. Opponents of the War on Drugs argue in favor of some form of decriminalization; that is, the use and possession of drugs would not be illegal, but manufacture and sale would not be legal. Defenders of the war on drugs forcefully reject any notions of decriminalization, arguing that the critics really want legalization, that is, removing all criminal penalties. The debate over decriminalization of drugs runs as follows.

Pro	Con
Moralistic rhetoric can not hide the stark reality that the war on drugs has been a failure. Its only accomplishment has been to fill the prisons to overflowing (all too often with minorities).	The need to keep illegal drugs illegal rests on the basic premise that drugs severely damage the social fabric of the U.S.
The association of drug abuse with crime exaggerates an ambiguous pattern. Many persons who use recreational drugs never commit crimes and many criminals will commit crimes whether they are on drugs or not.	Drug addiction produces untold human suffering, with addicts losing their jobs, destroying their families, and dying young. Those who buy and sell illegal drugs are more likely to commit crimes.
Drug use reflects escapism from the mushrooming social problems of our nation. Until we attack the root cause of drug use and drug abuse, little will be accomplished.	People use drugs because they have a desire for intense pleasure and instant rewards. Drug users should just say no. But for those who don't seek treatment, arrest, conviction, and punishment is the only way to demonstrate that such behavior is socially unacceptable. Moreover, an emphasis on arrest and punishment will deter others from selling and using drugs.
In treating the ills of drugs, law enforcement must take a secondary role to treatment and rehabilitation. Spending money on drug prevention and treatment of substance abuse is much more cost effective than continuing to waste taxpayer dollars on building more prison cells to house nonviolent offenders.	A failure to wage a vigorous war on drugs will result in too many young persons using drugs and becoming addicts. The war on drugs will succeed if society is willing to exert the effort necessary and spend more on law enforcement, particularly drug interdiction efforts.

On the pro side, Bertram and Sharpe argue that many drug treatment centers, police departments, and courts are opposed to the war on drugs, which has essentially failed. They see the treatment of drug abusers and the legalization of drugs as alternatives to the punishment of drug users.

On the con side, Joseph Califano argues that some people believe that the legalization of drugs would reduce crime, but drug use increases the likelihood of criminal activity. Legalization, he states, would be particularly damaging to children.

World Wide Web Exercises

1. Using the search engine of your choice, enter the search term **war on drugs** and locate two or more organizations that address this topic. To what extent do the Web sites differ in the mixture of proposed solutions to the problem of drugs? In particular, what relative emphasis do they place on punitive policy, education, and/or treatment? To what extent are these differences best understood in terms of the crime control versus due process model of criminal justice?

2. In recent years, groups in several states have attempted to make the medical use of marijuana legal. Use the search engine of your choice and enter the search term **marijuana + medical** to locate at least one article on each side of the issue. To what extent do arguments for and against the medical use of marijuana parallel those used in debating the war on drugs?

InfoTrac College Edition Exercises

1. An earlier article, "The American Drug Panic of the 1980s" by Goode and Ben-Yehuda, argued that the war on drugs in the U.S. is best understood as a moral panic. Using the search term **narcotics, control of,** locate two or more articles that analyze the war on drugs. Do the results of the studies support or contradict the assertion that the war on drugs is a moral panic?

2. Using the search term **narcotics, control of,** locate two or more academic articles that analyze the impact of the war on drugs. To what extent are the problems associated with Prohibition similar to or different from those associated with the war on drugs?

War Ends, Drugs Win; Resisters Say We're Fighting the Wrong Battles

Eva Bertram and Kenneth Sharpe

The war on drugs has by all accounts failed. Yet our national dialogue about how to address this failure is trapped in a dead-end, partisan debate over who stands tougher against drug use and dealing. The concept of legalizing drugs has sparked some significant discussions and controversy—but primarily among limited circles of academics and analysts. At the local level, citizens periodically signal an openness to rethink the war on drugs—witness the passage of initiatives in California and Arizona allowing the medical use of marijuana—but more consistently they demand a "get tough" approach.

Focusing on the limits of these public debates, however, misses an important part of the current struggle over drug control: Opposition to elements of the drug war is quietly cropping up in courthouses, police departments, hospitals and treatment centers across the country. Perhaps most striking, that opposition is coming from those who might be expected to be the drug war's most ardent supporters. On its front lines, the war is sowing the seeds of its own opposition.

The resistance among criminal justice officials, treatment providers and others involved in the drug war takes different forms. Some simply defect; others seek modest reforms emphasizing treatment rather than punishment. Still others challenge the fundamental goals of the drug war through harm-reduction programs. Together, they tell a story about the possibilities and politics of drug reform.

Source: *The Nation*, January 6, 1997 v264 p. 11. Reprinted by permission.

Dissenters among judges, police, federal and local officials and military leaders are forming a growing corps of drug war defectors, signaling a loss of confidence in the policy at the highest levels. Frustrated by the impossible task of interdicting, arresting, prosecuting and jailing an endless stream of traffickers, dealers and users—while other serious crimes go unpunished and drug abuse continues unabated, many have publicly criticized the drug war, or even chosen to go AWOL.

In April 1993, for example, the *New York Times* reported that two of New York City's most prominent federal judges announced "that the emphasis on arrests and imprisonments rather than prevention and treatment, has been a failure, and that they were withdrawing from the effort." Court officials estimate that in 1993 some 50 of the nation's 680 federal judges are refusing to hear drug cases. . . .

Former San Jose, California, police chief Joseph McNamara compares waging war on the drug supply to "throwing sand against the tide." A growing number of his peers agree. Some 60 percent of police chiefs polled in a March 1996 nationwide survey believe that current anti-drug efforts have been ineffective. . . .

Even top federal law officials have challenged the drug war strategy. In December 1993 Surgeon General Joycelyn Elders said it was possible that "we would markedly reduce our crime rate if drugs were legalized" and called for further study; that position, among others, cost Elders her job. . . .

The public criticism of drug war defectors has legitimized a wider debate. Others in the treatment community and criminal justice system have chosen to challenge failed policies not by defecting from the drug war but by reforming it to shift the emphasis from punishment to treatment. The failure to lower drug abuse has convinced many treatment providers that the law-enforcement emphasis of current policy is misguided. Some 70 percent of federal drug war funds are invested in enforcement, and only 30 percent in treatment and prevention. Providers are fighting to make treatment a full and equal partner with law enforcement in the war on drugs. They want access to treatment for all who seek it, and urge greater attention to the needs of particular groups such as pregnant addicts and H.I.V.-infected drug users.

They face an uphill battle. The stigma against drug users is deeply rooted, and there is widespread sentiment against using government funds to treat rather than punish those who have chosen to use illegal drugs. In response, many treatment providers make the strategic choice not to challenge the role of law enforcement. . . .

Many treatment advocates go further, turning the get-tough-on-drugs logic to their advantage by marshaling evidence that treatment is more effective than prison in preventing crime and reducing recidivism. "Riding the crime wave," notes one treatment professional, enables providers to "get the money we need."

Health care providers have found unlikely allies in the criminal justice system. Frustration with the drug war's revolving door has led many law-and-order advocates to conclude that substance-abusing offenders will cycle endlessly through the system—unless they receive treatment and health care. Reformers have organized not only for treatment in prison but also for treatment as an alternative to prison. In court-ordered "diversion to treatment" programs, drug offenders who commit nonviolent crimes are given the option of court-monitored treatment programs rather than prison. They are threatened with doing time, however, if they don't successfully complete these programs.

Not surprisingly, drug courts, as they are known, have drawn fire from antidrug warriors who object that users are lawbreakers, and the job of law enforcement is to punish—not coddle—them. "These are not the innocent drug addicts

they are made to seem," said a spokesman for New York State's former Senate majority leader, Ralph Marino. "If you're going to sink new spending into this area, we ought to deal with additional prison bed space." Because drug courts look "revolutionary," said Miami judge Herbert Klein, "it takes real clout to overcome ingrained bureaucratic resistance. . . . "

Despite significant gains in building political support, reformers in both the treatment and criminal justice communities point to a troubling paradox in their efforts. In practice, the goals of promoting health and punishing illegal behavior often come into conflict. Some reform advocates argue that selling treatment as a crime-fighting tool may win votes and funding for treatment—but it also reinforces the assumption that drug users are criminals. In the long run, this undermines public support for treatment. "Once we make drug addicts into the enemy," explained one treatment director, "society has a rough time taking them back in. Why would the public want to pay for more treatment if they're dealing with the enemy?" . . .

The strategy of treatment and criminal justice reformers is to publicly challenge the means (punishment) but not the end (no drug use) of the drug war. Harm-reduction advocates, in contrast, have chosen to take on the zero-tolerance goal of drug control itself. The objective of drug policy, they argue, should be to reduce the harmful consequences of drug use to the individual, his or her loved ones and the community as a whole.

The most vocal advocates of harm reduction are the public health and community activists who have had to challenge drug war policies in their battle against the spread of AIDS. More than one-third of all current AIDS cases are associated with injecting drugs. . . .

For more than a decade, AIDS-prevention activists have mobilized to discourage the practice of sharing contaminated needles through needle-exchange programs (NEPs), which provide sterile needles to addicts and encourage them to seek treatment. Mounting evidence demonstrates that NEPs can significantly slow the spread of AIDS and do not encourage increased drug use. But advocates are stymied by drug war policies banning the sale or possession of needles, and by a volley of rhetorical attacks and new laws prohibiting such programs. Concluding that we cannot "allow our concern for AIDS to undermine our determination to win the war on drugs," the Bush Administration said "there is no getting around the fact that distributing needles facilitates drug use and undercuts the credibility of society's message that using drugs is illegal and morally wrong." Clinton drug czar Gen. Barry McCaffrey concurs: "The problem isn't dirty needles; it's injection of illegal drugs. . . . "

The battle over needle exchange may be the most visible, but it is not the only effort under way to redirect drug policy toward harm reduction. From New York to California, methadone advocates are organizing to expand treatment for heroin addicts. Arguably the first harm-reduction tool adopted in the United States, methadone satisfies an addict's cravings without heroin's euphoric effects, enabling users to function and sometimes to overcome their addictions. . . .

The principle of harm reduction strikes at the core of the current approach to drug control. Conventional wisdom assumes that drug abuse and addiction are crime problems; in contrast, many harm-reduction advocates see them as public health problems, like heavy drinking or AIDS. Conventional wisdom assumes that drug use and abuse result from bad individual judgment or character; harm-reduction advocates emphasize the ways the social environment shapes these

choices. The drug-war solution to drug abuse and addiction is to threaten and punish those who use or deal drugs. Harm-reduction strategies, in contrast, would shift resources toward prevention and treatment, and would redefine and expand the scope of both.

Preventive education for harm reduction would seek to inform and influence individual choices, not only to discourage any use of dangerous drugs but also to educate those who will nevertheless experiment with and use drugs, teaching them how to minimize the harm they cause themselves and others—just as designated driver programs help reduce the harm of drinking. Prevention would also demand policies aimed at changing social environments that encourage abuse and addiction, including abusive family settings, peer pressures and joblessness. Treatment for harm reduction would make total abstinence only one goal along a continuum of care that would include many measures of success: more moderate use, safer use, the use of less dangerous drugs, reduction of criminal activity, ability to fulfill family and workplace roles, greater physical and mental health.

Not surprisingly, strategies to reduce the harm drug users cause themselves or others—without insisting on total abstinence or harsh punishment—draw fire from across the political spectrum, from parents' groups and church organizations to health officials and policymakers. Such opposition makes the prospects for building a broad-based harm-reduction movement daunting.

Fictions and Facts About Drug Legalization

Joseph A. Califano

When high priests of America's political right and left as articulate as William F. Buckley, Jr., founding editor of *National Review,* and Anthony Lewis, a columnist for the *New York Times* Op-Ed page, peddle the same drug legalization line, it's time to shout *caveat emptor*—let the buyer beware. For the boomlet to legalize drugs like heroin, cocaine and marijuana that they—and magazines like *National Review* and *New York*—are trying to seed among the right and left ends of the political spectrum, is founded in fiction, not fact. And it's our children who could suffer long-lasting, permanent damage.

Fiction: There's been no progress in the war on drugs.

Fact: The U.S. Department of Health and Human Services' National Household Drug Survey, the nation's most extensive assessment of drug use, reports that from 1979 to 1994 the number of current drug users (those using within the past month) has dropped from 24.8 million to 13 million, marijuana users from 23 million to 10 million and cocaine users from 4.4 million to 1.4 million. The number of hard-core addicts has held steady at around six million, a situation most experts attribute to the unavailability of treatment and the large number of addicts in the pipeline.

Source: *America,* March 16, 1996 v174 p. 7. © 1999 American Press, Inc. Used with permission.

Fiction: Whether to use drugs and become hooked is an adult decision.

Fact: It's children who choose. Hardly anyone in America begins drug use after age 21. An individual who does not smoke, use drugs or abuse alcohol by age 21 is virtually certain never to do so. The nicotine pushers understand this, which is why they fight so strenuously to kill efforts to keep their stuff away from kids.

Fiction: Legalization would be only for adults, legalized drugs would not be available to children.

Fact: Nothing in the American experience gives grounds to believe in our ability to keep legal drugs out of the hands of children. It's illegal for children to purchase cigarettes and alcohol. But today, three million adolescents smoke an average of half a pack a day: a $1 billion-a-year market. Twelve million underage Americans drink: a $10 billion-a-year market.

Fiction: Legalization would reduce crime and social problems.

Fact: Any short-term reduction in arrests from repealing drug laws would quickly evaporate as use increased; and the criminal conduct—assaults, murders, rapes, child molestations, vandalism and other violence—spawned by drugs like cocaine and methamphetamines would explode. The U.S.

Department of Justice reports that criminals commit six times as many homicides, four times as many assaults and almost one and a half times as many robberies under the influence of drugs as they commit in order to get money to buy drugs.

Here the history of our experience with alcohol can teach us. More state prisoners were drunk on alcohol than high on drugs when they committed their crimes, and America's number one criminal offense is driving while intoxicated (1.5 million arrests in 1993). Health and welfare costs would skyrocket if drugs were legalized.

Fiction: The American experience with the prohibition of alcohol supports drug legalization.

Fact: This ignores two important distinctions: Prohibition was in fact decriminalization (possession of alcohol for personal consumption was not illegal); and alcohol, unlike illegal drugs such as heroin and cocaine, has a long history of broad social acceptance dating back to the Old Testament and Ancient Greece. Nevertheless, alcohol consumption dropped from 1.96 gallons per person in 1919 to 0.97 gallons per person in 1934, the first full year after Prohibition ended. Death rates from cirrhosis among men came down from 29.5 per 100,000 in 1911 to 10.7 per 100,000 in 1929. During Prohibition, admission to mental health institutions for alcohol psychosis dropped 60 percent; arrests for drunk and disorderly conduct went down 50 percent; welfare agencies reported significant declines in cases due to alcohol-related family problems, and the death rate from impure alcohol did not rise.

Nor did Prohibition generate a crime wave . . .

Fiction: Greater availability and legal acceptability of drugs like marijuana, cocaine and heroin would not increase use.

Fact: This contradicts not only experience but human nature. In the 1970's we decriminalized marijuana. The Schafer Commission appointed by President Richard M. Nixon recommended decriminalization, as did President Jimmy Carter. The result? A soaring increase in marijuana use, particularly among youngsters.

Today we have 50 million nicotine addicts, 18 million alcoholics and alcohol abusers and 6 million illegal drug addicts. Experts like Dr. Herbert Kleber at Columbia University believe that with legalization the number of cocaine addicts alone would jump beyond the number of alcoholics.

That spells big trouble. In 1995 illegal drugs killed 20,000 Americans. Tobacco was responsible for 450,000 deaths; alcohol for more than 100,000. Studies at the Center on Addiction and Substance Abuse at Columbia University reveal that, of the $66 billion that substance abuse costs federal health and disability entitlement programs like Medicare and Medicaid, $56 billion is attributable to tobacco and alcohol.

Fiction: Drug use is an issue of civil liberties.

Fact: This is a convenient misreading of John Stuart Mill's *On Liberty*. Legalizers cite Mill to argue that the state has no right to interfere in the private life of a citizen who uses drugs; only when an action harms someone else may the state take action to prevent it. They ignore the fact that Mill's conception of freedom does not extend to the right of individuals to enslave themselves or to decide that they will give up their liberty. Mill wrote with blunt clarity: "The principle of freedom cannot require that he should be free not to be free. it is not freedom to be allowed to alienate his freedom."

Drug addiction is a form of enslavement. It "alters pathologically the nature and character of abusers," says Mitchell Rosenthal, M.D., the president of Phoenix House. Even Mill at his most expansive would admit that the state can take action not only to free an addict from chains of chemical dependency that take away the freedom to be all that God meant him or her to be, but also to prevent those bonds from becoming shackles in the first place. Indeed, a state devoted to individual freedom has an obligation to nourish a society and legal structure that protects individuals from the slavery of drug addiction. . . .

Certainly a society that recognizes the state's compelling interest in banning (and stopping individuals from using) lead paint, asbestos insulation, unsafe toys and flammable fabrics can hardly ignore its interest in banning cocaine, heroin, marijuana, methamphetamines and hallucinogens. Indeed, refusing to include drug use in the right of privacy, the Supreme Court has blessed state laws that prohibit even the sacramental use of peyote. With the exception of Alaska, state courts, like those of New York, have held that possession of marijuana in the home is not protected by the right of privacy.

Fiction: Legalization works well in European countries.

Fact: The ventures of Switzerland, England and the Netherlands into drug legalization have had disastrous consequences. Switzerland's "Needle Park," touted as a way to restrict a few hundred heroin addicts to a small area, turned into a grotesque tourist attraction of 20,000 heroin addicts and junkies, which had to be closed down before it infected the city of Zurich. England's foray into allowing any doctor to prescribe heroin was quickly curbed as heroin use increased.

The Netherlands legalized marijuana for anyone over age 15. Adolescent pot use there rose nearly 200 percent while it was dropping 66 percent in the United States. As crime and the availability of drugs like heroin and cocaine rose, and complaints from city residents about the decline in their quality of life multiplied, the Amsterdam city council moved to raise the age for legal purchase of marijuana from 16 to 18 and trim back the number of pot distribution shops in Amsterdam. Dutch persistence in selling pot has angered European neighbors because the Netherlands' wide-open attitude toward marijuana is believed to be spreading pot and other drugs beyond its borders. And Sweden, after a brief turn at permitting doctors to give drugs to addicts, in 1980 adopted the American policy of seeking a drug-free society. By 1988, Sweden had seen drug use among young Army conscripts drop 75 percent and current use by ninth graders fall 66 percent.

What is most disturbing about the arguments for legalization is that they glide over the impact such a policy would have on our children. The United States in 1996 is assuredly not the Garden of Eden of the Old Testament. Dealing with evil, including drugs, is part of the human experience. But there is a special obligation to protect our children from evil, and drugs are first and foremost an issue about our children. It is adolescent experimentation that leads to abuse and addiction.

Today, most kids don't use illicit drugs. But all children, particularly the poorest, are vulnerable to abuse and addiction. Russian roulette is not a game anyone should play. Legalizing drugs is not only playing Russian roulette with our children. It's slipping a couple of extra bullets in the chamber.

Should the Government Ban Cyberporn on the Internet?

"I was on my way to the White House when I encountered the topless woman," is how political columnist Leonard Pitts, Jr. (1998) encapsulates the problem of pornography on the Internet. Mistyping three letters led not to the official web site of the president's house, but a site promising access to all the "young teens, hot lesbians, and hard-core nymphomaniacs" for only $19.99 a month.

In just a few years the Internet has dramatically changed how the world communicates. This emerging technology has also greatly altered the longstanding pornography debate. For centuries governments have attempted to censor obscene materials. But by and large, pictures and books that appealed to the "prurient interest" were accessible in most communities, even though some effort was required. The Internet has dramatically changed accessibility; now allegedly obscene material is readily available (for a price though) by turning on the computer. And what pops up on the computer screen does not come wrapped in plain brown paper!

The arguments for and against some form of censorship on the Internet run as follows.

The opinion from Justice Stevens, written in neutral legal language, states the case for declaring the Communications Decency Act of 1996 an unconstitutional infringement on freedom of speech.

Congress responded in 1998 by passing the Child Online Protection Act, which was subsequently declared unconstitutional by a lower federal court. The statement from Enough Is Enough, employing fiery, moralistic rhetoric, makes the case for banning pornography form the Internet.

Pro	Con
Pornography is just about everywhere. This country now has over 20,000 outlets selling prosecutable, hard-core pornography, which would be found illegal by educated citizens in most American communities. In fact, there are more outlets for hard-core pornography in the U. S. than McDonald's restaurants.	The First Amendment protects freedom of speech. This Constitutional protection extends to unconventional speakers as well as those who reflect the political and social mainstream. Just because some find speech offensive is not a reason to suppress it.
Pornography is directly connected to crimes like rape and child molestation, and contributes to social problems like sexually transmitted diseases. Overall, pornography distorts societal values and fosters inappropriate attitudes (Enough Is Enough, 1999).	Congressional efforts to ban cyberporn are so vague that they exert a chilling effect on free speech. The economic costs imposed by the law will place an unconstitutional restraint on free expression. The content of speech reaching electronic mailboxes should not be limited to that which would be suitable for a sandbox.
The introduction of pornography to the information highway has made home computers the fastest growing and primary mode of distribution of illegal pornography. Laws must be passed that limit what children (and even adults) may inadvertently find on the Internet.	Emerging technologies will go a long way to ameliorate this problem. In the future, parents will be able to buy software programs that block objectionable Web sites from their children's computer screens.

World Wide Web Exercises

1. Using the search guide category http://dir.yahoo.com/Society_and_Culture/Issues_and_Causes/Civil_Rights/Censorship/Censorship_and_the_Net/Communications_Decency_Act/ locate two or more organizations on either side of the debate. Analyze the groups involved, using the concepts developed in the earlier article by Neubauer on interest groups.

2. Use the search engine of your choice and enter the search term **communications decency act** to locate at least one article on either side of the debate. Analyze the nature of the argumentation in terms of the concepts presented in the article in the Appendix entitled "Ground Rules for Proper Debating."

InfoTrac College Edition Exercises

1. After entering the search term **telecommunications act of 1996,** limit the search with the term **pornography.** Locate at least one article on each side of the issue. To what extent are the arguments similar to or different from those raised in the articles?

2. Using the search term **pornography laws, regulations,** locate at least one article on each side of the issue. To what extent is the debate over pornography best understood in terms of the ideological differences expressed by the crime control model versus the due process model of criminal justice articulated in the earlier article by Packer?

Making the Internet Safer for Children and Families

Statement of "Enough Is Enough"

Enough Is Enough respectfully submits this statement to the Senate Commerce, Science, and Transportation Committee to express our support for proposed legislation to require schools and libraries utilizing federal funds to install filtering and blocking technologies.

At its loftiest, the Internet is a useful tool, providing individuals access to academic research and historic documents they would otherwise never have the opportunity to see. Such access to information is a wonderful benefit of this relatively new technology. As with all innovations, however, the Internet also has a distinctly negative aspect.

At its basest, the Internet allows individuals to post and access the most antisocial and deviant materials imaginable. There are currently an estimated 100,000 commercial and noncommercial Internet sites containing graphic, hard-core pornography (Sterling Solutions, personal communication, March 2, 1998). Due to the legal loophole created by the Supreme Court's decision to strike down the indecency provision of the Communications Decency Act, children currently have startlingly easy access to the free material available at these sites. These sites may be found deliberately, by doing a word search for "sex," or inadvertently, by doing a word search for "toys" that results in "Horny Housewives and Their Boy Toys," or typing "whitehouse.com" instead of ".gov" and receiving a pornography site. The fact that obscenity and child pornography are illegal on the Internet does not eliminate their existence, nor does it prevent children from seeing, and being affected by, these images.

A great deal of research indicates that pornography has significant impact on the attitudes and values of adult males. A sampling of such findings includes:

1. Increased media viewing is associated with more stereotypical views, especially about gender, and exposure to "consistent and repeated stereotypical gender images shapes cognitive structures" (Allan and Coltrane, 1996). In other words, what individuals see affects how they think. When individuals view pornography, they become accustomed to viewing women in the manner in which pornography portrays them.

2. Individuals use pornography to inform and teach them about sexual behavior (Duncan, 1990; Duncan and Donnelly, 1991; Duncan and Nicholson, 1991). "The characteristic portrayal of women in pornography [is] as socially nondiscriminating, as hysterically euphoric in response to just about any sexual or pseudosexual stimulation, and as eager to accommodate seemingly any and every sexual request" (Zillman and Bryant, 1984). Pornography teaches individuals that degrading, humiliating treatment of women is a desirable sexual behavior.

3. At increasing levels of explicitness and depersonalization, an increase in sexual fantasizing occurs, and fantasies are more likely to be hostile and aggressive. Among consumers with established hostile-aggressive attitudes, a strong correlation exists between the consumption of depersonalized pornography and the amount of fantasizing by the consumer (Malamuth and McIlwraith, 1988, p. 766).

4. Due to the dehumanizing nature of pornography, exposure to even nonviolent pornography often leads to sexually callous attitudes (Saunders and Naus, 1993), including acceptance of rape myths, or the belief that rape victims are partially or even primarily responsible for sexual assault. The link between acceptance of rape myths and exposure to pornography stems from the premise that "pornography commodifies sex, that women become objects used for male pleasure, and that as objects of desire, they are to be acted on . . . [there is] acceptance of sexual behaviors as an objectified experience" (Allen, Emmers, Gebhardt, and Giery, 1995, p. 8).

5. "A nonrapist population will evidence increased sexual arousal to media-presented images of rape," because pornography typically depicts women responding positively when subjected to force (Donnerstein and Linz, 1986).

6. "Frequency of readership of sexually explicit magazines in a state [makes] a significant contribution to the prediction of rape rates" (Malamuth and McIlwraith, 1988, p. 754). Moderate exposure to pornography makes males less likely to convict for rape, and less likely to give a harsh sentence to a rapist if in fact convicted (Garcia, 1986, p. 382).

7. When the body physiologically responds to stimuli, the message to which it responds is rewarded, hence reinforced. Because pornography physiologically arouses the message recipient sexually (Allen, Alessio, Emmers, and Gebhardt, 1996), the antisocial messages about women, relationships, and behaviors of pornography are reinforced.

8. The ramifications of viewing pornography through the Internet are further magnified because research has shown that subjects who are computer literate and view computers in a positive manner tend to absorb information more quickly and consider that information more interesting than if that same information had been presented to them on paper (Wang, 1989, p. 1400).

Given the significant negative impact pornography has on adult males, common sense would indicate that pornography has an equal, if not greater, negative impact on children. The question, therefore, is not whether children, particularly curious adolescents, should be taught that such images are unrealistic, unhealthy, and harmful, or whether their parents should teach them to avoid these images on the Internet—both these questions must be answered with a resounding "yes." The question is whether the responsibility for protecting children from pornography should be entirely up to the diligence of parents and the self-discipline of children.

Children growing up in this "information age" must have the opportunity to learn in an age-appropriate manner. Adults have a duty to provide an environment for children in which they can develop critical thinking skills safely, without being assaulted by materials which they are in no way prepared to understand or process. The problem is not that children receive one antisocial message to counteract an abundance of prosocial messages; the problem is that the messages sent to children are increasingly antisocial. Those who would have us believe that confronting the images widely available on the Internet is somehow healthy for children, and will assist them in learning to distinguish between useful and useless, good and bad, moral and immoral, are ignoring the mountains of data proving children are significantly affected by images.

American society cannot afford to abandon its tradition of protecting children. Children are simply not equipped to handle many of the images they see on the Internet. Included in the social contract upon which this country was founded is a duty for citizens to ensure the safety of children. All members of society have a stake in the future of the culture, and the well being of children is inextricably linked to the well being of future society. Therefore, society must recognize that parents, despite all their efforts to teach and protect their children, simply cannot be with them 24 hours a day.

Society does seem to recognize a collective responsibility to protect children through laws prohibiting the sale of alcohol and tobacco to minors, and such responsibility is not abdicated when dealing with new technology. Parents must be assured that their efforts to teach and protect their children are not being undermined while their children are at school and that schools, acting *in loco parentis*, are doing everything within their power to support the positive values of parents and society. This certainly includes ensuring that Internet access is safe and protected, so children are not exposed to images that would shock most adults.

Public libraries, despite assertions by their trade group, the American Library Association (ALA), also have a duty to meet community standards when selecting materials for their shelves. This duty is not removed simply because the "shelf" in question is a cybershelf. Libraries who have attempted to reflect their communities' standards, in such areas as Loudoun County, Virginia and Kern County, California, have faced the opposition of organizations like the ALA, ACLU, and others. These self-proclaimed "civil liberties" groups believe as a matter of policy that children should have access to anything including, according to the ALA's Judith Krug, "pornography and bestiality" (Weinberg, 1997, p. 17). This ivory-tower mentality is in direct contrast to the views of librarians across the country who believe that filtering technologies do indeed reflect the standards of the communities they serve, communities who provide tax dollars that allow the existence of a public library.

Requiring certain conditions be met in order to receive tax dollars is neither inappropriate nor unprecedented. To place reasonable conditions, consistent with the values held by the vast majority of Americans, in this case, the protection of children, on the expenditure of tax dollars is appropriate. Making financial assistance contingent upon responsible choices does not prevent schools and libraries from utilizing the Internet; indeed, these institutions may use the Internet regardless of whether they receive federal funds. Rather, the reasonable condition of providing safe Internet access to children simply provides conditions under which these institutions may choose to accept tax dollars.

In conclusion, this legislation is the legitimate recognition of a civilized society's responsibility to protect innocent children from exploitation. Taxpayers are reasonable to expect their tax dollars be spent responsibly, and safe Internet access for children is one aspect of responsible spending. This legislation places no undue burden upon schools and libraries, but rather holds these publicly-funded institutions accountable for their choices in applying for and utilizing federal funds. Such an expectation is logical, reasonable, and necessary in the protection of children. We urge this Committee to stand courageously for this legislation to protect America's children. We stand ready to work with this Committee to provide information on the easy availability and significant harms of Internet pornography, as well as available solutions to protect children.

Reno, Attorney General of The United States, et al. v. American Civil Liberties Union et al. (No. 96-511 (1997))

Two provisions of the Communications Decency Act of 1996 (CDA) sought to protect minors from harmful material on the Internet. The U.S. District Court for the Eastern District of Pennsylvania struck down the law as unconstitutional and the government appealed.

[Justice] Stevens delivered the opinion of the Court.

At issue is the constitutionality of two statutory provisions enacted to protect minors from "indecent" and "patently offensive" communications on the Internet. Notwithstanding the legitimacy and importance of the congressional goal of protecting children from harmful materials, we agree with the three judge District Court that the statute abridges "the freedom of speech" protected by the First Amendment. . . .

The Internet

The Internet is an international network of interconnected computers. . . . The Internet is "a unique and wholly new medium of worldwide human communication."

The Internet has experienced "extraordinary growth." . . . About 40 million people used the Internet at the time of trial, a number that is expected to mushroom to 200 million by 1999.

Individuals can obtain access to the Internet from many different sources. . .

From the publishers' point of view, it constitutes a vast platform from which to address and hear from a worldwide audience of millions of readers, viewers, researchers, and buyers. . . . Publishers may either make their material available to the entire pool of Internet users, or confine access to a selected group, such as those willing to pay for the privilege. . . .

Sexually Explicit Material

Sexually explicit material on the Internet includes text, pictures, and chat and "extends from the modestly titillating to the hardest core." These files are created, named, and posted in the same manner as material that is not sexually explicit, and may be accessed either deliberately or unintentionally during the course of an imprecise search. "Once a provider posts its content on the Internet, it cannot prevent that content from entering any community." Thus, for example, "when the UCR/California Museum of Photography posts to its Web site nudes by Edward Weston and Robert Mapplethorpe to announce that its new exhibit will travel to Baltimore and New York City, those images are available not only in Los Angeles, Baltimore, and New York City, but also in Cincinnati, Mobile, or Beijing—wherever Internet users live. Similarly, the safer sex instructions that Critical Path posts to its Web site, written in street language so that the teenage receiver can understand them, are available not just in Philadelphia, but also in Provo and Prague."

. . . Though such material is widely available, users seldom encounter such content accidentally. "A document's title or a description of the document will usually appear before the document itself . . . and in many cases the user will receive detailed information about a site's content before he or she need take the step to access the document.

Almost all sexually explicit images are preceded by warnings as to the content." For that reason, the "odds are slim" that a user would enter a sexually explicit site by accident. Unlike communications received by radio or television, "the receipt of information on the Internet requires a series of affirmative steps more deliberate and directed than merely turning a dial. A child requires some sophistication and some ability to read to retrieve material and thereby to use the Internet unattended."

Systems have been developed to help parents control the material that may be available on a home computer with Internet access. A system may either limit a computer's access to an approved list of sources that have been identified as containing no adult material, it may block designated inappropriate sites, or it may attempt to block messages containing identifiable objectionable features . . . the evidence indicates that "a reasonably effective method by which parents can prevent their children from accessing sexually explicit and other material which parents may believe is inappropriate for their children will soon be available."

Age Verification

The problem of age verification differs for different uses of the Internet. The District Court categorically determined that there "is no effective way to determine the identity or the age of a user who is accessing material through e-mail, mail exploders, newsgroups or chat rooms. . . . "

The Telecommunications Act of 1996 was an unusually important legislative enactment. . . . Title V—known as the "Communications Decency Act of 1996" (CDA)—contains . . . the two statutory provisions challenged in this case. They are informally described as the "indecent transmission" provision and the "patently offensive display" provision.

The first . . . prohibits the knowing transmission of obscene or indecent messages to any recipient under 18 years of age. . . .

The second provision, . . . prohibits the knowing sending or displaying of patently offensive messages in a manner that is available to a person under 18 years of age. . . .

The vagueness of the CDA is a matter of special concern for two reasons. First, the CDA is a content-based regulation of speech. The vagueness of such a regulation raises special First Amendment concerns because of its obvious chilling effect on free speech. . . . Second, the CDA is a criminal statute. In addition to the opprobrium and stigma of a criminal conviction, the CDA threatens violators with penalties including up to two years in prison for each act of violation. The severity of criminal sanctions may well cause speakers to remain silent rather than communicate even arguably unlawful words, ideas, and images. . . .

The Government argues that the statute is no more vague than the obscenity standard this Court established in *Miller v. California,* (1973). But that is not so. In *Miller,* this Court reviewed a criminal conviction against a commercial vendor who mailed brochures containing pictures of sexually explicit activities to individuals who had not requested such materials. . . . Having struggled for some time to establish a definition of obscenity, we set forth in *Miller* the test for obscenity that controls to this day: "(a) whether the average person, applying contemporary community standards would find that the work, taken as a whole, appeals to the prurient interest; (b) whether the work depicts or describes, in a patently offensive way, sexual conduct specifically defined by the applicable state law; and (c) whether the work, taken as a whole, lacks serious literary, artistic, political, or scientific value. . . . "

The second prong of the *Miller* test . . . contains a critical requirement that is omitted from the CDA: that the proscribed material be "specifically defined by the applicable state law." This requirement reduces the vagueness inherent in the open ended term "patently offensive" as used in the CDA. Moreover, the *Miller* definition is limited to "sexual conduct," whereas the CDA extends also to include 1) "excretory activities" as well as 2) "organs" of both a sexual and excretory nature. . . .

Each of *Miller's* additional two prongs—1) that, taken as a whole, the material appeal to the "prurient" interest, and 2) that it "lac[k] serious literary, artistic, political, or scientific value"—

critically limits the uncertain sweep of the obscenity definition. The second requirement is particularly important because, unlike the "patently offensive" and "prurient interest" criteria, it is not judged by contemporary community standards. . . . This "societal value" requirement, absent in the CDA, allows appellate courts to impose some limitations and regularity on the definition by setting, as a matter of law, a national floor for socially redeeming value. The Government's contention that courts will be able to give such legal limitations to the CDA's standards is belied by *Miller's* own rationale for having juries determine whether material is "patently offensive" according to community standards: that such questions are essentially ones of fact.

In contrast to *Miller* and our other previous cases, the CDA thus presents a greater threat of censoring speech that, in fact, falls outside the statute's scope. Given the vague contours of the coverage of the statute, it unquestionably silences some speakers whose messages would be entitled to constitutional protection. That danger provides further reason for insisting that the statute not be overly broad. The CDA's burden on protected speech cannot be justified if it could be avoided by a more carefully drafted statute.

We are persuaded that the CDA lacks the precision that the First Amendment requires when a statute regulates the content of speech. In order to deny minors access to potentially harmful speech, the CDA effectively suppresses a large amount of speech that adults have a constitutional right to receive and to address to one another. That burden on adult speech is unacceptable if less restrictive alternatives would be at least as effective in achieving the legitimate purpose that the statute was enacted to serve.

In evaluating the free speech rights of adults, we have made it perfectly clear that "[s]exual expression which is indecent but not obscene is protected by the First Amendment. . . . "[W]here obscenity is not involved, we have consistently held that the fact that protected speech may be offensive to some does not justify its suppression." Indeed, . . . "the fact that society may find speech offensive is not a sufficient reason for suppressing it."

It is true that we have repeatedly recognized the governmental interest in protecting children from harmful materials. . . . But that interest does not justify an unnecessarily broad suppression of speech addressed to adults. As we have explained, the Government may not "reduc[e] the adult population . . . to . . . only what is fit for children. . . . "[R]egardless of the strength of the government's interest" in protecting children, "[t]he level of discourse reaching a mailbox simply cannot be limited to that which would be suitable for a sandbox. . . . "

The District Court found that at the time of trial existing technology did not include any effective method for a sender to prevent minors from obtaining access to its communications on the Internet without also denying access to adults. . . . By contrast, the District Court found that "[d]espite its limitations, currently available user based software suggests that a reasonably effective method by which parents can prevent their children from accessing sexually explicit and other material which parents may believe is inappropriate for their children will soon be widely available. . . . "

The breadth of the CDA's coverage is wholly unprecedented. . . . the scope of the CDA is not limited to commercial speech or commercial entities. Its open-ended prohibitions embrace all nonprofit entities and individuals posting indecent messages or displaying them on their own computers in the presence of minors. The general, undefined terms "indecent" and "patently offensive" cover large amounts of nonpornographic material with serious educational or other value. . . .

Under the CDA, a parent allowing her 17-year-old to use the family computer to obtain information on the Internet that she, in her parental judgment, deems appropriate could face a lengthy prison term. . . . Similarly, a parent who sent his 17-year-old college freshman information on birth control via e-mail could be incarcerated even though neither he, his child, nor anyone in their home community, found the material "indecent" or "patently offensive," if the college town's community thought otherwise. . . .

Part XI

Debating the Criminal Justice System

Faced with the problem of soaring drug prosecutions, insufficient jail space, and the absence of intermediate sanctions programs, two judges sought to implement a drug court. Their efforts required the active cooperation of a number of other agencies (as well as the acquiescence of others). At the center of these efforts was the drug court team consisting of a judge, treatment provider, district attorney, and public defender. Also involved were pretrial services (a division of probation), Spanish interpreters, and the Sheriff's in-custody treatment program. Overseeing the program was a steering committee as well as the Countywide Criminal Justice coordination committee (Torres and Deschenes, 1997).

The implementation of drug courts in Los Angeles County illustrates the difficulty of changing the "criminal justice system." To be sure the Los Angeles County criminal justice system is unique, if for no other reason than pure size. It is arguably the largest in the world. This area is home to over nine million people representing virtually every racial, ethnic, and religious group on the face of the planet. Every year the citizens report over 700,000 crimes. In turn, over 17,000 full-time sworn police officers make 450,000 arrests, which are prosecuted by 988 district attorneys, with over 20,000 inmates held daily in nine different jails.

But apart from the issue of scope, the types of challenges the two judges faced in trying to change the "system" are not unique. Whether the population served is 9,000 or 9,000,000, change requires the actions of numerous separate agencies. Newspaper stories highlighting the gaps and cracks in the criminal justice system are fairly commonplace. While not necessarily typical, they do serve to dramatize why it is important to examine the criminal justice system with a broad perspective.

Trying to gain a perspective on the criminal justice system is important because virtually all of the most pressing issues in debating crime occur at the junctures between separate and independent organizations. Whether efforts are aimed at reducing violent juvenile crime, increasing the prosecution of domestic violence offenders, or implementing a drug court, coordinated efforts by different parts of the system are required.

Viewing criminal justice as a "system," though, is a challenge in itself. One key finding that emerges from viewing the system from a broad perspective is how large it is. Federal, state, and local governments spend more than $103 billion for civil and criminal justice (an average of $397 for every resident of the country). Moreover, those who work in the criminal justice system typically focus on the immediate tasks in front of them. Seldom do they have the time to view the system from the outside looking in.

In debating (and analyzing) the criminal justice system, four key characteristics stand out: heavy workload, fragmentation, lack of coordination, and isolation.

Heavy Workload

A key feature of the contemporary criminal justice system is the large workload. Every year in the United States,

- law enforcement officials make over 15 million arrests;
- state courts process over 85 million cases;
- jails detain almost 600,000 suspects;
- prisons incarcerate over 1,300,000 inmates; and
- probation and parole officials supervise over 4,000,000 people.

Thus, to some the most critical consideration is that the system is overworked, with too many cases being processed by too few officials.

Fragmentation

The second key feature of the criminal justice system is fragmentation. Literally tens of thousands of separate federal, state, and local agencies are involved in law enforcement, courts, and corrections. Most of these agencies are governmental, but others are private. Again, some statistics (primarily nonfederal) provide documentation.

- 18,769 state and local law enforcement agencies employ over 660,000 sworn officers.
- 2,343 prosecutors' offices are staffed by 71,000 attorneys, investigators, and support staff.
- 17,000 courts are presided over by 28,000 judges supported by thousands of clerks, bailiffs, secretaries, court reporters, etc.
- 3,304 jails employ 227,000 guards and support personnel.
- 1,500 correctional facilities are staffed by 347,320 prison guards and administrators.

Lack of Coordination

A third key feature of the criminal justice system in the United States is the lack of coordination. The fragmentation of the system into numerous separate and independent (sometimes fiercely so) agencies means that the work of police, courts, and corrections is seldom coherent. Most immediately, the lack of coordination produces tensions and conflicts. In a given locale, for example, it is typical to find that some law enforcement agencies do not readily cooperate with others.

The tensions and conflicts inherent in the criminal justice system are most obvious when officials play the criminal-justice blame game. When something goes wrong, officials are quick to defend their own agencies while publicly condemning the misdeeds of other components of the criminal justice system. In the meantime, the general public expects somebody to be responsible for running the "war on crime." Instead, they find bickering between criminal justice officials more interested in blaming others than working toward a solution.

Isolation

The final characteristic of the criminal justice system in the United States is isolation. Over the last century, a variety of factors have contributed to an increasing separation of criminal justice agencies from the larger community. For example, the emphasis on police professionalism (which grew out of a concern about police corruption) created a barrier between police officers and political institutions. Likewise, as the law has become more complicated, judges and lawyers have become more isolated from citizens. And based on the time-honored American principle of NIMBY (Not in My Back Yard), correction facilities have been built in geographically remote areas, far from the cities where most inmates live.

In ending the book by taking a broad overview of the criminal justice system, we examine two issues. The first topic for debate asks, boldly: "Is the Criminal Justice System a Failure?" While many people, almost instinctively, respond in the affirmative, a closer examination reveals that assessments of "failure" are often contradictory, reflecting competing ideological positions.

The second topic shifts from the debate format to the broader endeavor of "Analyzing the Criminal Justice System." We examine two commonly mentioned changes in the criminal justice system: community-oriented policing, and harsher sentences for drug offenders. While these "reforms" are very different, the articles emphasize the difficulties of spanning numerous criminal justice agencies.

World Wide Web Resources

Web Guides

http://dir.yahoo.com/Government/Law/Criminal_Justice/

Searching the Web

drug court, injustice

Useful URLs

Bureau of Justice Assistance Evaluation Web Site: BJA provides planners, researchers, and local practitioners with resources for evaluating criminal justice programs.   http://www.bja.evaluationwebsite.org/

Criminal Justice Education: Provides information and links on researching, educating, and career preparation in the fields of criminology and criminal justice.
http://www.asweb.unco.edu/depts/sociology/plreich/

Justice Information Center: Extensive resources on criminal and juvenile justice provided by the National Criminal Justice Reference Service (NCJRS).
http://www.ncjrs.org/

National Archive of Criminal Justice Data: Archives, processes, and provides access to computer-readable criminal justice data collections for research and instruction.   http://www.icpsr.umich.edu/NACJD/

Fun Sites

Anatomy of a Murder: A Trip Through Our Nation's Legal Justice System: Fictional account of a defendant's criminal prosecution with detailed information about the process of the justice system.
http://library.thinkquest.org/2760/homep.htm

Justice: Denied: Monthly magazine which profiles the wrongly convicted and seeks assistance to free them. Also features current information about the justice system and prominent national cases.   http://www.justicedenied.org/

The Injustice Line: True reports of injustice in the U.S. and elsewhere, plus extensive links to other civil rights sites.   http://www.injusticeline.com/

RiteAway: Dedicated to assuring prompt, equal, and quality assistance and treatment for victims of crime or injustice.   http://www.riteaway.org/

Think Again: Artists who strike back at mainstream ideas that perpetuate injustice.
http://www.agitart.org/

Nonviolence Networks: Purpose is to train and educate future generations of youth to resolve conflict and to effectively address social injustice.
http://www.nonviolence.net/

InfoTrac College Edition Resources

Basic Searches

criminal justice system, criminal justice administration, drug courts

Issue 19

Is the Criminal Justice System a Failure?

- **Justice Overruled: Unmasking the Criminal Justice System** *(by Burton Katz)*
- **Don't Pee on My Leg and Tell Me It's Raining** *(by Judy Sheindlin)*

- *Protecting Yourself from the Criminal Justice System in the 1990's*
- *Texans for Equal Justice*
- *The Failure of the Criminal Justice System*
- *Injustice Studies*

These are the titles of some of the books and Web sites I discovered while searching the Internet using the phrase **criminal justice system**. To be sure, some of the sites provide information on how the system works. But as these provocative titles make clear, public discussions of the criminal justice system are often linked with words like *failure* and *injustice*. Indeed, this is a prime theme on radio talk shows.

The apparent broad consensus that the criminal justice system is a failure (and probably unjust as well) begins to break down, though, when one probes some of the specifics offered. The adherents of the crime control model and proponents of the due process model differ as to why the system is a "failure" and therefore offer clashing remedies. Consider, for example, the meaning of "injustice." The crime control model quickly points to guilty defendants who have been acquitted. The due process model, on the other hand, immediately singles out innocent suspects who have been convicted. Consider also the issue of equal justice under law. The crime control model portrays allegations of racism as an excuse for lawbreaking. The due process model, not surprisingly, views racial injustice as a primary problem.

In short, allegations that the criminal justice system is a failure and/or unjust mask underlying disagreements about what are the shortcomings and what are the injustices. Competing schools of thought differ on the specifics of particular issues (the exclusionary rule and deterrence, to name just two). Perhaps more fundamentally, different camps offer competing agendas. Thus, rather than provide the pro and con debate format used throughout this book, I have selected two works that represent contrasting thinking within these two broad camps. Let's call it:

The Ten Top Ways to Correct the Failures of the Criminal Justice System

Crime Control Model *Guilty: The Collapse of Criminal Justice*	Due Process Model *National Criminal Justice Commission*
Simplify and clarify search-and-seizure law.	Decrease the reliance on prisons as the primary response to criminal behavior.
The *Miranda* ruling should be abandoned.	Replace the war on drugs with a policy of harm reduction.
Speedy-trial statutes should be abolished because they only protect the guilty.	Balance criminal justice spending with resources spent on other civic activities.
The right to an attorney should not be a factor in the investigative stage, but only in the pretrial and trial stages.	Restore the internal balance of the criminal justice system so judges have more discretion at sentencing, and victims of crime receive better treatment by the court system.
The jury should be instructed that they may consider the defendant's failure to testify during trial.	Commission an independent clearinghouse to gather and report objective criminal justice information to the public.
Defendants seeking pretrial discovery should be asked to place a written version of their story in a sealed envelope.	At all levels of government, create crime councils to develop a coordinated anti-crime strategy
Peremptory challenges should be limited to three or fewer to avoid stacked juries.	Reduce violence by using innovative approaches developed in the field of public health, and reduce the harmful effects of violence by passing gun-control legislation at the federal level.
Unanimous jury verdicts should be replaced by ten-to-two or eleven-to-one verdicts in criminal trials.	Commit ourselves to reducing poverty in order to reduce street crime.
American judges should be allowed a more active role in the courtroom to assure that the process is swift, and sure.	Eliminate racial bias and reduce racial disparity within the criminal justice system.
Reevaluate our fundamental philosophy and procedures because an ever increasing number of major criminal cases have been reversed on technical (and often irrational) grounds.	Shift ourselves from an agenda of "war" to an agenda of "peace."

The excerpt from *Guilty: The Collapse of Criminal Justice* highlights disorder in the courts. The author, Harold Rothwax (a longtime judge in New York), argues that reducing the rights of criminal defendants will result in more guilty defendants (O. J. Simpson, for example) going to prison.

The article "Key Findings" stresses the need for a fundamental shift in the direction of U.S. crime policy. The author, the National Criminal Justice Commission (a self-appointed bipartisan commission), stresses the need to spend money not on prisons but on crime prevention.

World Wide Web Exercises

1. Use the search engine of your choice and enter the search term **criminal justice system.** Identify two or more sites that offer a critique of the failures of the criminal justice system. To what extent do these critiques present contrasting diagnoses of what is wrong?

2. Choose a search engine and enter the search term **injustice + crime.** Locate two or more Web sites that provide different perspectives on the topic. Do these sites define injustice in similar or different ways? Do they use individual cases to bolster their positions? Are they more likely to define injustice from the perspective of the victim or the defendant?

InfoTrac College Edition Exercises

1. Using the search term **Harold Rothwax** and/or **Harold J. Rothwax,** read two or more reviews of Judge Rothwax's book *Guilty: The Collapse of Criminal Justice.* Do the reviews offer similar or different reactions to the book? To what extent can reactions be understood within the opposing concepts of the crime control and due process models of criminal justice?

2. Using the search term **drug courts,** identify two or more articles that discuss implementation of drug courts. In what ways are the experiences similar to or different from those of Los Angeles County (discussed in the section opening)? What do these findings suggest about obstacles to criminal justice reform?

Key Findings

National Criminal Justice Commission

Failure

The American criminal justice system has grown spectacularly in recent years. This growth has failed to make the nation safe.

The number of people locked up has tripled since 1980. There are now 1.5 million people in prisons and jails nationwide. An additional 3.6 million people are on probation or parole. . . .

To sustain current increases in incarceration, the nation must open three 500-bed prisons every week.

The expansion of the justice system has had little, if any, effect on crime. Crime rates have been stable or slightly declining for the last twenty years. . . .

Overall, high rates of incarceration have little or no correlation to rates of crime. States with high rates of incarceration may or may not have high rates of crime. States with low rates of crime may or may not have high rates of incarceration.

The best that can be said is that the enormous increase in law enforcement caused a marginal decrease in crime. The worst that can be said is that the expansion did nothing for crime, but caused terrible collateral harm on society by draining money and ruining lives.

Costs

The criminal justice system is extraordinarily expensive. Taxpayers are getting a poor return on their investment.

Source: National Criminal Justice Commission. "Key Findings" http://www.ncianet.org/ncia/ Used with permission.

The nation spends about $100 billion annually on law enforcement—more than the entire combined federal budgets for Head Start, job training programs, AFDC, Housing Assistance and Food Stamps. . . .

While the real money spent on the "safety net" has decreased, the money spent on the "dragnet" has risen. Law enforcement has become a primary government response to social and economic stress.

The average cost of incarcerating a single prisoner for a year is $22,000. The average cost of building a new prison cell is $54,000 excluding debt service on money borrowed to finance construction. The average cost of incarcerating a 20-year-old for life is $1.8 million.

Prison costs are rising faster than any other category of state spending. Increases in prison spending average twice as high as increases in education spending. . . .

Scare Tactics

People use the crime issue for personal, financial or political gain. They play on people's desire for safety to sell them things they do not need.

The crime scares of recent years have been a fiction. The current appearance of solving the crime problem is nothing more than politicians heightening people's fears in order to assuage them. Crime rates have been essentially stable since the 1970s.

Politicians use a "bait and switch" scam in which they treat rare and horrifying crimes as if they are typical—switching voter outrage at the horrible crime to punishment of lesser and nonviolent offenders.

Most offenders are not dangerous. Eighty-seven percent of offenses reported nationwide are nonviolent; only three percent of reported offenses result in any injury.

There are simply not enough serious violent offenders to account for the massive increases in law enforcement. 84 percent of the increase in admissions to prison since 1980 were nonviolent offenders.

A representative sample of state prison inmates showed that 53 percent were convicted of crimes that Americans deem "petty"—such as shoplifting $10 of merchandise or smoking marijuana. In the federal system, over one-fifth of the prisoners are classified as low grade drug offenders—people with no prior commitment, no record of violence and no involvement with sophisticated criminal activity. . . .

It is politically safe for politicians to attack criminals because nobody likes them and nobody defends them. There is no natural counter-lobby to assert itself against the crime control lobby. Focusing civilian fear on crime is a politically safe distraction from issues like health care or deficit reduction that attract lobbyists from every angle.

Fear of crime is different from crime itself. To improve our crime policies, we must move perceptions closer to reality.

Race

The criminal justice system falls most heavily on minorities.

Relative to their populations, there are seven times as many minorities in prison as whites.

In many cities, about half of young African-American men are under the control of the criminal justice system . . . Almost one in three young African-American men in the age group 20–29 is under criminal justice supervision on any given day.

Rates of offending are higher in impoverished minority communities, but not high enough to explain the disparity. Rates of offending in middle-class minority communities are the same as the general population.

Racial disparities are better explained by disparate enforcement practices than higher rates of crime in minority communities. . . .

As minorities move through the system, they encounter slightly harsher treatment at every step. Marginal disparities at arrest are combined with marginal disparities at the bail decision, the charging decision, the verdict and the sentence—by the end of the process, the disparity is considerable.

Involvement in the system starts a vicious cycle. A person arrested once is branded an ex-offender for life. The person is pointed to as an example of how many people in the neighborhood are bad, or how many are repeat offenders. Having a criminal record also makes it more difficult to find a job.

Social Disorder

The "tough" model of crime control breeds social disorder and civil disharmony, which, in turn, leads to crime. The criminal justice system cannot be used to conform all antisocial behavior, from mental illness to teenage rebelliousness.

In some urban areas, so many young men are removed by the criminal justice system that it is increasingly difficult to maintain the two-parent family as a bulwark against crime.

Prison has ceased to function as an effective deterrent in some communities because it is overused. Many young men regard time in prison as a rite of passage. As ever more young men are incarcerated, the ethos of the correctional facility—the accommodation to violence, erosion of sensitivity, generalized hostility—have come out to the streets and made them more dangerous.

Women and children have suffered disproportionately from the imprisonment binge. Women represent the fastest growing classification of prisoners nationwide, with most offenses being nonviolent property offenses such as shoplifting, check forgery or substance abuse.

Incarcerating women often separates children from their primary care givers. Three-fourths of women in prison are single mothers with sole custody of an average of two children. Imprisoning the mother for a minor offense—even for a short period—harms the innocent child.

Searches and seizures that were unthinkable a generation ago are now commonplace. Incidents of overzealous enforcement like Ruby Ridge and Waco provide a glimpse of the kind of power routinely used by the police in minority communities.

Solutions

The problems can be solved; America can be made a safer place to live. We know the proven, cost-effective solutions; we need only choose to use them.

There are effective noncustodial ways to punish marginal offenders. Intensive probation, boot camps, in- or outpatient drug rehabilitation and community service are just a few of the options. Many of these options are much less expensive than prison and more effective at reducing recidivism.

If just half of the nonviolent prisoners were not incarcerated, about $8 billion would be saved annually on custodial operating costs alone. This money could be used to fund less expensive punishment and prevention programs that in the long run can prevent crime with fewer negative collateral effects on communities.

Under this scenario, the savings generated each year for crime prevention significantly exceeds all the money the 1994 federal crime control act allocates to crime prevention over six years. . . .

Crime prevention programs are cheaper and more effective at fighting crime in the long run than incarceration. We need to broaden our definition of "crime-fighting" to incorporate nontraditional means to improve public safety.

Early Childhood Development

The Head Start program returns about $7 in benefits for every dollar invested. Children born in poverty who attended a Head Start preschool program have half as many criminal arrests, higher earnings and property wealth, and a greater commitment to family than similarly situated people who did not attend a program. Head Start reaches fewer than half of the eligible children due to funding constraints.

Drug Treatment

A comprehensive study of drug treatment in California found that every dollar spent on substance abuse treatment saved taxpayers over seven dollars in reduced crime and health care costs. The study also found that the level of criminal activity by program participants decreased by 66 percent following treatment; the number of crimes involving a weapon or physical force decreased by 71 percent. . . . Current capacity of drug treatment facilities nationwide is inadequate to handle the need for treatment.

Recreation

Teenagers will find ways to entertain themselves—by breaking windows and drinking liquor if not by playing ball. Parks and recreational opportunities like midnight basketball are proven effective at reducing crime. . . .

Education

Education is the route to decent jobs and out of crime. In 1991, for the first time in U.S. history, cities spent more on law enforcement than education. Jurisdictions around the country are cutting education budgets because they lack sufficient funds while unquestioningly setting aside huge sums for law enforcement.

Job Training

Vocational training for adolescents and dislocated workers can help reduce crime by enhancing employment opportunities.

The Labor Market

Job training is useless if there are no jobs. . . . We must make a national commitment to genuine full employment.

Judgment Day: A Demand for Common Sense in the Courtroom

Harold J. Rothwax

What have we learned from the O. J. Simpson trial about the pursuit of justice in our society?

- That power and money have the effect of creating elaborate screens that hide the truth.

- That jury selection is hostage to peremptory challenges that, with the help of scientific jury experts, can mold a jury in the hope that it will be swayed by emotion and innuendo, not fact.

- That trial by media is a real specter in the age of unrestrained tabloid journalism.

- That clever defense attorneys, coupled with passive judges, can fashion "evidence" out of innuendo.

- That the only person who is protected from having to explain himself and his actions is the very person who is accused of the crime—and who may know the most about it.

- That juries are fragile bodies, subject to emotion, suggestion, and speculation and that often juries are comprised of citizens who lack the capacity to intelligently evaluate evidence.

- That the American courtroom is dangerously out of order.

A criminal trial is society's way of seeking justice when the life and liberty of its citizens are jeopardized. Can we be satisfied that this happened in the Simpson trial? The answer is a resounding no!

I am not afraid to say what is unquestionably true: that justice was not done in this case. O. J. Simpson is free. He will never be criminally prosecuted for these murders again. And society is left with the bitter taste of perverse justice. By law, Simpson is not guilty. Our system, however, is guilty, and it is the people who are punished.

This is my thirty-seventh year in criminal law—twelve years as a defense attorney and twenty-five years as a trial judge presiding over criminal cases. For as long as I can remember, practicing criminal law and being involved with this process is what I wanted to do. Nothing, it seemed to me, could be more exciting and stimulating, intellectually and personally, than being present at a meeting between the state and its citizens at moments of extreme conflict. And nothing could be more important.

But I am often discouraged. Over the last thirty-five years, since the advent of the Warren Court (which reacted to abuses that existed at that time), we have witnessed changes in constitutional interpretation and procedural statutes that have substantially altered the balance of advantage in criminal cases to favor the accused. As a result, we have made unduly elaborate and effective the means of blocking the proof of guilt.

The stories in *Guilty: The Collapse of Criminal Justice* have illustrated how complex, arbitrary, irrational, and incomprehensible our law can be—how, increasingly, it resembles a lottery. We now exclude highly reliable and probative evidence routinely, and we impose unnecessary, unreasonable, and arbitrary limits on the power of the police. We authorize our lawyers to engage in truth-defeating trickery and distortion.

This book is replete with cases where an obviously guilty, and often violent, criminal goes free.

Source: From *Guilty: The Collapse of the Criminal Justice System* by Harold J. Rothwax. © 1996 by Harold J. Rothwax. Reprinted by permission of Random House, Inc.

These results, and the shoddy reasoning that is frequently relied on to support them, should be intolerable in a civilized (and menaced) society with a highly developed system of law.

In spite of what must be an increasing awareness of these defects and deficits, we somehow, against all the evidence, continue to repeat the mantra that ours is the "best" system in the world. Whether we say this out of arrogance, ignorance, or inertia is unclear.

To the citizenry, the system is largely unknowable and inaccessible—and we have been taught from earliest childhood to view it with reverence and without question. My law school students are quick to mock the Ten Commandments—or at least some of them—but the first ten Amendments to the Constitution, the Bill of Rights, is holy writ and not to be questioned or critically examined.

Those working within the system are self-interested or have institutional interests they are determined to defend. They are often quick to question the motives, values, or competence of those who would challenge things as they are. Some principles, procedures, and practices are held to be sacrosanct.

This book is a call to look at our system afresh: to see it clearly; to review its workings; to rethink its present principles, prescriptions, and practices; and to ask *whether we have* the "best" system—or whether we deserve better.

Although we are a democracy, we have deferred these questions to our high priests (the judges), who tell us the meaning of our bible (the Constitution). Perhaps because it seems so difficult to change it, we are disinclined to question it. And when dissident voices are raised, there is a concerted cacophony that is quick to question their motives and values.

Because of the power of precedent, even the U.S. Supreme Court is reluctant to overrule holdings where it has doubts as to whether its decisions serve their intended purposes. That's how the exclusionary rule and the *Miranda* rule, among others, become fixed and immovable icons in our temple of justice. It appears that we are locked in place.

England, in the light of its experience, has done away with the peremptory challenge and the unanimous verdict and now permits a jury to draw an adverse inference from a defendant's silence, but we have not even begun to seriously contemplate such changes. There is a scarcity of comparative studies of the criminal justice systems of the British Commonwealth, Scandinavia, and the countries of Western Europe. The fine scholars who work in this area are largely ignored by the legal profession and legislators. A feeling of superiority in relation to these systems possesses us. As Professor Rudolf Schlesinger has written, this feeling "seems to grow in direct proportion to the ever-increasing weight of the accumulating evidence demonstrating the total failure of our system of criminal justice."

The public dissatisfaction with the administration of criminal justice today is well founded. It reflects a proper perception that our courts have substituted formalism for fairness, and, in the process, they are burying the truth. There is also, I believe, a growing, though as yet unexpressed, dissatisfaction on the part of our trial judges.

Not long ago I attended a judicial conference where one of the subjects on which we were lectured concerned a notice statute. The statute required the prosecutor to provide notice to the defendant, within fifteen days of his arraignment, of any statements the prosecutor intended to introduce at trial and of any prior identifications that he would be relying upon. The highest appellate court in New York had construed the statute to *preclude* the prosecutor from using this evidence if the notice was filed after the fifteenth day or, even if filed in a timely fashion, if it was incomplete in the details it provided. Even if the defendant had not been harmed or prejudiced in any way, the appellate court held that the evidence—the truth—had to be kept from the jury. As a result of these rulings, many violent felons have been released. . . .

For two hours we listened to three erudite instructors talk about when such notice is required and what the notice must contain. At the end of their talk, I rose to thank our teachers for their presentation, and went on to bemoan the fact that as we approach the end of the twentieth century, American jurists had to be preoccupied by such arcana. I said it was obscene that we were releasing those charged with serious crimes, without regard to the evidence of their guilt, because a notice was a day late or a fact short. There was no relationship or proportionality between the remedy and the "wrong." None of our core values were expressed in such a jurisprudence. It was a search for perfection without regard to consequence. We were exalting formalism at the expense of substance and safety. It was wrong.

To my surprise, my colleagues in the audience responded enthusiastically to these remarks. A number of them later approached me and told how frustrated they feel by the meaningless obstacles that are strewn in their path. These are judges who take their jobs seriously. Unfortunately, the system gets in the way.

There are no simple solutions to the disorder of our courts. But I believe that our courts would work better if we made the following ten basic changes:

1. The vast and unknowable search-and-seizure laws, based loosely on the Fourth Amendment, must be simplified and clarified to prevent a guessing game on the street and in the courtroom. As long as the law remains unknowable, there is no justification for the mandatory exclusionary rule.

2. The *Miranda* ruling is an unnecessary overreaction to past abuses that videotapes and other technology can now preclude, and it should be abandoned.

3. Speedy-trial statutes, based on a precise formula of days and weeks, only protect those who are most interested in getting away with crimes and manipulating the system. Reasonableness, not a ticking clock, should determine speed.

4. The right to an attorney should not be a factor in the investigative stage, but only in the pretrial and trial stages. Asking questions and receiving answers from a suspect is a legitimate aspect of crime-solving.

5. If it appears from the evidence that the defendant could reasonably be expected to explain or deny evidence presented against him, the jury should be instructed that they may consider his failure to do so as tending to indicate the truth of such evidence.

6. If defendants seek pretrial discovery from the state, they should be asked to place a written version of their story in a sealed envelope before receiving that discovery to preclude manipulation and lying.

7. Peremptory challenges should be limited to three or fewer to avoid stacked juries.

8. Unanimous jury verdicts are less likely to speak the truth than majority verdicts, and should be replaced by ten-to-two or eleven-to-one verdicts in criminal trials.

9. American judges should be allowed a more active role in the courtroom to assure that the process is swift, sure, and according to the laws of evidence.

10. The fact that, in recent years, an ever-increasing number of major criminal cases have had decisions reversed on technical (and often irrational) grounds, unrelated to our core values, demands we reevaluate our fundamental philosophy and procedures.

Finally, we should return to the premise that the criminal justice system is engaged in a search for the truth. For without truth, what can be the point of lofty principles? Without truth, how can our society properly maintain the ideals, values, and principles upon which it was founded? If, as Disraeli said, justice is truth in action, it's time for us to act.

Issue 20

Analyzing Criminal Justice Reforms

Discussions of reforming the criminal justice system tend to alternate between two contradictory positions. On the one side are the prophets of eternal doom, who emphasize that nothing works. On the other side are the forces of eternal optimism, who have discovered the latest "magic bullet" that will be the cure-all. What these two camps share in common is a lack of realistic expectations. The skeptics who argue that nothing works often base their assessment on unduly high standards. A single person who doesn't make it through drug court is held up as a example of why the entire program should be scrapped. Conversely, proponents of the "magic bullet" seem to feel that even minor changes will have dramatic impact.

In this final section, rather than examining the debate over criminal justice reform it is best to step back and try to analyze efforts at reform. The formulation and implementation of criminal justice policy must wrestle with the following four trends: increasing workload, increasing fragmentation, efforts at greater coordination, and decreasing isolation.

Increasing Workload

One of the great contradictions of the last decade is that as crime has decreased, the number of police arrests has increased, the volume of court cases has risen, and the prison population continues to skyrocket. Most directly these recent trends reflect the impact of the war on drugs. More broadly, though, the increasing workload is a response to the political pressures discussed in the opening. The three major themes in debating crime are:

• "there oughta be a law";
• the penalties should be tougher;
• more efforts should be devoted to prosecution.

It is reasonable to expect that workload will increase irrespective of crime rates.

Increasing Fragmentation

A second likely trend resulting from debating crime is increasing fragmentation. As demands increase, the response of the criminal justice system is greater specialization. Creations of drug courts are among the most prominent examples. Others include special courts (and police squads) to handle domestic violence, and units to conduct mandatory pretrial drug testing. In short, one can expect the creation of more, not fewer, criminal justice agencies.

Greater Coordination

To a certain extent, increasing fragmentation will be partially offset by efforts at greater coordination. The notion of "system" is now firmly engrained into the thinking of the public and many (but certainly not all) criminal justice officials. Indeed, federal and state grant money is often premised on coordination of various members of the local criminal justice community. At least in terms of law enforcement, these efforts at creating task forces, working groups and the like, are virtually demanded by the changing living patterns of Americans, including the decline of central cities coupled with the sprawl of suburbs

Decreasing Isolation

Another important pattern that will affect the criminal justice system of the future includes efforts to decrease isolation. Today, discussions of criminal justice reform emphasize the importance of community. Community policing is an important trend in law enforcement. Community prosecution and community courts are likewise significant new developments for the judiciary. Similarly, the concept of community corrections is a reaction to the swelling number of persons under correctional supervision. Whether this emphasis on "community" will ultimately redirect the system, or will disappear as merely the latest buzzword, remains to be seen. Nonetheless, viewing the criminal justice system in relation to other social institutions—schools, for example—is of critical importance.

The message of this last section is that analysis of criminal justice reforms requires an understanding that workload, fragmentation, coordination, and isolation are key factors in the criminal justice system.

The first article, "Ceremonial Justice, Loose Coupling, and the War on Drugs in Texas, 1980–1989," illustrates how the police, courts, and corrections systems in Texas adapted to the war on drugs. Results show that drug arrests remained a small proportion of total law enforcement efforts. Thus, the war on drugs was waged primarily in the courts. Convictions resulted in the incarceration of more offenders, yet inmates were released early to maintain compliance with population caps.

The article, "Core Challenges Facing Community Policing: The Emperor Still Has No Clothes," offers a critical assessment of a major effort to change law enforcement in the United States. The authors, Robert Taylor, Eric Fritsch and Tory Caeti (of North Texas University), caution that changing the institution of policing also requires changes in many other governmental systems.

World Wide Web Exercises

1. Use the search engine of your choice and enter the search term **community oriented policing**. Locate two or more articles that discuss the topic. To what extent do they

adopt an advocacy or analytical position? On the basis of the readings and the Web sites discuss this innovation in terms of the four concepts presented in the text: increasing workload, increasing fragmentation, greater coordination, and decreasing isolation.

2. Using the search engine of your choice, enter the search term **drug courts.** Locate two or more articles that discuss the topic. To what extent do they adopt an advocacy or analytical position? On the basis of the readings and the Web sites discuss this innovation in terms of the four concepts presented in the text: increasing workload; increasing fragmentation; greater coordination; and decreasing isolation.

InfoTrac College Edition Exercises

1. Using the search term **criminal statistics** locate two or more articles that discuss the workload in the criminal justice system. Does it appear that workloads will increase or level off? Which of the three perspectives discussed in this book—ideology, politics, and sociology—best explain increasing workloads?

2. Using the search term **narcotics, control of,** locate two or more articles that discuss whether the war on drugs is a success or failure. What types of statistics do they use to document their case? To what extent do the articles employ contrasting definitions of failure (or success)?

Ceremonial Justice, Loose Coupling, and the War on Drugs in Texas, 1980–1989

**James Marquart, Madhava Bodapati,
Steven Cuvelier, and Leo Carroll**

The War on Drugs in Texas was officially declared even before [the federal war on drugs]. . . . On May 10, 1980, Governor William Clements made the following remarks before a graduating class of new state police officers: ". . . it's time that we get the dope off the streets and put the pushers in our jails, and I'm ready to lock them up."

This speech was the first salvo in an antidrug crusade that lasted throughout the 1980s (and continues unabated today). . . . New laws were approved that both expanded enforcement activities and established harsher penalties for dealers and users. The legislature in 1981 enacted laws to shut down "head shops," incarcerate offenders up to 99 years for selling drugs to minors, institute fines of up to $1 million for those financing narcotics trafficking as well as seizure of their property, and to raise the minimum sentence for several drug offenses from five to ten years. . . .

The rapid escalation of the drug war in the 1980s taxed the resources of the Texas criminal justice system on every level. The strain was greatly aggravated by another constraint imposed on the state by a federal court in the landmark prisoner's rights case *Ruiz v. Estelle* (1980). . . . The cornerstone issue in the suit was overcrowding. . . . From 1981 onward, the Texas prison system entered into a "compliance phase" in which

the state implemented numerous court-ordered requirements. . . . In 1985 the court recognized that demand for prison space was quickly outstripping supply and established prisoner population limits, set forth in the "Crowding Stipulation," at eleven existing prisons. Most of these units had to be "depopulated" (inmates were transferred to other nonaffected prison facilities) in order to comply with the decree.

The federal court was not alone in dealing with the rising demand on prison bed space. The state legislature in 1983 passed the Prison Management Act or PMA. This controversial law specified that the state prison system not operate in excess of 95 percent of capacity. The prison system was required to shut its doors until enough prisoners (especially those eligible for parole) were released to maintain the legally specified capacity. In other words, the "back door" was opened, like a safety valve, to relieve population pressures at the front door. . . .

The Police Response to the Antidrug Crusade

Between 1980 and 1989, the number of drug arrests by state and local police in Texas increased by 69.4 percent from 38,981 to 66,027. Although this increase indicates a marked growth in drug enforcement efforts by these agencies, it is only about half the percentage increase in drug arrests recorded by state and local police nationally over this same time period. . . . State and local police in Texas, then, seem not to have become as involved in the War on Drugs as their counterparts in other

Source: James Marquart, Madhava Bodapati, Steven Cuvelier, and Leo Carroll (1993 October). Ceremonial Justice, Loose Coupling, and the War on Drugs in Texas, 1980–1989. In Dae H. Chang (Ed.), *Crime & Delinquency*. Reprinted by permission of Sage Publications, Inc.

states. In part, this may have resulted from Texas's strategic geographical location for the war, which made it a focal point for federal interdiction efforts. It was also, perhaps, due in no small measure to the great demands placed on Texas police by increases in serious crime that occurred simultaneously with the War on Drugs and were perhaps part of it. From 1980 through 1984, the number of index (Uniform Crime Report [UCR] Index) crimes known to police nationwide dropped by 11.4 percent but those in Texas rose by five percent. Then, from 1984 through 1989, although the nation as a whole was experiencing a 20 percent increase in the number of known index crimes, Texas experienced an increase of 47.3 percent....

Thus, although Texas police certainly seemed to have responded to public sentiment by stepping up their drug enforcement activity during the 1980s, they did not do so to the extent that most other state and local police did. Dramatic increases in the level of serious violent and property crime, itself perhaps part of the drug problem in a border region, seems to have severely taxed police resources. The dual demands placed on the police by the sheer volume of serious crime in the late 1980s, on the one hand, and the call to get tough on drugs, on the other hand, appear to have impeded the efficiency of the police in apprehending serious offenders.

The Judicial Response: Convict and Imprison

Although the number of drug arrests by Texas state and local police increased by 69 percent during the 1980s, the number of felony convictions for drug crimes increased by 329 percent, from 5,393 in 1980 to 23,126 in 1989. The number of felony convictions for other than drug offenses also increased at a rate greater than that for arrests, but at nowhere near the pace for drug offenses....

[B]y the end of the decade, arrests for drug offenses in Texas were more likely to result in a felony conviction than were arrests for serious property crime, and nearly as likely to end in felony convictions as arrests for serious violent crime. The War on Drugs in Texas was clearly being fought more intensely in the courts than on the streets, and the major tactic employed by the

courts was to indict and convict as felons, drug offenders who previously would have been tried as misdemeanants.

That previously minor offenses were more likely to have been treated as felonies during the 1980s probably also explains why the median sentence length did not increase.... [D]espite the War on Drugs and the general get-tough-on-crime sentiment prevailing in the state, and despite the fact that in Texas, district trial judges are elected officials, the median sentences imposed by judges remained virtually constant.

What seems a plausible explanation is that this lack of change in average sentence length was an unintentional by-product of the increase in the number of felony convictions. That is, offenders who in the past would have pleaded guilty to a misdemeanor and received jail time or probation were, by 1989, much more likely to be convicted of a felony and to receive a prison sentence, but a short one. These shorter sentences balanced longer sentences for more serious offenses, with the result that the median remained about the same.

The Response of the Prison System

That the number of prison admissions increased is scarcely surprising in light of the data presented above concerning the increase in arrests and felony convictions. But the magnitude of the increase would not have been as great had not the courts also become more severe in their disposition of felony convictions. Just as the ratio of arrests to felony convictions fell over the decade, so also did the ratio of felony convictions to prison admissions. In 1980 there were 3.1 felony convictions for every prison admission. By 1989 this ratio had declined to one admission for every 2.3 convictions. This decline in the ratio of convictions to admissions occurred to about the same degree in each major category, suggesting that Texas judges responded to the call for a War on Drugs by making war on crime in general.

The dramatic increase in the number of prison admissions quickly overwhelmed the capacity of the prison system to provide inmates with sufficient space and services.... Despite the construction of 20 new facilities during the decade, adding about 4,000 beds per year to its capacity, the system was not able to expand sufficiently to accommodate the tidal wave of new admissions. As a result, between February 1987 and September 1987, the prison system closed 21 times. The PMA hastily became a back-door prison population control device. Prisoners were paroled early to maintain the system at 95 percent capacity. "Good time" policies were also liberalized to quicken the pace of early prison releases.

In 1980 just over 7,000 inmates were released on parole in Texas. In 1985 the figure grew to almost 9,500. By 1989 some 30,000 were released from state prisons on parole. According to Jack Kyle, chairman of the Texas Board of Pardons and Paroles, "during this period of time [mid-1980s] parole in Texas became an open door. . . ."

The results of the early release policies are clearly evident. . . . Violent offenders released in 1980 had served a median of roughly 40 percent of their sentence; those released in 1989 served only 26 percent. . . .

The overused cliché of prisons being a revolving door became a reality by the end of the decade in Texas. To a great degree, the antidrug crusade in Texas had become an example of symbolic justice as incarcerated felons were quickly released from prison to make room for the next cohort. . . .

The impact of the PMA, and especially the scheduled admissions policy, created another unintended but nonetheless explosive consequence. . . . The combined effects of prison closures and the implementation of the allocation formula created a massive backlog of state prisoners in the county jails. The Texas Commission on Jail Standards estimated that in November 1989, Texas' largest county jails contained about 10,700 convicted felons (or "paper ready") awaiting transfer to state prisons. By October 1992, this backlog increased to 20,100 convicted felons and had placed a severe burden on local resources. The state, however, was required, as the result of litigation by several large Texas counties, to reimburse the counties for the costs (estimated to be tens of millions of dollars annually) of housing state prisoners. To relieve the population pressure in the jails, the state began, in 1989, to parole offenders . . . In other words, a segment of convicted offenders, particularly those with sentences of five years or less, never make it to the prison system.

Conclusion and Discussion

Our analysis makes clear the loosely coupled nature of the criminal justice system in Texas, and how this loose coupling facilitated the maintenance of stability in the face of major environmental changes posed by the War on Drugs. State and local police in Texas stepped up their enforcement of drug laws during the 1980s, but drug arrests remained a small proportion of their total enforcement effort. At the same time, the Texas law enforcement community encountered increases in serious violent and property crime. In the face of these dual environmental demands, police efficiency in clearing serious crimes declined.

Although the police were faced with competing demands, this was not true of the courts. In Texas, prosecutors and district trial judges are elected officials. Indeed, it is hardly surprising that the War on Drugs in Texas was waged more intensely in the courtrooms than on the streets. Offenses that in 1980 were treated as misdemeanors became, during the decade, more likely to be treated as felonies. And felony convictions were, in 1989, more likely to result in incarceration than was true 10 years earlier.

Although the state prison system was expanded over the 1980s, authorities resorted to accelerating good time and using early paroles to accommodate increased demand in maintaining compliance with the court order. In consequence, the percentage of sentence served by released offenders declined sharply. Not only had the prison system become a "turnstile" but incarceration lost its significance as the state's most punitive form of punishment. . . .

In sum, the Texas criminal justice system maintained its overall stability in the face of the demands placed on it by the War on Drugs by instituting a form of ceremonial justice in which offenders were arrested, convicted, imprisoned, and then quickly released and returned to the community. The War on Drugs in Texas was transformed into a symbolic crusade, one with potentially high costs in terms of public safety.

Core Challenges Facing Community Policing: The Emperor Still Has No Clothes

Robert W. Taylor, Eric J. Fritsch and Tory J. Caeti

For the past decade, we have witnessed the rhetoric and reality of changes in American law enforcement stemming from the perceived implementation of community policing. Fueled in large part by a few select works and studies beginning in the late 1980s . . . law enforcement has been trying to change from a closed, incident-driven and reactive bureaucracy to a more open, dynamic, quality-oriented partnership with the community. No one can argue with the virtues of quality service expressed in the tenets of community policy, nor can they disagree with the mission and philosophy of proactive, information-based organization committed to community problem solving, to safeguarding basic human and constitutional rights, and to public scrutiny and accountability. After all, these are the lofty goals that police in a democratic society have always heralded.

Indeed, the philosophy of community policing is value-laden with all the "good" virtues expressed by people governing themselves. The problems with community policing are *not* with the philosophy and mission, but rather with the implementation of change. . . .

Illustratively, we still argue about the definition of community policing. In some cities it is the addition of a bike patrol or extra officers assigned to the DARE program or being the leader in a Neighborhood Crime Watch meeting. The problem, of course, is that community policing has been defined in so many different ways that the evaluation of specific programs has been benign.

The result is that "what works" in community policing is relegated to a few initiatives highlighted in a few, select cities across the country. The vast bulk of the literature on community-oriented policing is anecdotal and more apt to read like propaganda. To date, there is a paucity of methodologically sound, empirical research assessing the effectiveness of community-oriented policing.

Do we really see most of the changes once espoused by community policing advocates? How many departments have actually changed the entrance requirements for new officers to reflect the changes in the police role? How many have changed recruit training from a military-oriented academy to a curriculum more in tune with the new role demanded by community policing? How many departments have flattened their organizational pyramid and placed more decision-making in the hands of the officers? How many chiefs have turned the organization "upside down" and have committed to participatory dialogue with officers as a major part of their management style? How many departments have actually changed their organizational culture? How many departments have structurally changed on a citywide basis? Unfortunately, we submit to you, only a very select few! . . .

To be successful, community policing must confront and hurdle five core challenges in the future.

Challenge #1

There is precious little empirical evidence that supports the idea that community policing has a positive impact on community perception of the police or crime reduction.

Source: *ACJS Today,* Vol. XVII, May, 1998, pp. 1–5. Reprinted by permission of the Academy of Criminal Justice Sciences.

Few studies point to successful programs of change. Even the millions of dollars recently spent by the Community-Oriented Policing Office (COPS Office—U.S. Department of Justice) on evaluating community policing focus on specific programs rather than on holistic studies of the concept itself. This problem hints at the politicalization of the process. But much more importantly, how do we measure prevention of crime? How do we document all that has gone on in the last ten years? How can we be sure that "community" policing ventures were more important in reducing a specific crime compared to more "traditional" tactics such as saturation patrol, directed investigations, zero tolerance, and strong enforcement of curfew and truancy laws. Quite simply, we cannot . . .

Challenge #2

Community policing demands a systemic change in all of city government.

Community policing requires changes in not only the police but also in the other components of the criminal justice system. Indeed, community policing requires an entire city-wide change toward community government. City services must be coordinated, and cooperative ventures between governmental agencies must be developed. The police cannot be an isolated group within a city trying to address major social problems without the combined commitment and resources of the entire city. Police must be able to pass the "baton" to other agencies more appropriately designed to address many social problems, often times first encountered by the police. Contrary to public opinion, the police *cannot* be all things to all people. They have a very specific set of skills and accompanying training, and are well equipped to handle crime-related problems. Broadening the mission of an organization that was having difficulty with a narrow mission to begin with may have not been prudent. Long-term counseling, social work, trash pick-up and inspirational speaking may not be the best fit for the police; and perhaps they should not be. These are most certainly not reflective of the

curriculum in current police training academies. Community-oriented policing may have to face the realization that the police will never be able to shake the perception that they are responsible for crime control. As discussed, police still hire the same type of individuals, and, for the most part, train them the same way they were trained 20 years ago . . .

Challenge #3

The implementation of community policing is more "academic" than actual.

Real efforts to involve the community have been mixed at best. Police officials note difficulty in getting good turnouts or participation in their community policing efforts. Whose interests does community policing represent? It would seem on initial inspection that, like other forms of government, interest groups have the ear of the police. What community policing advocates should be asking is "are we representing the community, or only the most vocal, visible members of it?" The charge that community policing works best in areas that don't need it rings, unfortunately, true. Then, there are significant ethical questions concerning the risk of corruption and favoritism. If the principal goal of community policing is to bring order to the community, and if different segments of the community have different views of "order," whose "order" will prevail? What if one segment's preferred "order" compromises the legal rights of another segment? If community policing is to be successful, it must work in the core, ghetto areas of our cities, where crime, poverty and disorder are most pronounced, and where political factionalization is most apparent. . . .

Challenge #4

Community policing has been too "politicized."

Unfortunately, community policing has become the buzzword of the last decade. If a department was not involved in community policing then it was labeled backward, stationary, nonprogressive, or worse, Neanderthal. The few scholars and practitioners that questioned the concept were branded "heretics" and unenlightened. . . . One chief of police recently indicated (on a private basis) that he believed community was "bull____" invented by a few well-meaning individuals to try something new. Unfortunately, he also admitted that he (like many of his colleagues) could not afford to be public about community policing. There simply is too much at stake . . . [including] free officers and free federal money for those involved in community policing. Community policing is now big business, and those individuals managing police departments understand, all too well, the political ramifications of heading a movement against what is deemed as somehow more progressive and better than the status quo. . . .

Community policing was never envisioned to be short term . . . And make no doubt about it . . . community policing is headed on the path of being a political scapegoat. . . .

What will happen when federal grants that support community policing cease? . . . As federal money becomes much more difficult to obtain and cities start to bear the burden of financing extra officers and programs themselves, community policing will face much more scrutiny and criticism. New political leadership will most assuredly point to the great financial costs of community policing in an attempt to justify their own position. Community policing will be further politicized as national debate focuses on the search for a new president. What will be the empirical evidence of success? . . .

Challenge #5

Community policing is riding the facade of success.

Politically, community policing can only be justified as "successful." Crime is down, violent acts in most major cities are down, unemployment is down, the number of youth between ages 14 and 21 is down and the general economy is doing well. Unfortunately and most dangerously, some police

chiefs and most politicians are taking credit for these statistics. Policing needs to be very careful! What will happen after we have built a public expectation that the police can do all things for all people? What will happen when the wave crests . . . when unemployment starts to creep up, the economy shrinks, inflation builds, cutback management highlights the federal agenda, and the new "boom" generation hits the criminal justice system? Will tension further increase between minorities and police and erupt in frustration and riot? During these times, will the police still be able to afford storefront operations, graffiti patrols, crime watch, DARE programs, and other community policy projects? Or, will the police be mandated to respond more effectively to 911 calls?

The issues facing community policing are no different than the issues confronting policing in general. Where do we go from here? The answer is quite simple: We continue to press forward in a positive manner, understanding that change is difficult and evolutionary. Police need to refine the concept of what good policing is and "tweak" their departments to meet existing cultural and organizational demands. We no longer need the buzzwords of community policing, but we desperately need the strong leaders that have taken bold risks in an attempt to find out "what works and what doesn't." We still need those individuals courageous enough to try something new, to bridge a new communication and information age, and to open up a new dialogue with communities of the future. In essence, we need to understand that team policing of the 1970s and community policing of the 1990s represent only the beginning stages of change and that the process has only just begun. Community policing advocates a necessary and important reform. Its recognition of the close relationship of crime to other social problems is a big step in the evolution of American policing. Our immediate job is to safeguard the many worthy efforts of the community policing movement by squarely facing the challenges posed, understanding the inherent nature of police in our society today.

Appendix: Ground Rules for Proper Debating

Dictionaries equate the word *debate* with words like *discussing, arguing,* or *disputing.* Such definitions, however, provide only an imperfect guide to public forums where debates seem to involve *quarreling, asserting,* and *ignoring.*

Some public exchanges are little more than quarrels with loud shouting and occasional threats of violence. Here, arguers think the winner is the person who shouts the loudest or perhaps the longest. Somehow the ruder you are the better the debater. Other public dialogues involve heavy doses of asserting without proving. Advocates make exaggerated or unsubstantiated claims. Bold statements do serve to energize those who already believe, but without documentation others remain skeptical. Finally, some public forums involve little more than ignoring the opponent. Every four years, for example, the nation is able to watch "debates" between candidates for president. But these are often not true debates because there is no true give and take. Rather, each side is allowed to recite a standard campaign speech without being forced to confront the arguments or evidence of the opponent.

Academic debates differ from these public exchanges, loosely characterized as debates, in important ways. *Debating Crime: Rhetoric and Reality* has hopefully provided an overview of the public debate. The task of the appendix is to stress the importance of proper debating in an academic setting. As will become obvious, some techniques that are effective in public advocacy are not acceptable in university classrooms.

Most immediately college debate is more formal and more structured than what is loosely labeled "debate" in public forums. The figure below provides a short overview of basic debating. But more important than the formalities of college debating is its underlying purpose. Instead of quarreling, the emphasis is on reasoned analysis (Freeley, 1996). Proving, not asserting, is the norm. Toward this end, in a true debate one is forced to confront the arguments of one's opponent.

Basic Outline of a Debate

RESOLVED	
Affirmative	**Negative**
Statement of the Problem	
The affirmative seeks to prove the existence of a significant problem that requires remedial action.	The negative seeks to prove that the problem does not exist or the scope of the problem has been overstated.
Presentation of the Plan	
The affirmative seeks to prove that the proposed plan will solve the problem.	The negative seeks to prove that the plan won't solve the problem.
Benefits of the Plan	
The affirmative seeks to prove that the benefits of the plan outweigh any disadvantages.	The negative seeks to prove that the disadvantages of the plan outweigh any possible benefits.

College debate is most often associated with oral presentations. But debate need not be limited to speech classes. Written presentations are also appropriate. Moreover, apart from oratory, preparing to debate is no different from conducting good research and constructing strong arguments. What follows is an attempt to briefly summarize some important dos and don'ts.

Research the Topic

The first step is selecting a topic. In some settings you have no choice because someone else has decided on the topic. But if you have a choice, then by all means select a topic that interests you. Toward that end, you might want to review the issues discussed in this book before deciding how to invest your time. After some preliminary research you need to move on to the next step.

Define the Issue

In debating, as in any analysis of a social problem, it is important to begin by carefully specifying the problem. An essential starting point, therefore, is a definition. As we have seen throughout this book, most debatable crime issues have elastic definitions. Often, different sides work from contrasting definitions. In a structured debate it is important to be clear and precise about terms.

Debate topics are stated as resolutions. For example, the collegiate debate topic for 2000–2001 is: RESOLVED: That the United States federal government should significantly increase protection of privacy in one or more of the following areas:

employment, medical records, consumer information, search and seizure. Note that the resolution is stated so that the affirmative has the burden of proof. A good topic statement is also even-handed, stating the proposition for debate in a way that does not favor either side.

Narrow the Topic

After arriving at a working definition, it is important to narrow the subject. Good debate topics have a scope to them (bad ones are way too narrow and specialized). But because they have a scope, it is necessary to do some broad-based research. Not all of this exploratory research will necessarily show up in the final product, but this broad-based inquiry will help to put the issue into perspective. It will also identify a number of dimensions of the problem.

The purpose of exploratory research is to narrow the topic to something that is doable and manageable. The librarians at Broward Community College in Florida have done an admirable job in placing pathfinders on the Internet, one of which is reprinted in the box that follows.

Police Brutality Pathfinder

Definition

"The excessive use of force by those whose duty it is to use force if necessary to maintain law and order. From the early 1960s to the 1990s, the issue of police brutality repeatedly strained relations between the police and racial minorities." (*American Justice*)

Narrow the Subject

- Is police brutality a serious problem?
- Is police brutality against minorities, juveniles or the poor a serious problem?
- How can the extent of police brutality be measured?
- Is the mission of police officers clearly defined and understood?
- What are the causes of police brutality?
- Is racism a factor in police brutality?
- Does job stress contribute to police brutality?
- Can police self-defense be mistaken for brutality?
- How can police brutality be reduced?
- Should civilian review boards supervise police misconduct?
- Would community policing reduce police brutality?
- Would better training of police reduce police brutality?
- Would a police corps be an effective means of reducing police brutality?
- Research specific instances of police brutality, such as William Lozano or Rodney King.

Source: http://ucl.broward.cc.fl.us/pathfinders/policebrt.htm

---

Stick to the Topic

In preparing the argument (either pro or con) it is critical to stick to the topic. Some arguments remind me of frogs skipping from one hot rock to another, never landing in one spot very long. It is better to stick to two or three points than adopting a scatter-gun approach. In sticking to the topic here are two pitfalls to avoid.

Associated Logic

Hopping from topic to topic is sometimes referred to as "associated logic"; the arguer mentions an issue and then associates it with other events and trends. Typically, the arguer uses vague concepts to link a number of social problems and fails to offer any specifics. Some conservatives, for example discuss moral issues in this way, starting (perhaps) with pornography but then quickly mentioning promiscuity, gambling, prostitution and the like without establishing a clear link between any of these social problems. Likewise, some liberals address feminist issues by suggesting a seamless blending of sexual assault, domestic violence, and child abuse without delineating how these problems may (or may not) be interrelated.

Hell in a Handbasket

Falling into the trap of associated logic is often related to *hell-in-a-handbasket* arguments, which take the form of arguing that numerous and mounting social problems means that society is going to hell in a handbasket. This type of argument typically reflects a nostalgia for an idyllic past. It ignores problems faced by past generations and exaggerates today's problems. Ultimately, the only solution appears to be turning back the clock. Hell-in-a-handbasket arguments run the risk of condemning all social change.

Avoid Alarmist Rhetoric

A persuasive argument is one that presents the case in a logical way, with evidence supporting the major propositions. Weak arguments, on the other hand, are ones that rely on alarmist rhetoric. For example, phrases like "any right-thinking American" has no place in college debate. Conservative commentators are fond of labeling their opponents as socialists or, worse yet, communists. Not to be outdone, liberal commentators label their opponents as Nazis and point to vast right-wing conspiracies (Potomac Institute, www.us.net/phoenix).

Overall try to avoid what I call the "alliteration trap." Striking a nice-sounding phrase is fine, but at times such phrases either get in the way of a strong argument or are so overused that they become trite. Among phrases falling into that category that regularly appear in the crime debate are "shocking numbers," "alarming increase," and the like. I know they are the favorite stock-in-trade of today's journalists, but they have been used so often that they have become banal.

Avoid Logical Fallacies

A fallacy is a deceptive argument, one that attempts to make a point not by proof but by guile or trickery. One set of fallacies is that referred to as *logical fallacies*. These fallacies pose as logical proof, but upon close examination they prove nothing at all (Wood, 1995). Here are several logical fallacies that tend to occur in debating crime.

Begging the Question

A begging-the-question fallacy is characterized by the arguer restating the claim (sometimes in different language) but not offering any proof for it. For example, "Capital punishment deters crime because it keeps criminals from committing murder" simply restates the same idea, only in other words. Perhaps my favorite is the title of an article by Enough is Enough, "Illegal Pornography is Illegal." This is admittedly a catchy phrase, but it has no meaning. It begs the question because it assumes that there is a clear definition of pornography when in reality this is one of the slipperiest concepts the U.S. Supreme Court has ever tried to define.

Straw Man

A straw-man argument is one in which the arguer sets up an irrelevant idea, refutes it, and then claims victory. Most often, straw-man arguments take the form of stating the opponent's case in the weakest possible way and then demolishing it. By way of illustration, the debate over lowering the threshold for drunk driving (Issue 5) featured an exchange over eating a slice of pizza and drinking a few beers. In my analysis, both sides are guilty of misstating the opponent's position (and trivializing the issue in the process).

Post Ho Ergo Propter Hoc

Translated from the Latin, *post hoc ergo propter hoc* means "after the fact, therefore because of the fact." This is a fallacy because there is no proof that a given event at time one caused an event at time two. For example, some link Supreme Court decisions in the mid-1960s with a subsequent rise in crime. While it has become common to blame all manner of social ills on Supreme Court decisions, if you are going to argue this proposition you will need more proof than a simple time sequence.

Avoid Ethical Fallacies

Ethical fallacies are aimed at attacking character or using character instead of evidence as proof. Here are several ethical fallacies that often appear in debating crime.

Ad Hominem

An *ad hominem* argument attempts to dismiss the soundness of an idea by attacking the character of its source. Discrediting the character of the person (or group) also adds an emotional tone to the argument. Recall, for example, the article by Wayne LaPierre that sought to discredit gun control by associating it with President Clinton. *Ad hominem* arguments often attack the motives of the other side, suggesting that the proposal is really a small part of a larger, and more sinister plot. Some *ad hominem* arguments are veiled appeals to prejudice.

Guilt by Association

Guilt-by-association arguments suggest that people's character can be assessed by examining the character of their associates. In debating crime, groups will often try to discredit an idea by associating it with "unpopular" groups. At times, conservatives will attempt to discredit liberal proposals by using phrases to the effect that this is just another "left-wing proposal of the ACLU" or "part of the misguided feminist agenda advanced by NOW." And at times, liberals will attempt to discredit conservative ideas by associating them with the other right-wing proposals of the National Riffle Association or the John Birch Society.

Poisoning the Well

Poisoning-the-well arguments attempt to discredit the other side before one even hears the counter-argument. On a personal level, they take the form of telling a person not to believe a word that Judy says because she is a habitual liar. Thus, nothing she says can ever be true. In public forums, poisoning-the-well arguments often take the form of stating one's position as fact, and labeling the opponent's arguments as myth. Liberals and conservatives are equally culpable on this score. For example, the ACLU statement on the death penalty (in this book) takes this form, as does the National Rifle Association "Fact Sheet: 'Junk Lawsuits' Against Gun Makers" (www.nraila.org/research/19990825-LawsuitPreemption-001.shtml).

Avoid Emotional Fallacies

Emotional fallacies introduce irrelevant, unrelated, and distracting materials into an argument. Here are two examples:

The Bandwagon Appeal

The bandwagon appeal is based on the dubious premise that we should adopt a given policy change because everyone else is in favor of it. Results of public opinion polls are often used to bolster bandwagon appeals. Arguments in favor of the death penalty, for example, often mention that a majority of those polled are in favor of executions. Even if true, this is not necessarily a reasoned argument for adoption. Moreover, poll results showing strong majority support often mask important public disagreements on specifics (which is especially true of public opinion on capital punishment).

Testimonials

Arguments based on testimonials are a more specific version of the bandwagon appeal. The arguer urges adoption because experts or famous persons have endorsed the idea. This might be a good reason for consumers to buy shampoo but not for changing criminal-justice policy.

At times, testimonial arguments reference unnamed "experts." A case in point is this recent press release: "In developing the 'Higher Risk Driver' plan, MADD consulted with highway safety experts and researchers, treatment professionals, public policy advocates and others at the local, state and national levels." Not only aren't we told who these experts are, what their credentials might be and most importantly what they recommended—it could very well be that these "experts" recommended *against* the final plan.

The flip side of asking your audience to adopt a policy based on support from prestigious persons is attacking your opponent's experts as unworthy of attention. Thus, it is improper refutation to attempt to discredit studies reaching a different conclusion from the one you prefer by simply labeling them as "so-called" experts, or "pseudo" experts.

Slippery Slope

The slippery-slope fallacy is a scare tactic that suggests that if we allow one thing to happen, we will immediately be sliding down the slippery slope to disaster. Arguments about "taking away our constitutional rights" often take this form. Thus the arguer will suggest that if the government takes away our Second Amendment rights (or our first or fourth or fifth) then they will shortly take away our other rights under the Constitution.

World Wide Web Resources

Web Guides

http://dir.yahoo.com/Social_Science/Communications/Forensics/Debate/

Useful URLs

Propaganda: Propaganda analysis home page.
http://dir.yahoo.com/Social_Science/Communications/Forensics/Debate/

Debate on the Web: Geared to policy debaters.   http://www.cross-x.com/

Forensic Resources on the Web: Information geared to the National Debate Tournament.   http://www.wfu.edu/NDT/homepage.html

Debate Central: A good, basic site from the University of Vermont.
http://debate.uvm.edu

References

Allan, Kenneth, and Scott Coltrane. 1996. "Gender Displaying Television Commercials: A Comparative Study of Television Commercials in the 1950s and 1980s." *Sex Roles* 35: 185–203.

Allen, M., D. Alessio., T. M. Emmers, and L. Gebhardt. 1996. "The Role of Educational Briefings in Mitigating Effects of Experimental Exposure to Violent Sexually Explicit Material: A Meta-analysis." *The Journal of Sex Research* 33: 135–141.

Allen, M., T. M. Emmers, L. Gebhardt, and M. Giery. 1995. "Exposure to Pornography and Acceptance of Rape Myths." *Journal of Communication* 45: 5–26.

American Civil Liberties Union. 1982. *The Rights of Crime Victims*. New York: Bantam.

Barnes, Patricia. 1998. *Domestic Violence: From a Private Matter to a Federal Offense*. Levittown, PA: Garland Publications.

Bates, Eric. 1999. "CCA, the Sequel: The Largest Private Prison Firm Continues Its Pattern of Abuse and Profit." *The Nation* (June 7) 268: 21.

Beck, Melinda, Gerald Lubenow, and Martin Kasindorf. 1981. "Nancy: Searching for a Role." *Newsweek* (February 22).

Bernard, Thomas. 1992. *The Cycle of Juvenile Justice*. New York: Oxford University Press.

Berry, Jeffrey. 1997. *The Interest Group Society*. New York: Longman.

Bivens v. Six Unknown Federal Narcotics Agents. 403 U.S. 388 (1971).

Bonczar, Thomas, and Allen Beck. 1997. "Lifetime Likelihood of Going to State or Federal Prison." U. S. Department of Justice, Office of Justice Programs.

Brown, Lee P. 1995. "Why the United States Will Never Legalize Drugs: Protecting Our Children." *Vital Speeches* 61: 628–30.

Bureau of Justice Statistics. 1997. "Criminal Victimization Rates (1994) in the United States." U. S. Department of Justice, Bureau of Justice Statistics.

———. 1993. "Correctional Populations in the United States, 1992." U.S. Department of Justice, Bureau of Justice Statistics.

———. 1997. "Police Use of Force." U.S. Department of Justice, Bureau of Justice Statistics.

———. 1998. "Violence by Intimates." U.S. Department of Justice, Bureau of Justice Statistics.

Carter, David. 1985. "Hispanic Perception of Police Performance: An Empirical Assessment." *Journal of Criminal Justice* 13: 477–500.

de Young, Mary. 1997. "The Devil Goes to Day Care: McMartin and The Making of a Moral Panic." *Journal of American Culture* 20: 19–26.

Dilulio, J. 1993. "Rethinking the Criminal Justice System: Toward a New Paradigm." In *Performance Measures for the Criminal Justice System*. Washington, D.C.: U.S. Department of Justice, Bureau of Justice Statistics.

Donnerstein, E., and D. Linz. 1986. "Mass Media Sexual Violence and Male Viewers." *American Behavioral Scientist* 29: 601–618.

Duncan, D. 1990. "Pornography As a Source of Sex Information for University Students." *Psychological Reports* 66: 442.

Duncan, D., and J. Donnelly. 1991. "Pornography As a Source of Sex Information for Students at Northeastern University." *Psychological Reports* 78: 782.

Duncan, D., and T. Nicholson. 1991. "Pornography As a Source of Sex Information at Southeastern University." *Psychological Reports* 68: 802.

Enough Is Enough. 1999. "Illegal Pornography is Illegal." www.enough.org

———. 1999. "Reefs & Rocks." http://enough.org/reefs.html

Epstein, Gail, and Cyril Zaneski. 1998. "Southern Gun Culture Blamed for Explosion of School Killings." *New Orleans Times-Picayune* (March 29).

Estrich, Susan. 1987. *Real Rape*. Cambridge: Harvard University Press.

Fairchild, Erika. 1981. "Interest Groups in the Criminal Justice Process." *Journal of Criminal Justice* 9: 181–194.

Federal Bureau of Investigation. 1996. *Uniform Crime Reports*. Washington, D.C.: U.S. Department of Justice, Federal Bureau of Investigation.

Feld, Barry. 1998. "Abolish the Juvenile Court: Youthfulness, Criminal Responsibility, and Sentencing Policy." *Journal of Criminal Law, & Criminology* (Winter).

Freeley, Austin. 1996. *Argumentation and Debate: Critical Thinking for Reasoned Decision Making,* 9th Edition. Belmont: Wadsworth.

Friedman, Lawrence. 1993. *Crime and Punishment in American History*. New York: Basic Books.

Gallup Poll Monthly. 1995. October.

Garcia, L. T. 1986. "Exposures to Pornography and Attitudes About Women and Rape: A Correlative Study." *AG* 22: 382–383.

Gest, Ted. 1995. "The Great Gun Debate: Get the Picture?" *U.S. News & World Report* 119 (July 17): 6–8.

Gilliam, Frank, Shanto Iyengar, Adam Smith, and Oliver Wright. 1996. "Crime in Black and White: The Violent Scary World of Local News." *Press & Politics* 1: 6–23.

Greenfield, Lawrence, Patrick Langan, and Steven Smith. 1997. "National Data Collection on Police Use of Force." U. S. Department of Justice, NCJ-165040.

Greenfield, Lawrence, et al. 1998. "Violence by Intimates: Analysis of Data on Crimes by Current or Former Spouses, Boyfriends, and Girlfriends." Washington, D.C.: U.S. Department of Justice, Bureau of Justice Statistics.

Heinz, Anne, Herbert Jacob, and Robert Lineberry, eds. 1983. *Crime in City Politics.* New York: Longman.

Hubert, Bob. 1999. "Storm Brewing Over Killing by Police." *New York Times* (February 11).

Hunzeker, Donna. 1995. "Grown Up Time." *State Legislators* 21 (May): 14–18

Kamisar, Yale. 1978. "Is the Exclusionary Rule an 'Illogical' or 'Unnatural' Interpretation of the Fourth Amendment?" *Judicature* 78: 83.

Kass, John. 1999. "And You Wonder Why Police Officers Become Embittered." *Chicago Tribune* (March 17).

Kerr, Peter. 1986. "Anatomy of an Issue: Drugs, the Evidence, the Reaction." *New York Times* (November 17).

Kinder, Donald, and Lynn Sanders. 1996. *Divided By Color: Racial Politics and Democratic Ideals.* Chicago: University of Chicago Press.

Levine, Harry, and Craig Reinarman. 1988. "The Monkey on the Public's Back." *Newsday* (January 4).

————. 1988. "The Politics of America's Latest Drug Scare." In R. Curry (ed.), *Freedom at Risk: Secrecy, Censorship, and Repression in the 1980s.* 251–8. Philadelphia: Temple University Press.

Logan, Charles. 1993. "Criminal Justice Performance Measures for Prisons." In *Performance Measures for the Criminal Justice System.* Washington, D.C.: Bureau of Justice Statistics.

Logan, Charles. 1996. "Public vs. Private Prison Management: A Case Comparison." *Criminal Justice Review* 21: 62–85.

Los Angeles Times. 1994. "Asians Are Automatically Labeled Gang Members" (December 12).

Malamuth, N., and R. McIlwraith, 1988. "Fantasies and Exposure to Sexually Explicit Magazines." *Communication Research* 6: 753–771.

Mann, Coramae, and Marjorie Zatz. 1998. *Images of Color, Images of Crime.* Los Angeles: Roxbury Publishing.

Mapp v. Ohio. 367 U.S. 643 (1961).

Marion, Nancy. 1995. *The Politics of Criminal Justice.* New York: Harrow and Heston.

Melone, A., and R. Slagter. 1983. "Interest Group Politics and the Reform of the Federal Criminal Code." In S. Nagel, E. Fairchild, and A. Champagne (eds.), *The Political Science of Criminal Justice.* Springfield, IL: Charles C. Thomas.

Miller, Jerome. 1994. "From Social Safety Net to Dragnet: African American Males in the Criminal Justice System." *Washington and Lee Law Review* 51: 479.

Nathan, Debbie, and Michael Snendeker. 1995. *Satan's Silence*. New York: Basic Books.

National Institute of Justice. 1994. "The Future of Minority Law Enforcement Executives in the State of Florida." Washington, D.C.: U.S. Department of Justice, (NCJ 153059).

Neubauer, David. 1999. *America's Courts and the Criminal Justice System,* 6th Edition. Belmont: Wadsworth.

Oreskes, Michael. 1990. "Drug War Underlines Fickleness of Public." *New York Times* (September 6).

Pitts, Leonard. 1998. "Tripping Through Cyberporn Maze." *New Orleans Times-Picayune* (October 15).

Russell, Katheryn. 1998. *The Color of Crime*. New York: New York University Press.

Sampson, Robert, Stephen Raudenbush, and Felton Earls. 1997. "Neighborhoods and Violent Crime: A Multilevel Study of Collective Efficacy." *Science* 277: 2–25.

Saunders, R., and P. Naus. 1993. "The Impact of Social Content and Audience Factors on Responses to Sexually Explicit Videos." *Journal of Sex Education and Therapy* 19: 117–131.

Sexton, Robert. 1996. "The Economics of Juvenile Crime." *Investors Business Daily* (May 21).

Singer, Simon. 1996. *Recriminilizing Delinquency: Violent Juvenile Crime and Juvenile Justice Reform*. Cambridge, England: Cambridge University Press.

Song, J. 1992. "Attitudes of Chinese Immigrants and Vietnamese Refugees Toward Law Enforcement in the United States." *Justice Quarterly* 9: 703–19.

Sorrentino, Joseph. 1996. "A Felony's a Felony, Whether You're a Kid or Adult." *USA Today* (June 11).

Stone, Christopher. 1999. "Race, Crime, and the Administration of Justice." *NIJ Journal* 239: 27-32. Washington D.C.: U.S. Department of Justice, National Institute of Justice.

Suro, Roberto. 1998. "Suits Against Guns Use Tobacco Model." *The Washington Post* (December 24).

Torres, Sam, and Elizabeth Piper Deschenes. 1997. "Changing the System and Making It Work: The Process of Implementing Drug Courts in Los Angeles County." *Justice System Journal* 19: 267–290.

Tuch, Steven, and Ronald Weitzer. 1997. "Racial Differences in Attitudes Toward the Police." *Public Opinion Quarterly* 61: 642–64.

Wang, Z. 1989. "The Human Computer Interface Hierarchy Model and Strategies in System Development." *Ergonomics* 32: 1392–1400.

Walker, Samuel. 1982. "What Have Civil Liberties Ever Done for Crime Victims? Plenty!" *ACJS Today* 10: 4–5.

———. 1998. *Sense and Nonsense about Crime and Drugs,* 4th Edition. Belmont: Wadsworth.

Weed, Frank. 1995. *Certainty of Justice: Reform in the Crime Victim Movement.* New York: Aldine de Gruyter.

Weeks v. United States. 232 U.S. 383 (1914).

Weinberg, S. 1997. "One Public Library That Is Not an Adult Book Store." *Culture Wars* (October).

Wilkins, Julia. 1997. "Protecting Our Children from Internet Smut: Moral Duty or Moral Panic?" *The Humanist* 57 (September 4).

Wood, Nancy. 1995. *Perspectives on Argument.* Englewood Cliffs, NJ: Prentice-Hall.

Zillmann, Dolf, and Jennings Bryant. 1984. "Effects of Massive Exposure to Pornography." In N. Malamuth, and E. Donnerstein (eds.), *Pornography and Sexual Aggression.* 115–142. Orlando, FL: Academic Press.

Index